AF480662

NOT a Father's Daughter

Elizabeth Rodenz

The Storybook House

Copyright

All rights reserved.

Except for use in a review, no part of this book may be reproduced in any form without written permission of the author. Neither the author, nor publisher, assumes any responsibility for the use or misuse of information contained in this book.

10 9 8 7 6 5 4 3 2 1

ISBN: 979-8-99372-490-4

LCCN: 2025926433

Library of Congress Cataloging-in-Publication Data:

patriarch	feminism
psychology	psyche
patriarchy	Jungian psychology
archetypes	ego
masculinity	collective unconscious
relationships	

Cover by Stonepatch Design LLC

Printed and published in
the United States of America 2026

Dedication

To those who eased my journey, inspired and supported me, and accepted me as I am and to those who have made my journey difficult. I have learned from all of you.

You Have No Enemies

You have no enemies, you say?
Alas! my friend, the boast is poor;
He who has mingled in the fray
Of duty, that the brave endure
Must have made foes! If you have none,
Small is the work that you have done.
You've hit no traitor on the hip,
You've dashed no cup from perjured lip,
You've never turned the wrong to right
You've been a coward in the fight.
Charles MacKay

"Ours is not the task of fixing the entire world all at once, but
of stretching out to mend the part of the world that is within our
reach... One of the most calming and powerful actions you can
do to intervene in a stormy world is to stand up and show your
soul. Soul on deck shines like gold in dark times. The light of the
soul throws sparks, can send up flares, builds signal fires, causes
proper matters to catch fire."
Clarissa Pinkola Estes

Table of Contents

Part One

Getting My Wings

A Father's Daughter

From birth you are adored and loved
Sent to your father from heaven above
For a nod or a smile, you deny your desire
That which puts your soul on fire
Demands for more you cannot rebuff
Whatever you do is never enough
  Who are you really?

Pleading, won't you let me do more
Never questioning what's in store
As you are denying the life you crave
Doing all for applause and praise
Never asking what would you do
If no one's pushing and pulling you
  Who are you really?

The king demands, "Spin straw into gold"
"I cannot do it," was far too bold
Pleasing the fathers in your life
Filling you with angst and strife
Their approval and blessing you cherish
Not knowing, how soon you will perish
  Who are you really?

Always doing the patriarch's bidding
Never asking if it is fitting
Using his mirror to define yourself
Hoping not to be put on the shelf
Carrying the water for the men in your life
Never risk throwing the dice
  Who are you really?

To the Reader .... A Few Words

"I must be a mermaid, Rango. I have no fear of depths and a great fear of shallow living."
Anais Nin

Until I began my journey of discovering what resided deep within, I did not understand my words and actions. At times I knew immediately what to say or do and did not put my words or actions through a filter. I did not worry or think "Oh, I should not say that." "I should not do that!"

Yet, I cannot recall ruminating or attempting to refine those thoughts. How I responded is what I felt compelled to do or say. A force just bubbled up without warning, or a magnet was pulling me in a particular direction.

There were times when I was alone in my thinking. Outnumbered, so I must have been wrong. But there was something within saying, "No, Elizabeth, you are not," and always saying "You are allowed a different point of view. You do not have to go along!"

By reflecting on my life's journey, I came to realize that I had no agenda. My actions were authentic. I had no inkling of trying to please, nor did I fear being chastised.

Being that one voice can be a lonely existence. Psychologist, Carl Jung, stated, *"Loneliness does not come from having no people about one, but from being unable to communicate the things that seem important to oneself, or from holding certain views which others find inadmissible."* That rings so true for me.

By putting those memories down on paper, patterns of behavior, rather than disjointed bits and pieces are revealed. Those times are over; no opportunity to make other choices.

Maybe that is a good thing. I am more drawn to reflect and that is a never-ending journey. I often say, "When I get there, THERE will have moved." THERE will be some other element that will become conscious, but I thought it was time to share.

There is no template. There are no ten steps, no seven things to help us live our lives. People are messy, and there is no "quick fix" or "one size fits all."

Instead, I have chosen to accept the complexity of the individual and the issues facing us in the world and tackle them from a variety of angles.

In this part of the book, I use memoir to reveal and illustrate the life of a woman who unknowingly showed no signs of acquiescing to dogma and dictates. I report these unforgettable memories as best as I remember them. You may even find yourself, your stories, time and time again, between the covers of this book.

By sharing my stories and what I have gleaned from my journey, you too at a minimum, may be inspired to reflect on your life's journey, admit to some truths, and discover what is buried within.

I did not write this book to tell you what to think. I did so to take you on a journey, so you can take from it what will serve you in this moment and in the future.

The bits and pieces of this book have been swirling in my head most of my life and finally coalesced. And the universe was no longer nudging me, it was screaming, "Elizabeth, speak out!" So, a few years ago I began to put pen to paper for this book, *NOT a Father's Daughter*. It was like a magnet, pulling me in, and although I was not sure where I was going, I was aching to write. Now, I am grateful for that journey.

Life goes by in a blink, so let's get started.

One
What is Buried Within

"What I am looking for is not out there, it is in me."
Helen Keller

There's a Native American myth that I wish to share.

The Creator gathered all of creation and said, *"I want to hide something from humans until they are ready for it. It is the realization that they can create their own life and their own reality."*

The eagle said, *"Give it to me; I'll take it to the moon and hide it there."*

But the Creator said, *"No! One day they will go there and will find it."*

Then the salmon said, *"Give it to me; I'll hide it in the bottom of the sea."*

"No!" said the Creator, *"They'll get there too."*

Well, the buffalo came and said, *"Give it to me; I'll bury it in the plains."*

The Creator said, *"No! They will cut into the skin of the earth, and they will find it even there."*

But then Grand Mother mole came. She has no physical eyes to see on the outside but has spiritual eyes and the capacity to see on the inside, and she said, *"Put it inside them; they'll never find it there."*

And the Creator said, *"It is done."*

The challenge of our life becomes how to find what the Creator buried within each of us. So, the journey of discovery begins!

Two
A Father's Daughter

"Well-behaved women rarely make history."
Eleanor Roosevelt

In the fairytale, *Rumpelstiltskin*, the miller says to the king that his daughter can spin straw into gold. Why would he make such a claim? To elevate himself in the king's eyes, to win favor….? At the same time, he has put his daughter in peril if she refuses or cannot perform. And please note that in the fairy tale the "daughter" has no name, no identity of her own.

Not wanting to disappoint her father and afraid of the king's punishment of death, the daughter never says, *"Oh, I can't do that."* She stays silent. When Rumpelstiltskin appears, she quickly accepts his offer to achieve that feat.

By not denying her father's words and not pushing back and telling the king she cannot spin straw into gold, she allows herself to be used by her birth father and the king for their own purposes. And every time she has to enlist Rumpelstiltskin's help to spin that straw into gold, she denies and surrenders more of herself. In time, once she awakens, she will be asking, *"Who am I really?"*

This fairy tale demonstrates what a *Father's Daughter* is willing to do to please the fathers in her life. The image that appears before me is a puppeteer pulling the strings that make a woman move this way and that way. And as he is pulling the strings of her life, she does not object because she desires to please and seeks approval and attention.

"

She never stops to wonder what is happening to her life, who she is becoming, and what she is losing. And that relationship with her birth father, she repeats with the other *fathers* in her life who attempt to pull the strings.

As the *Father's Daughter* matures, she attaches her destiny to the coattails of the men in her life and will do whatever is asked of her, never carving out her own life. She does so to acquire whatever gifts are offered, but in time the price may be too high.

A *Father's Daughter* covets her fathers' approval and does not seek to find their flaws. If flaws appear, she will ignore them. Surely, she did not attach herself to the wrong star!

A *Father's Daughter* is not seeking marriage and children. She is seeking a career, but at the same time she does not support gender equality. She believes in her ability to succeed because she is the exception. She is not like other women.

Margaret Thatcher, also known as the Iron Lady and the first woman Prime Minister of Great Britain, had many traits of a *Father's Daughter Archetype*. She revered her father and said of him, "I just owe almost everything to my father...."

Her steadfast refusal to place her weight behind the battle for equality is well documented. She had only one woman in her cabinet – Baroness Young, a close friend, who was considered an enemy of gay rights. When asked why no other women, Thatcher said she could not find any other competent women. A reminder that she was in office for eleven years, and no other woman did she appoint during that time.

Not all women are *Father's Daughters*, as the title of this book indicates. Not every woman is willing to march to the tune of the "fathers" in her life. Instead, a woman may choose to follow her own path. The backlash for following her own desires may be reprisals and denied opportunity, so a female of any age could believe that serving the fathers could be less painful. Maybe? Maybe not?

And we cannot forget the men who get tangled into the web of their father's desires—a man wanting to live the life he desires but is being prodded and poked to fulfill his father's dictates, and maybe his mother's expectations. The main question you must ask if you are in this situation is: Whose life do you want to live? One that has been dictated to you or one of your own choosing?

Starting at a very young age, my actions and words surpassed any conscious knowing and reasoning. But it is now very clear I was sending messages as young as eight to anyone who would listen that archetypally I was not a *"Father's Daughter."* And I came to realize that I had no desire to be, although throughout my life I had a close and loving relationship with my own father and supportive relationships with other men in my life.

Many of my stories that follow are to illustrate how a woman responded when encountering a puppeteering father—a woman who wanted to live her life as she desired.

Three
He's Just a Man

*"As a child, I felt myself to be alone, and I am still,
because I know things and must hint at things which
others apparently know nothing of, and for the most
part do not want to know."*

Carl Jung

At times I believed that someone was guiding me, and it was not someone in human form. I envisioned a hand on my shoulder, assuring me, saying "Yes, that way. I've got you." As a young child, I looked to the heavens. Maybe my father's mother was taking care of the daughter he loved.

I had the same vision in my teens. I dismissed the earlier notion of someone in heaven. Yet, I still believed something or someone was directing me. Later in life, I decided that because those feelings were so memorable, I had to pay attention. I needed to understand why, even at a young age, I was unyielding, stood steadfast, or declared a thought that came from nowhere, but yet somewhere.

Then I did not have the understanding and the words. But I did come to believe that this powerful force was within me, understood me, and supported me and my notions.

Two awakenings of my youth stand out vividly. At the time I thought they were so unlike me. I was not expressive or fussed or had loud emotional outbursts.

Although my parents ensured we were never hungry, we never had money for "extras." The only books in the house were my mother's Bible and our Church prayer books. Wanting to read something other than school books,

I read the Bible again and again. Certain passages spoke to me and comforted me. Others left me wondering and confused. But by reading what connected to me in a personal way, I found solace.

In time, I felt I had my own relationship with God through those words. The priest and his sermons never gave me that feeling. At that time in school, students were asked to pick a passage from the Bible for morning prayer. I did not have to ask Mom or just pick anything. I knew exactly what I wanted to read: *The Beatitudes.*

One of my earliest memories of my resolve took place in the church. Mom said that I had to go to confession. I was to tell the priest all my sins—what I had done wrong. For days, maybe longer, I struggled with what I was going to say. I was a kid of eight years old. I could not go in and say, "I have no sins. I did nothing wrong."

The church was telling me I had sinned, and I was bad. It did not matter that I had not and was not. I decided to tell the priest I swore, which I had not. I also said I pinched my sister, which I might have done. I had difficulty tolerating her outbursts because they upset my mother.

I walked into the confession booth and confessed my two sins, knowing I was lying about the one and not convinced correcting my sister's behavior, the only way I could, was a sin. I am still amazed that I went along with this dogma, but I do know that the response that followed was triggered by many things. One of them is that I was angry I was made to lie.

I walked into the pew, sat down beside my mother, and said, "Don't ever ask me to do that again." My voice was just above a whisper, but I am sure she heard my resolve.

A year later I refused confession again. When Mom asked why, these words flew out of my mouth. "He's just a man. I don't need him. I can talk to God on my own."

I was shocked by my words, but they rang true. If asked then, I could not have answered why. Most importantly, I could not explain why that decision seemed so right for me.

My mother tried a third time. This time she told me that if I did not take confession, the priest would not announce my donation at the end of the mass.

I thought that was such a mean thing to do—making a point of what people gave in the donation basket and what they did not. It forced people who wanted to receive accolades to give more money, and it would force those who could not give to give more or feel embarrassed. So, that was not going to motivate me. I never went to confession again.

We do not live in a society that prepares us to say "no" to any demand. And we do not live in a society that rewards and respects those who do not conform. But confession, at such a young age, seemed unreasonable to me, and I was willing to say so. Forgiving gave people permission to keep sinning, harming others. Is that why there is so much sinning throughout the world? You can confess, and it will be forgiven with little effort.

As a child, the consequences for refusing confession were negligible. The priest was threatening me, but for a threat to be effective, it must be something any one of us would wish to avoid. Not announcing my donation had no meaning to me.

I could have acquiesced, but I did not. I could have asked why, but I could not. My mother could have chastised me and called me stubborn, but she did not. I believe my mother had a knowing about me, and maybe because I was so steadfast, she left it alone. Unfortunately, I never asked her about that, so I am left to wonder.

At the ages of eight and nine and then ten, I was unaware as to why my reasoning was so clear. Why shouldn't I have direct access to God? We pray to him, so why can't we confess to him? Is he that frightening? And telling me that I had sinned and had to comply was cruel.

What I said was what I believed. I did not frame that thought, "he's just a man" prior to that time. It happened in a nanosecond. And I believed that rejecting confession was right—at least right for me.

Why was I so steadfast and had the courage to stick with my convictions? Oh, one could say I was stubborn. Why else would I, a little girl, be so adamant? But I was not stubborn or argumentative in general. I was a quiet child, and as such, I never argued with my parents.

My actions and words were not an indictment of God or any spiritual being. It was an indictment against an institution that wanted to control an aspect of my life. The confessional sends the message I must have sinned. I also heard that a man had the power to forgive my sins. I had declared he did not.

I was Unwilling to bow down to dogma that I could not embrace. I was UNwilling to accept the priest's dictates and any punishment. And it surprises me to realize now that I was not seeking the priest's approval or anyone's approval in the church nor was I worried about disapproval.

I did not recognize then that my behavior would extend beyond the priest and the church. As a young girl, I could not look beyond those moments, but later when I did, revelations were in abundance.

I take no credit or blame for my behavior. I was being true to myself. In time I came to identify the patterns of my behavior that flowed throughout my life.

That "knowing" clarified why I did not fear the repercussions of my actions and why I did not have any regret. Only then did I begin to embrace the essence that was me and the soulfulness that resided within.

Four
You Run Like a Girl!

The second incident of awakening came when I was ten years old. Neighborhood children were playing ball. I was not always comfortable doing so. I had spent the first eight years of my life with any illness that came along, but that day I joined in.

Dad, who was watching, rushed up to me after I ran the bases and said, "Elizabeth, you run like a girl."

"Dad, I AM a girl!" flew out of my mouth. That stopped him from saying anything else.

Once again that response amazed me. I had not hesitated, and I spoke with conviction. It was clear that Dad was saying I needed to run differently. What other way was there to run but like a boy? He was not saying I should run like a bunny or a dog.

Upon hearing those words, some young girls, wanting to please their fathers, might say, "So, teach me how to run?" That might imply I was willing to change the way I ran to please my father or was embarrassed by the way I ran. I was not. I was running like a girl, and I was a girl. I realize now that I believed that his loving me should not be dependent on how I ran.

It was fortunate Dad never talked to me again about my running. I guess what I said rang true or maybe a slap-in-the-face reminder, although not my intent, that I was a girl. That was not going to change, no matter how I ran. I was declaring that I was fine being a girl and unwilling to do something different. And if he wanted to teach me to run differently, he should have done so without saying, "Elizabeth, you run like a girl!"

Those watching my relationship with my father might say I was a *Father's Daughter*. We were bonded at my birth and beyond, were easy together, and discussed issues that spoke to both of us, although we did not always agree. We had a strong connection that nothing eroded during our fifty-three years together.

But most importantly, I was not like the young daughter in the tale Rumpelstiltskin — at least at most of the important junctures in my life. I was not willing to spin straw into gold to please my "fathers."

Yet, there were times later in my life when I did NOT follow the "knowing" that resided within. At those times I was not true to myself, and I acquiesced because I felt forced or desired to avoid conflict. And the times I acquiesced to the "you should" of society, I later became disappointed in myself and my choices. At all other times I was unwilling, and I came to realize I had declared that unwillingness at a young age in the church, and again when I declined the opportunity to learn how to run differently.

Eventually, I discovered that my responses were instinctual. That was why I was quick to speak. And I never wanted to be a boy or wanted to act like a boy. I never wished that I were born male, despite the disregard and the challenges women experience.

I also came to realize that I do not march to the beat of everyone else's drum, but I did want to understand my choices and actions throughout my life.

Some men and women might not applaud or even approve of my journey — the times I followed my own "knowing" and did not give into the forces around me. But then I am not writing this book for approval. Yes, approval could be affirmation, but my journey has taught me that approval should not be a strong enough force to sacrifice my very being and speak only about what is popular or what sells.

Looking back on my childhood and adolescence has been revealing. It was a time before society tried to put its big hand over my mouth, shoved me into a corner, and told me "Go along to get along," and so on.

It may be helpful for you to reflect on a happening in your life when you were UNwilling to conform. Were you punished or praised?

Also, reflect on a time when you did conform. Did you garner approval? Was the approval everlasting, or did you have to conform repeatedly?

Did you regret acquiescing?

And if you do regret those times, what would you do now in a similar situation?

Five

I Want to Date

"…her wings are cut and then she is blamed for not knowing how to fly."
Simone de Beauvoir

Mr. Collins, the minister who proposed to Elizabeth in *Pride and Prejudice*, could not believe she said "no" to his marriage proposal. Because of his station in life and her lack of prospects, surely, she would say yes. When she said no, he believed she was toying with him. Why wouldn't she want to marry?

Then Darcy could not believe Elizabeth would say no to his marriage proposal and demanded an explanation. Why were both men surprised? Because surely Elizabeth would want to marry and any man would do.

In the film, *The Help*, Skeeter's mother says to her, "Eugenia, your eggs are dying," insisting that her daughter had to date, get married, and have children. She yells out, "My obituary will read, 'Charlotte Phelan dead. Daughter unmarried.'"

Skeeter shouts, "Maybe I won't marry," horrifying her mother.

Although boyfriends were present in my young life, I have come to realize that most of the time I was swept away by the tide of expectations. Society said that I should desire a boyfriend, so I went along until I didn't. I did not question the wisdom of such a decision, but I realized in time that I wasn't enthusiastic.

That I accepted a boy's attention because I had to do what was expected had not occurred to me then. But on reflection, it was definitely true. Boys expressed an interest, and I did what young girls were supposed to do—agree, although I am sure I was not always grateful.

Early on, children and teenagers are encouraged to have friends. There are smiles all around if they have a special someone. The message is clear: The attention and acceptance of others makes you special; you are worthy. If you are alone, what is wrong with you? Why don't you have a friend or a date for the dance? Boys receive the same message, which doesn't make dating life easier for them either.

I was seventeen and still had not dated. Dad thought I was too young, and all boys were *jerks*. And my mother had not pushed me into dating, although she always ensured I had nice clothes and dresses for special occasion dances.

A few months into my senior year of high school, Walt started walking me to my classes. We met at school events, but we never went on a date. Then Walt asked me to go to the Christmas dance. I mentioned the dance to Mom.

"You'll have to ask your dad."

I guess they both thought he had the last word. That evening, I said, "Dad, a boy has asked me to the Christmas dance, and I want to go!" He did not argue, just grunted.

Announcing I WANTED to date was a critical juncture in my life. I was starting to bend to the expectations of society. I started to believe that I must be interested in boys and date, especially during the era in which I grew up. It is also true for many women today, probably more so than some would want to believe.

Later in life I became secure in my belief that "he" did not have the right to choose and insist, that I did not have to say yes because he asked, and that acquiescing should not be on my to-do list. No, no, no!

Six
Perry Mason and Me

*"Sometimes people don't want to hear the truth
because they don't want their illusions destroyed."*
Friedrich Nietzsche

As a young girl, I watched the television series, *Perry Mason*. Not because I thought Perry was attractive or I wanted to marry someone like him. I wanted to be him. I wanted to be an attorney, but my acquired mindset reared its ugly head, and said to me, "Elizabeth, you have no father or uncle who is an attorney, you are a girl, and your family has no money."

My mind had been co-opted by the forces around me. Yet, I was unaware of that or the impact. That programming was subtle, layer after layer. And although I had a flicker of ambition, I had allowed the collective to limit my expectations and put an end to that dream at a young age.

There are probably women today who still have similar thoughts. They put roadblocks in their way. There are also women who believe they must be an attorney or....

During my senior year my mother said, "Elizabeth, you should go to college. You would make a great English teacher." My mother, who always championed my efforts, had spoken.

A university had opened a satellite campus about ten miles away from our home. I could go there for two years and live at home. Then I would transfer to the main campus.

I grew up in a small coal mining patch in western Pennsylvania. Neither of my parents had a high school degree. Neither of them knew what I had to do to enroll in college. They had not guided or encouraged me in that direction until Mom spoke out. Until that time, a high school degree was sufficient, and I went along with those expectations.

Even though I had excellent grades and was on the honor roll, the guidance counselor had not encouraged me. I had not taken the college boards or two of the math courses for college. The mountain seemed too high to climb in my senior year. And maybe, just maybe I was afraid to dive into unknown waters. And maybe, just maybe those voices about being a "have not" were still ringing in my ears. So, I dismissed the idea of attending a university.

I limited myself by what I did not know, what I did not have, and lack of guidance. I had not realized that I had gifts that would serve me if I were willing to leap. Also, an uncle told my father that I should be a secretary as his daughter had done. Fortunately, his daughter did go to a business school, so Dad also went along with that idea.

It was fortunate that in the interim, the business school had become a junior college. I told my father I wanted to attend for two years to obtain an Associate's degree. I was insistent on the two years, although I had no idea why I would need that degree. I just knew that was what I should do. Dad agreed.

Unconsciously, I was starting to chart a course I had never imagined. I was breaking away from the die I had cast by looking at my limitations. Fortunately, through the years, I learned that it is not where you begin. It is the roads you travel and how true you are to yourself on that journey.

While looking for a job after graduating, my father wanted me to work nearby, in the town where he worked. He could give me a ride to work every morning and bring me back in the evening. Hmmm…. I wanted to work twenty-five miles away in the city where I had gone to college for eighteen months. Disappointed by my decision, my father pouted for a while, but I held my ground. He broke the ice a week later.

We never spoke of it again. For over four years, he drove me to the bus every morning and picked me up each night, sometimes waiting up to an hour if the bus were late. He did this without complaint. He never once asked me to quit that job and take another nearby. The message was clear. I wanted to be in charge of my life, and he had decided to stay silent.

At the same time, I was unaware that focusing on my limitations, with a good dose of confusion and doubt, had dimmed my ambition and the expectations I had of myself. I bent to the voices around me. I lost the dream of being an attorney because society had sent me the message that I was a "have not," and I believed I was to stay that way.

Yet, there were times when my spirit burst forth, and my soul was soothed by the work I was doing. And yes, at times, I did break the chains that bound me, but not always. My life became a series of circuitous paths. But maybe those paths gave me gifts that I would not have received otherwise.

Seven
Judge Me Not

"If you have yet to be called an incorrigible, defiant woman, don't worry, there is still time."
Clarissa Pinkola Estés

My first job after graduating was at a bank. It was an entry-level job in the administrative pool. My one friend worked for the company in the next building, so every week we had lunch. Her job seemed ideal; while mine seemed lacking.

The woman in charge of the administrative pool, Miss B, was an older woman. Her attitude towards me was surly. Her face puckered, and her words sharp. When I asked a question, she was dismissive. I was never sent out as a replacement in another department or for an interview so I could get a permanent position. But she did send every one of my colleagues.

Reflecting on that time, maybe she regarded my reserved demeanor and shyness as backwardness. Maybe I signaled to her that I was weak and an easy target. Someone she could torment who would not fight back. I did not speak out or draw attention to myself, displaying any confidence. But then there wasn't anything to grab my attention or enthusiasm.

Psychologist Carl Jung believed that an adolescent on the way to adulthood needs a "terrible mother" or "terrible father" to test one's mettle, and Miss B was mine. I wanted to prove to her that I was not as clueless as she thought. But by not sending me out as a substitute when someone was on vacation, I had no opportunity to do so.

I did not need Miss B to "like" me, and I did not need to like her, but I believed there was no reason for her to be irascible, with a sharp edge to her voice. I felt like Cinderella—a suffering servant. I never remember being angry with her, but I was disappointed in her disregard for me. Not because she did not support me, but because she was so outwardly hostile to someone she did not know. Being committed to my decision, I just had to wait for the day I could get out.

One day I was asked to replace someone in the International Department for a week. I did well and made a good impression by solving a difficult situation. When I returned, Miss B said, "Well, at least you didn't embarrass yourself."

A few weeks later Miss B sent me to interview for a permanent job in Trust, Wills, and Estates. She said, "I don't think he will want you. Mr. M has turned down everyone I have sent him." I guess she needed to get in one more shot at me.

There was no one else left to send, so I was it. Much to my surprise, I was verbal and comfortable during my interview. I had something to say and said it, and to Miss B's surprise, he hired me.

I was on my way to what was unclear. But life evolves for most of us without fulfilling our expectations. And if you do have them, disappointment could be hanging on every tree branch.

Eight

Possessive Before an ING

"This has always been a man's world, and none of the reasons that have been offered in explanation have seemed adequate."

Simone de Beauvoir

Mr. M was friendly and easy to work for most of the time. He walked around with his chest puffed out literally and had learned the art of "shmoozing," but I never observed wisdom, passion, conviction, and tenacity. He did the perfunctory, and often he would remind people that he graduated from Princeton and name drop.

One day I presented him a letter for his signature, which he returned to me with a correction in heavy ink. He wanted me to change the word, "your," to "you." I said, "Mr. M, the correct word is YOUR." He put his hand to his head as he often did when he was confused. I went on, "The possessive case is used before ING in this case. You—the nominative case is incorrect."

Of course, I am sure I confused him more. I went into my drawer and pulled out my manual, which I knew backward and forward. I quietly showed Mr. M the rule. He relented.

I did what I believed was my job. Why allow something to be wrong? Also, I did not expect him to make such a fuss. But this incident, in its small way, activated and revealed my courage because I did not fear any fallout.

To clear my head, I took a walk. Mr. M came to me when I returned to my desk and said, "I hired you to do the job. I should have trusted you to do it. It won't happen again." Then I knew he was starting to see me as more competent than he first thought.

In time, Mr. M started to give me opportunities that would serve me throughout my life, although he did so unknowingly. There was a kind, elderly lady, Miss S, who called him now and then to chat about her estate. She needed someone to hold her hand, someone to talk with. He made me call her because he did not have the patience or kindness. And he got paid the big bucks!

One day Miss S stopped by the office. He sent me out to meet her. There was no such thing as coaching, and if there were, he would not have done it anyway. "Just go talk with her," he said. Not helpful!

Miss S and I had a nice chat, and from that day forward, she would stop by and always asked to see me. She had found someone who listened, gave her time and attention, and addressed her concerns about her estate, which was all she wanted. He acted as though she wanted one of his limbs or an organ.

This opportunity gave me confidence and experience to work with other clients, as well as hone my communication skills. Mr. M thought he was helping himself, getting out of something he did not want to do, but he was helping me. Yet, I knew that helping me did not interest him.

In time Mr. M extended my duties. I had learned and understood the language of Wills and Trusts, often finding errors in the drafts he did or mentioning items that were left out. So, he started asking me to call the attorneys and go through those documents and probe and ask questions when needed. He believed he had bigger fish to fry. For me, the fish were just the right size.

One of his responsibilities was meeting and orienting the trainees who rotated throughout different areas of the bank. I always greeted them and checked in on them at times. Often, he found me in the conference room, explaining this, that, and the other. I knew Mr. M thought this responsibility was beneath him, and he was ignoring them. In time this also became my responsibility. That assignment gave me the opportunity to learn how to communicate in a way that kept an audience's attention—a new experience for me.

Again, he helped me unknowingly. These tasks and assignments also gave me badges of courage and helped me discover my value. It helped me prove myself to me.

And this all happened because of ING. Think of instances in your life when you wish you had spoken. Were you afraid of the repercussions? Have you not spoken and regretted it afterward?

Have you spoken up, believing the walls of Jericho would come down; yet, the walls still stood? Often what we imagine may be an insignificant blip on the screen.

I believe when Mr. M hired me, he saw ability and promise. His biases made him think that my position and not having a bachelor's degree was a measure of my intellect, which had limited his expectations of me. A credential is just that—a credential! It does not mean anything other than a degree was granted.

However, there is the assumption that degrees signify a person has abilities and expertise for that particular job. Maybe? Maybe not?

Nine
Bow? You Must be Kidding!

"A woman is like a tea bag. You never know how strong she is until she gets into hot water."
Eleanor Roosevelt

Christmas was soon approaching, and the president of the bank was to walk through our department to wish us a Merry Christmas. Mr. M called me to his desk and said that when the president walked by, he wanted me to stand up and bow. To this day, I would have loved to see the expression on my face.

"You want me to do what?"

"I want you to bow."

I was shocked. "Bow?" He nodded. I took a deep breath, and the words flowed. "I don't think so. I believe in treating everyone the same, from the janitor to the president. Everyone deserves the same respect. I don't bow to anyone."

I returned to my desk. Of course, I did not stand up and bow when the president walked through. I just sat at my desk, smiled, and wished him a Merry Christmas, as did all the other administrative assistants.

I surprised myself that I spoke up. I was surprised that I had the opportunity to do the work my boss was supposed to be doing and meeting some of the more influential people in the city. I was doing what my parents and I had never expected and definitely could not have imagined. I did not know I could, but my Mom was fond of saying, "Elizabeth! Can't couldn't do anything because can't didn't try!" I tried.

I did what I was supposed to do after I graduated—got a job, but that was where my obedience ended. I insisted on getting an Associate's degree and did not take the job five miles away from our home, as I was being encouraged to do by Dad. And although Dad wanted the best for me, he did not know what was best for me. And I was not going to follow his dictates because he was my father.

In time I had nice clothes, and even though I had the money to buy a car, I still took the bus for those many miles every day. On the bus I met Paul who was a husband and a young father. He always saw me with a book—still a bookworm, as I had been dubbed at an early age. We would chat about this and that and the other.

One day he said to me, "You should go back to college and get a bachelor's degree." He said this again and again. For how long I do not remember. In time I heard his words. I was no longer challenged in the job and knew there were no career paths I wished to take or could take without a bachelor's degree.

Finally, I made an appointment to speak with the admissions people at a nearby university. When I walked into my first university class, I remembered my mother's words, "Elizabeth, there isn't anything you can't do." I sometimes think I survived on those words, plus a wing and a prayer, as Mom would say. How serendipitous!

I guess I could look back on that time at the bank as wasted, especially wasting my potential. I could have regretted that I did not attend a four-year college directly from high school, especially since I received a Bachelor's degree and then a Master's degree and also a Ph.D. Instead, I chose to look at the opportunities I had because Mr. M was an absent boss.

Years later I saw Paul at a local restaurant. I was there celebrating. I had just defended my dissertation and would receive a doctorate. I went over to him and re-introduced myself, reminding him of that time—about fifteen years before—when he encouraged me to go back to college.

I said, "Not only did I go back to college. I am getting my doctorate. I want to thank you for believing in me."

He was delighted to hear the news. We spoke as we had done years ago—about this and that and the other.

I had not appreciated my mother's insight, certainly not at the time. I also did not fight for the opportunity to go to college in my senior year. Even though my mother encouraged me, I limited my possibilities by my socio-economic situation, shyness, reserved demeanor, and messages from the collective.

We do not make our journey alone. I will always be grateful for my father who stepped back and gave me a chance to display my courage; my mother who believed in me and thought there wasn't anything I could not do if I tried; Mr. M who unknowingly helped me get my wings; Paul, whose inspiration and nudge, gave me the courage to take flight.

Look around, be an inspiration, be a nudge for someone today.

Ten
A Daring Leap

*"The most common way people give up their power
is by thinking they don't have any."*
Alice Walker

I started my degree work by taking classes at night. When I had enough money saved to pay to be a full-time student, I resigned my position at the bank. I also wanted to leave my parents' home and move into an apartment so I would not have to travel by bus.

When I announced my decision, my father said he would pay my tuition, but he shouted he would not pay for an apartment. His declaration about the apartment did not deter me. I was so excited that I would have my own place near the university. No waiting for a bus every day, at least an hour-long ride each way, and a place to return to in between classes. I was in heaven.

I came home a few weeks later to visit my parents. Dad did not speak to me the entire weekend. His silence did not have the desired effect. I was not changing my mind. A few weeks later my mother asked if I were coming home. "No," I replied. "Why come home? Dad isn't speaking to me, and you and I can talk on the phone."

The next day Mom called and asked for directions to my apartment. My parents were coming to visit. Hmmm. What a surprise! My father never drove near the city, let alone into it. To him, it was like a foreign land.

When they arrived, Dad was laden with bags of groceries. He put them on the counter and started pointing out the meat and veggies they had brought. No words to mend the fences. Food did the talking for him, and I understood the language.

I felt blessed by my father's love. Yet, I did not covet his favor. For example, we would discuss politics, and we did not always agree. One time during a heated discussion, he said to me, "I'm older than you. I know about these things."

I said, "Dad, you will always be older than me, so that means you will always be right? I don't think so!"

I surprised him once again. Yes, it would be nice to know that he thought well of me, but Dad was not one to praise, so it was a good thing I did not seek his approval in words. He was not dogmatic, so I also never felt the need to agree with him or be indoctrinated with his way of thinking. My every move was not based on whether he approved or disapproved. I did what I did because I felt compelled to do it. My thoughts and my words were mine alone and not handed to me on a tablet by my birth father, or any other fathers.

Now, it was always evident that I returned my father's love and respected him, but he was not in charge of me and my life. And since he was not a patriarchal father, who thought he could and should control my life, he knew when to back away. But loving me did not stop him from thinking of me as a woman who did not, could not, know her own mind. That was a lesson I decided that he needed to continue to unlearn.

Eleven
The Bell Curve

"An understanding heart is everything in a teacher, and cannot be esteemed highly enough. One looks back with appreciation to the brilliant teachers, but with gratitude to those who touched our human feeling. The curriculum is so much necessary raw material, but warmth is the vital element for the growing plant and for the soul of the child."

Carl Jung

Betty Friedan, a feminist writer and activist, said, *"It is easier to live through someone else than to complete yourself. The freedom to lead and plan your own life is frightening if you have never faced it before. It is frightening when a woman finally realizes that there is no answer to the question 'who am I' except the voice inside herself."*

So, I became a high school teacher. My first teaching job was uneventful, and I left after two years to have a shorter commute. My second teaching job was near where I grew up. I was hired even though I was not a graduate of that school system.

Not only was I not one of them, I had a different teaching style. I had been influenced by a professor who advocated the open classroom concept. I was pragmatic enough to know I could not use that methodology, but I did embrace the idea that students should move at their own pace and that the classroom should be alive with possibilities, inspiration, and creativity.

Not every student came to my classroom with the same educational background and experiences, so they should not be subjected to a lock-step process or expected to learn the same way. That required me to use a variety of teaching strategies and interact with them one-on-one.

As a new teacher, I was assigned courses that no other teacher wanted to teach. Those classes included students struggling to survive in a school system that had declared them as second and third best. Many had been beaten down, limiting their expectations, and they had acquired the mindset that they could not achieve or only had to do the minimum.

For my economics class, there was a ten-year-old textbook, so I improvised and prepared materials and activities to engage my students. I used projects and tests to evaluate them. I told them that they were not allowed to get below a C on a test. I graded on percentages, so a C was 78 percent or better. If they got below a C, they had to meet with me, do some additional work, and take a second test that was more difficult. Yes, it would be more work for me, but I was betting on them.

By having that standard, I was telling my students that I believed they had the ability to get a C or better. I was also taking responsibility if they got below a C, and I would put in extra time as well. On the first test, two students got a D, but from then on, not one student got a D or F. I would pay for that in time.

Then one of my female students came to me and told me she was pregnant and was leaving school. She was a lovely young girl of fifteen and an excellent student. Soon she would have a child to raise, and most likely she would not return to graduate from high school. And that would limit her opportunities to get a job or have a career or have enough money to raise her child.

I asked her about the father, who was also her age. He had abandoned her. Not his problem! The boy would walk away with no responsibility, so writing a check had to be in his future. I then suggested that she get child support from him.

Of course, he was too young to have a job and pay child support, so his parents would have to write the check until he was of age. I connected her and her parents with an attorney, who did get her child support.

Not soon after another student came to me. It was a case of incest. I connected her with an attorney and the right authorities, and they got her out of the house.

Then, one day, the principal called me to his office. His first comment was, "Where are the Ds and Fs? Why are the students getting such good grades?"

First, I said that some of the students were very bright, and the course that the guidance counselor had scheduled was too easy. They should be taking the higher-level course. I also told him about my rule—no Ds or Fs.

"What about the Bell Curve? You have to give as many A grades as F grades, B grades as D grades; the majority get Cs."

I am sure I was glaring at him as I said, "First, I don't give grades. They earn them. Second, the Bell Curve is the worst travesty perpetrated on students. Why do there have to be bad grades? If I teach and they learn, why should they be penalized?"

Mr. P did not have an answer to that question, so then he switched to my relationship with my students, faulting me for helping two young girls who had sought me out.

"You should have sent them to the guidance counselors."

"They know there are counselors. If they trusted them, they would have gone there. They didn't. If I had turned them away, and they did not go to a counselor, then those two girls probably would not have gotten the help they needed.

"A teacher is more than a disseminator of information. If you take away my caring, then why should I be in teaching? I'm not a robot and that is what you are asking me to be."

I believe the lightbulb lit, and he realized in no way was I going to be remorseful or agree that I had done something wrong. He also knew that I had committed no crime. I was to conform to rules that existed in his mind and the minds of others. Those were rules that did not serve the welfare of students.

The matters were dropped. No repercussions. Later that year, when I heard that a teacher was leaving, I went to that principal and asked for a change in one of my assignments. He did not hesitate.

My thoughts and actions were not preplanned. I had no idea that I had done something that warranted being called to the principal's office. I was not going to allow someone to dictate rules and standards that did not yield anything beneficial. I refused to follow guidelines that would not inspire or motivate my students and which put limitations on them.

What was uppermost in my mind was that students were in my care, and I did not become an educator to allow them to fail.

This incident solidified to me my philosophy about teaching. I was not going to support a system that was designed to ensure the minority would rise to the top, while the majority languished. And they were languishing because they were not expected to succeed. That was what the Bell Curve was dictating.

The Bell Curve is an iniquitous system designed to keep the majority of the students from receiving a higher grade, even if they are performing at a high level. So, why use this grading system? Maybe because there are those who want to preserve the social and economic class systems and do not embrace the ideal of opportunity for all.

Grading systems are designed to limit the competition for the few. They are designed to keep the majority out of the game. They are designed so those students with the lower grades would have no other choices but to labor.

There are teachers who brag about giving low grades, believing it is a testimony to how difficult their course is. Maybe it is a testimony to their arrogance and their inability to make information relatable and accessible to their students.

This system was also adopted in the workplace in the 1980s and 1999s. The major proponent of the Bell Curve was the former CEO of General Electric, Jack Welch. In that system the manager identified top performers at 20 percent, low performers at 10 percent, and average performers at 70 percent.

What does this say about management? What did it say about the methods used to hire employees if 70 percent are identified as "average" performers? And what about the failure of managers to support and guide employees?

Just like the Bell Curve used in the schools, it is expedient, and the manager has to do little if anything. And the majority of employees are left to languish without support and guidance. Many companies have abandoned this system, but again it must be asked why was it ever used in the first place? My first thought is money—how it was distributed—and it limited the majority's opportunities.

Do you agree with Betty Friedan that it is easier to live through someone else than to lead your own life? Do you also agree that by living through someone else and adhering to the demands of others, you let go of having your own life? Your life is dictated to you because of someone else's beliefs or dogma.

I appreciate that standing up for what you believe is frightening, especially if the punishments for doing so are riddled with too many negatives or bravery is lacking, or both. But sometimes you have to dive in.

I could not bow down to rules that were designed to elevate the few and diminish the majority, and I take no credit or blame for my actions. It was what I had to do, and only by reflecting and revealing what is buried within, would I figure out why.

Twelve
Three Minutes Late!

"To be ourselves causes us to be exiled by many others, and yet to comply with what others want causes us to be exiled from ourselves."
Clarissa Pinkola Estés

I left the second high school and took a position in my former high school. After four years of teaching in this school, I became department chairperson. I was the youngest teacher in a department of eleven teachers, and I had the least seniority. That had its challenges.

My workday started at 7:30 a.m. As department chair, I had no homeroom assignment so my teaching day began at 9:30. I am not a morning person and found myself racing into the parking lot, most days getting there just before 7:30. One day I arrived at 7:33 a.m. The principal was outside, saw my late arrival, and made a note.

Later that day a note requesting that I see him was in my mailbox. I walked to his office and kept telling myself that I would be silent, nod, and not say a word. When he spoke, I got amnesia. Maybe at that moment, it was the way he said it. But on reflection, I believe that it was for many reasons.

"So," I said, "If I come in on time and leave on time, I'm a good teacher and will not be chastised by you? Is that how you gauge good teachers? I chair a department of eleven teachers, teach five classes, with three different preps, and chair two clubs. That includes the yearbook, so I stay four days a week until five or six o'clock."

Mr. C looked at me and started mumbling. "Well, yes, and if you would need to leave early for a doctor's appointment, I would make sure your classes are covered." Dah! He did not answer the question: What made a good teacher. And what did covering my class for a doctor's appointment have to do with what I said?

"But I wouldn't make an appointment when I'm to be teaching. I make my doctor's appointment after school hours. I don't want someone doing my job. I can do that."

I then walked out, amazed at what I had said and that I wasn't afraid to say it. Again, I had no desire to kowtow to him for favor or apologize. I also did not curry his good opinion because it would not be based on anything substantive, any knowledge of me as a teacher.

In addition, his chastisement was unwarranted. Three minutes! He had to be kidding! My role as an educator did not begin and end because of the time on the clock. It was folly for him to focus on three minutes rather than how well a teacher taught and what contributions a teacher made to the students, the school, and the community.

What was he going to do? Send me to detention for a week? But most importantly, why was it so important to him? The answer to me was clear. He lacked any willingness or ability to work with teachers in any substantive way. But he had to do something.

As a principal, he saw his role as a disciplinarian, and I guess that included teachers. He was to keep order and punish. It was well known that he advanced to the position of principal because he was large in stature. The School Board and upper administration chose male principals at both the middle school and high school who had an imposing manner. They thought, with their loud voices and presence, they would be able to handle the problem students.

There are several serious problems with that thinking. Most of the students were not problem students. Why was that more important than putting someone in that position who could work with teachers to create a more inspiring learning environment and interact and show interest in the students?

Mr. C had not become a teacher to teach. He had become a teacher as a means to coach and then to get an administrative position. There is nothing wrong with aspirations, but interacting with teachers is a critical skill to focus on when supervising teachers and that is what he should have been doing. To do that, you have to be a competent teacher first.

A few months later, Mr. C was to observe me teach a class. During my review meeting, he said, "Well, you don't stand behind the desk. You move around a lot."

Dah!!! "Well," I chuckled, "It's hard to hit a moving target."

He scowled because he had nowhere to go with that comment. I gave no reason because he did not ask me why I moved around. Maybe he did not care, or if I did explain, he would not understand.

I always considered the desk a divide between teacher and student. I walked around and got up close when they responded to a question or asked a question. I looked at their work, stopped and asked questions, checked to ensure they were not having difficulty. I wanted them to know that I was approachable, and they could talk with me.

These techniques were my ways to acknowledge them, signify their success and questions were important to me, and I was listening. It was a way of saying to them that I was vested in their learning. I was not standing behind a desk, wondering if they understood.

The principal had no other comments. I had to sign that I read the evaluation, which consisted of no narrative, and then left. He could not give me constructive feedback because he did not understand educating at its deepest level, at any level.

He could have asked other questions about the issues I faced, how I thought students were doing, did I need anything. But instead. there was silence. Doing the perfunctory minimum. Fill out the paperwork and move on.

My response to both these encounters again surprised me. The words just came out. As I write and reflect about these situations, I realize that I could speak out because I saw myself equal to the principal. His position held no meaning because he did not function in any way that was meaningful. This principal's inability to function in his position and his "Mickey Mouse" behavior compelled me to reject his chastisement and authority.

I was committed to my students. I wanted them to succeed in a school system that did not always plan for their success. I wanted them to live a productive life, and I wanted them to know they were capable and worthy. And there was also something within me that was shouting, "Don't hold back, Elizabeth! Stand up for what is right! Don't be bullied! You're here to make a difference!"

Estés' quote at the beginning of this chapter states that you have to decide whether to be exiled by others or exiled from yourself. Yes, my behavior caused me to be exiled from those who did only the minimum, did not embrace my values, or thought I was wrong-headed.

Maybe you can relate to the choice of speaking out for something you believe in. Maybe you have been exiled. Did you acquiesce or are you still pushing back?

Thirteen
The Drama Triangle

"And the day came when the risk to remain tight in the bud was more painful than the risk it took to blossom."

Anais Nin

Circumstances evolved, and I started to attend graduate school during the evenings to get my doctorate. Charlie, a professor who taught the last course I was required to take, asked me if he could be my dissertation advisor. He also offered me a consultancy fellowship, so I took a sabbatical. He then brought me a dissertation topic that captured my enthusiasm and imagination.

Charlie was a gift during that difficult year of writing my dissertation. He, Joe, another professor, and I would go out to different organizations to consult with the administration. We soon became known as the *Three Musketeers.*

One day at a meeting of all male administrators, the topic was leadership. As a doctoral candidate and a fellow, I was quiet and listened. The minute the meeting was over, Joe, a bear of a man, raced up to me and put his finger in my face. "You knew more about that topic than anyone at the table. Why didn't you speak up? Now, next time, speak up!"

I was shocked at first, but he had given me a gift. At our next consulting session, Charlie gave me a group of administrators to facilitate. I remembered Joe's words, so I facilitated, being present in word and deed. A break was called, and my group did not move. I was addressing an issue, and all were engaged, so I did not interrupt.

When I called a break, Joe came up to me (he watched over me) and said, "What the heck were you talking to them about? They never took their eyes off you."

"Well, I was telling off-color jokes to keep them interested," and I chuckled. I had heard his words and acted.

Charlie then decided to involve me in another group discussion where I was the main player. I walked into a room with a group of superintendents from local school districts and was presented a problem. I was to explain how I would handle a dispute between two employees.

The scenario was what I later named the "drama triangle." A (an employee) comes to C (management) tattling about B (another employee.) Person A portrays himself as a victim, the good employee, the one in the right, and expects Person C to take his side, be the rescuer, and fault Person B—the bad person.

The issue had not been expressed that way, but that is how I viewed it. It is how children often deal with their issues. Go to Mommy, Grandpa, teacher, and tell tales, wishing for someone else to rescue them from whoever they claimed was BAD. Isn't that what is happening on the world stage—people not accepting responsibility for their choices, scapegoating someone else, and expecting to be rescued?

I dealt with the situation believing that just because someone tattles on another does not make him a "good" person and the other person "bad." My solution consisted of fact-finding before taking action, speaking to each employee, asking probing questions, and not just jumping in and believing the first person.

I also recommended that after a session with each, they speak to each other to resolve the issues. Both parties had created the problem; they were the best to resolve it, if possible. If they rejected that suggestion or there was too much anger from one side or both parties, the administrator would meet with them and facilitate their discussion.

One of the administrators, John, argued that my solution was wrong and not expedient. "A" was in the right, and "B" was bad and in the wrong. He got loud and assaulted me with a bombastic and confrontational tone of voice.

I was calm and continued to state my reasons, without mincing words, pointing out that taking one side against another without fact-finding can create future problems. One reason for not taking sides is that once other staff members learn that if they get to the boss first, they will always be the person in the right and wronged by Person B.

One of the superintendents who I had consulted with was present and tried to support me. After getting pushed back several times by John, he decided not to say more. Maybe he realized he was not going to yield me anything different. Or maybe because he would have to interact with John in the future. Or there was nothing that would change John's mind. Whatever the reason, I was on my own.

I was upset by the tone of the encounter. It was heightened because John decided to tell me that the same scenario had been presented to another doctoral student prior to me. John revealed that he had a similar issue and had solved it the way my colleague had. Two against one. Isn't the majority always right? Not in my world. Not in our world. Evidence is everywhere.

It was then I realized that my arguing a different position made him look bad in front of the others. That was not my intention. I had no way of knowing the reason behind his adamant stance until that moment. And his only comment against my idea was that it was time-consuming. *"Just act—be a bull in a china shop,"* seemed to be his motto.

When I walked into the luncheon after the event, a professor came up to me, smiled, found me a chair, touched my arm, and said, "You have some b...." I knew because of who he was that it was a compliment. But he was wrong. By standing up to John, he considered me to be masculine. My response was not about masculinity because it is foolish to believe that courage, logic, and reasoning are only attributes exhibited by men. I was being true to myself and my philosophy about how to resolve conflict, but he did not understand that. To some, women who speak out and stand firm either have a male body part, or we are just nasty, horrible women.

Charlie, who was very supportive of me, apologized for what happened. He had put me in that situation, never imagining how John would act. For me, that was a given. I had seen John with his staff. He was a bully, pompous, verbose, righteous but not always right. My guess is he had probably gotten away with being a bully in the past. In front of a room full of his colleagues, he came up against someone who could not be bullied. Again, I did not have to be right, but I was entitled to a different opinion.

He was using the forum to prove himself right, puffing himself up. The ego will trip a person up every time. In retrospect, he revealed a lot to his colleagues, embarrassing himself more than his effort to embarrass me or prove me wrong, although he was incapable of realizing that.

When I was to defend my dissertation, Joe had a heart attack a few days before, and I went to see him in the hospital. He would not be there for my defense, and he knew I was concerned. "Look, you know that topic better than anyone at the table. Own it! You'll be fine!"

It warms my heart to remember both Charlie and Joe and how they embraced me into their twosome. I never experienced their need to be right. They were never righteous. They had inquiring minds and did not rush to judgment or a finality. They supported and inspired me, championed my efforts, and saw me as capable. I never felt less than them. What wonderful gifts they gave me, for which I am forever grateful.

In my novel, *Josephine: A Woman of Indomitable Spirit*, Josephine states:

"Growing up Gran had given me a daily dose of obedience and sweetness, cautioning me to hold my tongue. Although quiet, not one to speak out just to talk, I still don't want to say I agree when I don't. I don't want to keep my mouth shut because that's what a woman should do. I will not! I cannot! I choose not to!

"Maybe that's why Joseph and I butt heads now and then. Joseph wants me to silence my thoughts. But I'm not going to stay silent and walk away. He wants me to lose myself in him, believe and think as he does, want what he wants."

Like many women, Gran told Josephine to ensure harmony, she was to go along, but Josephine did not want to lose her voice. She did not desire to stay silent and walk away, losing herself in her husband, thinking and acting as he wished. She wanted to be free from the chains that attempted to bind her, free from the dictates of the father in her life in the guise of her husband, and I was stating by my words and actions so did I.

Josephine's story took place in the late 1800s, but aren't there women today who are pushed and pulled, expected to be demure, quiet, defer to the man, and not disagree? No, no, no!

Fourteen
You Know What's Wrong With You Women!

"Do not stop thinking of life as an adventure. You have no security unless you can live bravely, excitingly, imaginatively; unless you can choose a challenge instead of competence."

Eleanor Roosevelt

After fourteen years of teaching, including six years as department chair, and soon to have a doctorate degree, I desired an administrative post. My interest was in curriculum and instruction, giving me an opportunity to support and guide teachers throughout the school district.

The position of assistant director of curriculum and instruction became available in the district where I was teaching. I could step into that position after I received my doctorate. I would be the only administrator in the school district with that degree. As assistant director, I could influence needed instructional and curriculum changes.

Many principals did not counsel and coach teachers or could do so. It could benefit more students if I had a position to support and inspire teachers. I could be a sounding board, and I wanted new challenges.

In addition to writing my dissertation and working as a fellow during the year of my sabbatical, I had been speaking for a textbook publishing company at teacher conferences and universities on how to be a more effective educator.

I met with the current assistant director about applying for the position. He was influential in my last appointment and would be the new director. During our discussion, he seemed delighted with my decision and encouraged me.

A few days later I was in a restaurant having lunch with another doctoral student. The current curriculum director, who would move to superintendent, came up to me and said without a greeting, "Do you know what's wrong with you women? You want to move too quickly. Do you know how long it took me to get the position you want? I was an assistant principal and a principal first."

I did not blink. "How long did you teach?"

"Two years." Oh my! He barely got his feet wet.

"I've spent fourteen years teaching and six as a department chair, focusing on curriculum and instruction. I have a doctorate and extensive studies in curriculum. I have been speaking for a large publishing company on effective teaching at conferences and universities.

"What I have done is more relevant to this position than being assistant principal and principal. I did NOT spend my time checking potties and disciplining students. I had time to perfect my teaching and write curriculum."

Whew! That felt good. He was shocked and walked away. Again, I had no intention of saying what I did, mainly because I assumed I would have his support given our history. I just spoke the words that hit my head.

When he claimed that women want to move too quickly, he pricked something deep within. My words came out like a raging river, although my words fell on deaf ears. He said what many men think. Women are asking for too much, too quickly, when often it is quite the opposite.

In that instant I realized that what I had planned for my future and what I believed I wanted had to change. I would not beg this "father" for an opportunity. The die had been cast.

Women who wish to climb the ladder may plead for opportunities, hold their breath for a chance. And many women do that unconsciously. They are caught up in their endeavors and do not reason out that they are "ladies in waiting."

Some feel like they have been placed in a cage, looking out, and waiting for permission to come out and play. When women get those few opportunities, they often perform with gusto. They think they are given a gift, kudos from the boss, credit they have desired for eons. They may be grateful!

Women who work in the home 24/7 experience something similar. They wait for an invite to dinner, a thank you for a nice meal, an acknowledgement of what they do. They also want to be a good wife, so they do more and more, and they wait.

It can be stressful and oppressive when you are no longer challenged and your talents and abilities are stagnant. It is unfulfilling when it is mindless work, does not give you opportunities to excel, and most definitely when it limits opportunities for advancement or additional challenges. And how much talent is languishing because that talent resides within a woman?

And yes, I wrote proposals for new courses that got Federal funds for the school, which made the administrators look good. I was happy to do so. I was helping my students by offering new courses, updating curricula, and providing new equipment and materials. I knew that for the privilege of being employed, I was serving the "fathers" in my life, but I was also serving others.

The administration was fine with me in my cage, but when I reached for the opportunity that would challenge me and use all my skills, I was denied. But not for long!

Fifteen
FINALLY!

"Like the embroidery thread in my basket, I will not become tangled so tight that I lose myself. Joseph thinks I SHOULD bend to his will. Well, I have a WILL of my own…. Maybe I wouldn't have these thoughts if Joseph were different. Nay, I would have these thoughts."

Elizabeth Rodenz

Before I started my doctorate program, I was asked by people, who had observed me in various roles and applauded my speaking abilities, to run for the House of Representatives at the state level.

By the way, I had married after I received my degree, and my husband did not support this endeavor nor did my father. My father thought that comments about me would hurt my feelings. I disagreed. Just like with the priest, what sins had I committed? I know Dad was trying to protect me, but he did not know the real me. Then neither did I at that time.

My husband was concerned about the time I would spend at the state capitol, not being home with him, being his counsel, cooking, and caring for our dogs. And because I was engaged in my job, bringing in a paycheck, and supporting his career, there was no reason to change our situation. I could have pushed back. I did not! Instead, I enrolled in a doctorate at the university.

When I wanted to go to law school six years earlier, he had said we could not afford for me to quit my job and go full-time to school. The reality was we could have afforded it, but he liked the life my paycheck gave him. Yet, he had said I should have been the lawyer, not him. Again, I had not pushed back.

Yet, for a year and a half, I provided a home for him while he was in law school. At that time one paycheck was fine. I helped him study. I had made calm and secure the unbearable life that he was experiencing as a law student. He had dinner each night and a helpmate.

But when I wanted to fulfill a desire, he said no. So, I had to ask myself why did I go along? It could have been because I did not want to run for a public office or be a lawyer. That could be denial. Or possibly the truth. I loved teaching and maybe did not want to change my life, especially leaving my two lovely dogs to his care.

I did have job offers after I received my doctorate. One was a second-in-command administrative position. The school district was about forty-five miles away from our home. An assistant superintendent position was quite a coup. I had taught with the superintendent who was offering me this position at the school with the "Bell Curve."

Again, my husband said, "No!" He didn't want me to travel that far every day, especially when I had to stay late into the evening for a Board meeting. I knew he cared about me, and his reason, I am sure to him, sounded plausible. I suggested that I could stay overnight at a hotel on school board meeting nights. No, no again. I suggested we could move in between both work locations. Then we could share the commuting time. At the time he was ten minutes from his work. No, no again.

Our history came washing over me. Surely, divorce was not in my future. I had been programmed to keep our marriage intact. And my greatest fear was my parents' reaction. I believe I had not disappointed them up until then. But after much consideration, I decided I had to choose me.

A professor once asked me why people marry, and the words flowed out, "Because it's time."

He chuckled, "I've never heard a better explanation."

Deep down, I knew I had not wanted to marry. I had a history of breaking off with someone when the relationship got too serious and had broken an engagement. In time, I realized, that it wasn't marriage I was against. It was the fear of having my wings clipped. But the "should" of society reared its ugly head, and I gave in. I had married.

I have learned that people will make changes once the pain is too great. You may remember Anais Nin's quote. *"And the day came when the risk to remain tight in the bud was more painful than the risk it took to bloom."* Well, the day came. I could not continue to deny my desires. Each time my desires were crushed, I took another path. This time I would not, could not! The "ask" was too great!

I cannot take away that time. Instead, I choose to honor the lessons learned. And I do take responsibility for not taking a stand sooner.

My husband said to me, "I always thought you would be here." I had taught him that whatever happened, I would find a way to stay by taking another path. This time, I chose to leave.

I share this story not to blame him. Nor is it for revenge. I hold no animosity, and we probably could have stayed friends if…. This story is about me and my inability to act when I should have acted. This story also demonstrates the subtle and not-so-subtle ways a woman can become trapped in situations and relationships.

Other choices than those I made might have served me better. Some I look upon with disappointment in myself. Those disappointments were choices I made when I was not true to myself or was swayed by individuals or the collective.

And yes, my story demonstrates patriarchal behavior — a husband believing he had the right to weigh in as the decider of my choices. And this scenario is not unique to me, so I hope that it gives you courage to use your voice if you are facing a similar situation. And that is the only reason I tell this story.

Please step back and assess your worth. You might realize that you do not have to serve the "fathers" in your life. You will stop waiting and staying. You will cut the ties that bind or begin to set boundaries, say "No, thank you," and heed the voice that says, "No, not that way, this way."

My father and mother had taught me I did not have to turn myself inside out for love and approval. But in my marriage, I made decisions to keep it intact, decisions to avoid conflict and divorce. I could regret those choices, but regretting does not yield anything.

Time and again in the future, I permitted myself to choose me. I left my teaching position, parted with my husband, and moved to New York City for an editorial position with a publishing company.

I would be asked to serve other "fathers" in that new position. I would soon discover how I would respond to those "fathers." I never looked back. I will never regret the years I taught. My one sorrow was the students I left behind. I loved them all, but I needed to take flight once again.

Sixteen
Rocking the Boat

"A strong woman stands up for herself. A stronger woman stands up for everybody else."
Unknown

When I told my professor Joe that I was moving to New York City, he said, "It's fine to run away, as long as you know you're doing it."

"I'm not running away. I'm running to something."

I had heard the three most difficult things to do in life are moving to a new location, starting a new job, and severing a relationship. I decided to do all three at once. Was I up for it? Being away from friends and family would take a bit of adjustment, but for me, it was a MUST, something pulling me to that new life. So, I decided to run to something.

Surprising though, after I moved into my hotel room where I would live until I found an apartment, nothing about New York seemed to intimidate or surprise me. The first morning as I was walking down the Avenue of the America's on my way to work, I was thrilled that I was hearing other languages. How different from where I grew up. Within an hour, I threw myself into my work and never looked back.

Bob, the editorial director, told me that I was the only editor he had hired that did not praise the company's textbooks. I had not only pointed out to him what was wrong but what needed to change. I reminded him that there are plenty of people who find fault and speak of problems, but solutions are what was needed. He agreed.

55

At my first meeting, there were three levels of management—my manager, Gretchen; the editorial director, Bob; and the VP of the book division, Daniel. Daniel and Bob had interviewed and hired me, so I believed they did not want a "yes" person. Without hesitation, I advocated a complete rehauling of the textbook series.

Daniel was against this idea because of the cost. "Just cut and paste it," was his call. That meant just put in new pics, design a different cover, and use the same material and the same ineffective way of teaching.

I objected by saying, "Making money and doing what is right for students are not opposing forces. The content and instruction have to change. You are losing sales because teachers are not having success using the books. We need to present the material differently, which would make teachers more effective. In time, we would not lose sales. We may even get more sales because we would have a superior book."

I went on to explain the needed changes and got Daniel's agreement. Bob caught my arm after the meeting was over and said, "You know, Elizabeth, it's not a good idea to argue with Daniel so soon upon arrival."

"He did not hire me to agree. He hired me for my expertise. At the interview, you both knew I would not do the minimum. I would not agree because I must. I did not hide that. Why disappoint either of you?" I chuckled, and he smiled.

Later I learned from my administrative assistant that Bob had said to his admin, "She's going to rock a lot of boats, but I like her." I had an ally.

I was to convene a focus group to determine what other teachers perceived as problems with the textbooks. I hired an outside firm to conduct the discussion. The morning the focus group was to meet, I met Jerry, the head of the marketing department, in the elevator.

"How are things going?" he asked.

I answered, not realizing he might have an agenda. "Just fine! So excited about the focus group today."

He inquired to know more. I was happy to tell him. About a half hour later, Daniel walked into my office and closed the door.

I learned later that my assistant and those outside my office thought he was there to fire me. Daniel did not come to your office. He called you to his office. I did not know that bit so I was not concerned, thinking it was to be a friendly chat.

He asked me how I put together the focus group, who I contacted, how I got the names of the participants, and so on.

"So, you spoke with Wanda in marketing, and she got the names from the sales representatives."

I confirmed that, and he left the room. It was clear that Jerry was unaware of what was happening in his department. Thinking I had sidestepped his department, he had gone to Daniel and complained about me.

I marched to Jerry's office and sat down across from him without being invited in. He did not look at me, keeping his eyes on a paper he was pretending to read. I was brief and direct. "Jerry, I did nothing wrong. If you thought I did or had a question, why not talk to me? Don't go running off telling tales. It might save you some embarrassment."

I walked out and went to Bob's office. Again, I was brief. "I did something I thought you should know. I told Jerry he should speak to me if he had a problem with me. Not go telling tales."

He chuckled. "You don't have to protect me."

I smiled and walked out. I had not realized that people did not deal with each other directly. They used the chain of command. To me, that is tattling and unacceptable. It was the *drama triangle* all over again, and Daniel fortunately did not take the bait and fault me. Instead, he was willing to find out from me what happened. He did what I had proposed in my encounter with John, the bully administrator.

Something similar, although minor, happened with an assistant editor, Art. He and I usually stayed after hours, and we chatted about this and that. One day my manager told me that Art was complaining about the little clock in my office chiming on the hour. It disturbed his concentration. Gretchen told me she was embarrassed to tell me this, but Art's manager had complained to her for him.

I could not believe it. I thought we had a good relationship. So, after leaving Gretchen's office, I walked to Art's desk and asked him why he did not speak to me about the clock. He was shocked that I would address him about the issue. He mumbled and said he thought he should go through his boss.

"About a clock! From now on, if you have a problem with me, can you come to me?" He nodded, and I walked away.

One day Mary, my gem of an assistant, came into my office and said to me. "This is a laboratory for you, isn't it?"

Surprised at her comment, I asked her meaning. "Well, you observe and watch. I think all the antics of the people fascinate you. It's like we are part of your research."

I smiled at her for her insight. After writing a dissertation on leadership, I was intrigued by how managers work with their staff. But Mary's comment made me realize that I was intervening in a system I could not embrace as designed but wanted to understand.

I do not regard hierarchy, how it is commonly designed, in corporations and institutions as conducive to favorable results. I was not a fit. All people are equal in my mind. I do not limit them by their title or lack of one, education, salary, money, home, or other trappings. I take people as I find them and go from there.

At the same time, I believe in handling situations straight on, without an intermediary. Years later when asked about my management philosophy, I said without hesitation, "It shouldn't hurt."

Seventeen
Thorns Among Women

"The question isn't who's going to let me; it's who's going to stop me."

Ayn Rand

My boss, Gretchen, had a habit of holding court every morning when she was in the office. She was known for doing a monologue about the men out in the field (the sales field was dominated by men). She gave them degrading nicknames, rated their intelligence, and pointed out their faults. I would walk by and keep going, while my colleagues chuckled.

Interesting though, she coveted the male sales force when she was out in the field because they were the ones who requested her to speak, getting her out of the office. She wined and dined them on corporate money, and they used her because she was a good speaker. And although not substantive, she was funny and entertaining.

She had laryngitis a few weeks after I was hired, so I was asked to travel to do two of her presentations. Instead of helping me with the content, she called me into her office and told me her opinions of the salesmen and managers I would be meeting.

After speaking for a few minutes, she said, "You don't seem to be interested in what I am saying."

I guess my face revealed what I was thinking. "It's just that you have your history with them, and I want to have mine. I don't want your comments to affect how I regard them before I meet them."

My words rang true. My response said I was not comfortable with her harming the reputation of those in the organization.

In time Gretchen discovered there were requests from the sales field for me to speak at conferences and universities—requests she would have received if I had not been there. She considered herself the company's premiere speaker.

I had received a call from a regional manager to make sure I would be available for three speaking dates. I never received the requests so I went to the person who scheduled the speakers. I was told that my wings had been clipped— no speaking engagements could be scheduled for me.

Not sure why that happened, I went to Bob because Gretchen was out of the office. He was my champion because after only three months, he gave me a substantial raise. Bob said that Gretchen had told him that I was too busy to speak. I told him that if I were too busy, I would not schedule them.

He realized this was a surprise to me, and Gretchen had not discussed it with me. He said I could continue to speak if I had the time. He understood the dynamics, and neither of us had to name what was happening.

Eighteen
Mr. Penny

"Be the heroine of your life, not the victim."
Nora Ephron

Each morning Mary, my assistant and a partner in fun and work, got me coffee and a goodie at her urging. The three pennies returned to her she insisted on giving to me. Ugh…. Pennies… So, I started throwing them into an empty vase. It was soon filled to the top, beginning to overflow. Marilyn, a colleague, nudged me again and again about taking home the jar of pennies that was on my credenza.

"Someone will steal them," she would say.

One evening before leaving the office, hearing Marilyn's voice, I put the pennies in a paper bag to take back to my apartment. I jostled my way along 49th Street, holding the bag of pennies. People were coming at me from all directions, hurrying for home or something fun. Then, someone bumped into me. Down went the bag of pennies, scattered all over the street. There were hundreds.

My first instinct was to walk away and leave them. But, looking at the pennies piled high, I thought someone could slip on them and fall. I started to pick them up. People were hurrying by, stepping around me, but I held my ground.

Then, all of a sudden, two men were beside me, gathering the pennies into my purse. Once I had picked up the last penny, I had a chance to see the two men who had been helping me. We laughed about the incident, and they asked me to go for a drink and dinner. After their valiant rescue efforts, I could not say no.

Throughout our getting-to-know banter, I learned that Mike and James were working for the same investment company. Mike asked me about my work, so I shared a bit about my traveling and speaking at different conferences and workshops. I didn't give away too much. Mystery in a woman can be to her benefit. Let him wonder.

We parted an hour later, my telephone number on a piece of paper in Mike's hand, with a promise to call. I walked away thinking, "Where have I heard that before?"

I was known for my adventures of meeting people, ending with a twist that was often funny. Being a newcomer to the city, I had not learned the New York way of keeping people at arm's length. After telling about yet-another encounter, a colleague chuckled, "There are a million stories in New York, and you're trying to have all of them."

The following morning, I told Mary, responsible for the pennies, about the previous evening. She laughed and named him Mr. Penny. A day later Mr. Penny called and invited me to see a film that weekend. Thinking it would be fun to hang with someone and enjoy the city, I said yes.

My mother had run away to New York when she was fifteen and had lived with a group of girls. I had run away to New York and lived alone. I remembered all her stories about her friends, Far Rockaway, Central Park and ice skating, Roseland, and the Cotton Club. That New York didn't exist forty years later, but I had yet to experience this New York. Wanting to have those experiences, I was thrilled to have someone as a playmate.

Mike was easy to be with, and we talked about our travels and our careers and whatever hit our heads. We took walks in the park, went out to dinner, visited museums and old book stores, and took a turn at dancing. We were having fun, enjoying our time together and the sights of the city.

One night we met for dinner before I left for a business trip to the West Coast. It was his birthday, and before meeting me that evening, he had met a friend and had a drink or two. With a Cheshire grin, he mentioned that he had told his friend about me. His next remark almost sent me across the room. "So, this friend asked me, 'How old is this woman you're in love with?'"

Who's in love? Then he said, "How old are you?"

Mike had told me his age when he mentioned his birthday, so I knew he was thirty-three. Thinking he was the one who looked forty-two, I told him without hesitating that I was forty-two. That almost sent him across the room.

He was silent, so I added, "Does my age bother you?"

It was ten seconds TOO long before he said, "I dated a woman who had a sixteen-year-old son. She was forty."

He hadn't answered the question. When I said nothing, he said, "When I first met you, I thought you were about twenty-seven."

"And your point is that I've aged well?"

"Then I learned you had a doctorate, learned about your career. I started to think you were in your early 30s."

"That's nice to hear, I think."

I rushed through dinner and left to go home and pack. I had an early flight to San Francisco the following morning. Previously when I returned from a business trip, he would call within an hour of my arrival—anxious to get together. But this time, no call. So, about three hours later, I called him and said, "What's going on?"

"I saw someone while you were away," was his reply.

"Now, tell me something I didn't know!" was my quick reply. There was silence, so I hung up.

A few weeks later he called. "Take control," I said to myself and asked, "Do you have a problem with my age?"

His reply, "I don't know." Honesty!

I said in a calm voice, "Nothing will change. I'm still nine years older. I will always be nine years older. The problem with men is they think they can date someone younger, but women can't. You think you're going to age gracefully. Men get bald, fat, gray, paunchy, wrinkled, boring, grumpy. When you met me, you thought I was twenty-seven. I'd like to see you when you are forty-two."

Then I hung up. Whew! That felt good. About a month later, he called and asked me to come over to his apartment. Did he think I inherited a stupid gene? I hung up.

A few months later, he called again and asked me to see a play. Free ticket to an impossible-to-get play, why not? I wondered if he would talk about what happened. He never did. I was just to accept that things had changed for him.

Again, he called about a week later. That seemed to be a habit he couldn't break. Curious and still waiting for an apology, something, I agreed to a walk. But there was nothing there. I had shut down. I could not let myself be me. Any signal to him that all was behind us would not serve me well. And again, he did not speak about what happened.

He asked to start seeing me again, and I replied, "I haven't gotten any younger. Have you gotten older?" I also added that I didn't want to wake up and hear once again that he had decided I was NOW TOO-OLD.

I wasn't able to trust him, and, I was no longer interested. It wasn't because I had another choice. I just discovered over the years, it's more painful to be with the wrong person than being alone. Before dating him, I had dated a man who was twenty-seven. I was then forty. I would say to him, "I'm too old for you."

He would say, "You don't have THE PROBLEM. I have THE PROBLEM. You should be saying, 'I'm too young.'"

He had said again and again that my age was not a factor, and he proved it, sometimes daily. We had a fun romance until…. We did part. Not because of our numerical ages. We parted because in time I discovered that he was never going to grow up. Sad though, because he was brilliant and a romantic.

About a year later, I remember saying to a friend as she probed about the man I recently dated, "I have friends. I love my work and my apartment. If this is all I'm to have, that's fine." I said it with fervor, and I meant it.

A few weeks later, Dad phoned and told me that a guy named Mike had called the house. Dad had taken Mike's number and said to him that he would call and give me the message. I guessed that Mike had tried to contact me in New York and discovered my phone was disconnected. However, he knew where my parents lived, so he tracked down a telephone number using my last name.

I waited several weeks before I called him. In ways I was curious about his life and what had happened to him. Or maybe he had changed. Nay, that would make a good story, but then there's reality.

During our call he told me that he was now living near my parents, and maybe we could get together when I came to visit them. Again, I made it clear that nothing had changed. I was still the same person.

I have known women who take men back into their lives. Maybe because it's easier. "Better the devil you know than the one you don't." I understand that. For me, dating ranks high on my list of things I would choose not to do in my conscious moments, although there are times when I have been unconscious. Haven't we all?

Dating because we should or because we don't want to be alone. Dating because he seems nice or we want an arm to cling to. Continuing to see him, hoping things will get better, that one day he will be the man you need in your life, and he will be thankful for the person you are. And so on.

I realized at his birthday dinner that my age was a problem for him and that AGE was a predator that had invaded both of our minds. When he looked at my face, would I be thinking: Does he notice my crow's feet, a wrinkle, a gray hair, an age spot...? Questioning over and over, my age preying on my mind, and, of course, his mind.

I wasn't going to give him the right to make me doubt myself, to make me less. He wasn't going to get that kind of control over me. It wasn't that I had a problem with our parting. It was the way he did it, and the reason he did it.

I also believed our time together was past. Women, myself included, do what I describe as "staying at the party too long." We don't give up on relationships—not only with men but with our hairdresser, our doctor... and other women. We keep trying to make the relationship work.

At times we all have to stop letting others pull the strings. Declare we are not puppets. Not an easy lesson and not a lesson many want to learn. Not an easy journey and not a journey many want to take. Being attached to someone, anyone, seems easier until you become aware that it is not.

Mike came into my life for that short time for me to have that experience. It reminded me how resilient I was, how in charge of me I was. I didn't need to attach myself to someone else, and when and if I did, it would be for reasons of my own, not society or another person's mandate. I was in Mike's life to teach him a lesson—age is only a number.

I share this story with you because persistence can get us to give in, make a choice we don't want to make, but consider choosing yourself and your desires.

Nineteen
Not the End

"Dare to declare who you are. It is not far from the shores of silence to the boundaries of speech. The path is not long, but the way is deep. You must not only walk there; you must be prepared to leap."
Hildegard Von Bingen

My journey of reflection helped me understand some of my choices and revealed some truths about my struggles and decisions. I acquired insight into the reasons why I made the choices I did and why I rejected the dictates of a world that was trying to box me into their image and how I should act.

My ruminations revealed to me why at times I had difficulty fitting into the world. I came to understand why some women applauded me, and why some found me an enigma. Others questioned my choices, if only to themselves. My journey disclosed why some men supported my efforts and championed me and why I confused and befuddled others.

I have shared but a few of my life stories that are relevant to the salient messages in this book. As you may have observed I did not always seek the approval of the "fathers" in my life, especially if I did not find them worthy.

At times, especially at a young age, I did not understand why I said and acted as I did, nor could I frame it into a context. But in time I did become conscious of what resided deep within and that is a never-ending journey.

My goal throughout the stories I share is to demonstrate the continual patterns throughout my life and how I dealt with those who thought they could dictate what choices I were to make. And my reflections revealed glimpses of my authentic self that I did not understand at that time.

To reflect on your journey, start to observe behaviors that emerged throughout your life and kept repeating in numerous ways.

I do not share these stories to be a role model for who you should be and what you should do. You are unique. You should choose your own path and be true to who you are. Not a cardboard cutout of what others believe you should be. And taking this journey with me will be freeing, and you may be inspired to look at your life through a different lens.

Part Two

Coming Into the Light

Woman to Woman

Women are as different as colors in a box of crayons
Lumping them together—fool hardy, done for eons
"Women are…." two words that should never be spoken together
Easier than getting to know them, regard them as birds of a feather

What attracts men to women drives them crazy in time
Resentment and fear may take over with no reason or rhyme
Men lash out at women they profess to revere and love
What once attracted now repels, no longer from heaven above

Wives, mothers, daughters, sisters, the fairer sex they say
Words meant to keep them out of the way and at bay
Keeping men guessing—some of a woman's charm, until it isn't
Intrigued by a woman's deeds and mind, until he isn't

Women relegated to the shadows—a fate cast upon her at birth
Her gifts must be unfurled to a world that keeps denying her worth
Calling out oppression is just a beginning
Expecting help from others leaves women spinning

Smiling, nodding, going along are all ill advised
Behavior that signals a woman is unwise
Calling out a woman's plight confirms women are not free
Screaming out, stomping your feet, and shaking the trees

Not an everlasting solution, giving you peace of mind
Instead walk away from the chains that bind
Create the life you wish, never agonizing
Rejecting the alternative and never apologizing

To the Reader.... A Few Words

"She woke up every morning with the option of being anything she wished. How beautiful it was that she chose herself."

Tyler Kent White

Through my studies of Jungian psychology and other disciplines and integrating that knowledge with my experiences, I started to untangle some of what has puzzled me about human behavior. The interpretation and analyses that follow are my attempt to make the information relatable and accessible.

As you read, you may feel compelled to hold up a mirror. Sometimes you may think I am speaking to you. The words will jump off the page. You may realize that you have had similar experiences or recognize yourself and others.

You may delight in that knowing or experience upset, possibly at me, the messenger. And although not tied in a pretty bow, the knowledge and your reflections are gifts—gifts of understanding. That can lead to opportunity and maybe needed changes. But you must be ready and willing and have the courage to take this journey and ask yourself many questions, including:

What forces have pushed and pulled you this way and that way and why you resisted or acquiesced?

Why all of us do not have the same desires, crave a different life, wish to walk a different path?

Why do you....?

No one person and no words can inspire you beyond a moment. You must do that for yourself, but you cannot do that unless you are willing.

Your responses to the material and my interpretation will be based on who you are deep within because truth lies not within the written words but in the heart of the person who wrote them and the hearts of those who read them.

One
That Which is Buried

"Nothing in life is to be feared; it is only to be understood. Now is the time to understand more, so that we may fear less."

Marie Curie

Remember the story of the Creator who buried something within us she did not want us to know until it was time? Well, it is time!

Voices buried within me activated my actions and choices. Words that flew out of my mouth charted the course of my life. By choosing not to participate in the confession ritual, I was refusing dictates that I could not embrace. By refusing to bow to the bank president, speaking without any concern for repercussions, I was being true to myself. I did not know the forces that were pushing and pulling me, but my essence was on full display.

What was buried within was shouting at me, guiding and compelling me to take action, urging me to speak out. No deliberation! Spontaneity reigned!

When I would NOT acquiesce to forces around me, when I resisted bending and pretending, when I shut out the voices and followed my own instincts, I was rejecting dogma and the collective's dictates, which are forms of control and which force conformity.

Voices that ask you to conform are robbers of your soul. You must say NO to those forces to live the life you are meant to live. If you acquiesce to those forces, your very essence and your uniqueness are lost to you and to the world.

Two
The Acquired Mind

"To be nobody but yourself in a world which is doing its best, night and day, to make you like everybody else means to fight the hardest battle which any human being can fight, and never stop fighting."
E.E. Cummings

We all start out asleep. What the Creator buried within has yet to appear. And we remain asleep until we become unsettled, until something or someone nudges us out of our slumber like Rip Van Winkle.

We also start out as a part of a collective. The collective extends beyond your family to society, organizations, the workplace, and your friends. They have rules of behavior, values, and beliefs you are to embrace.

I also include all forms of media in the collective because of the pervasive influence they have on your reality, your life, your choices, and what you are expected to desire.

From birth and as you grow, the collective pushes and pulls you to shape what the Taoists call the *acquired mind.* Once the mind is acquired, it tells you what you are to value and the choices you should make. So, instead of staying true to who you are, you kowtow to those outside voices and forces. They pull you this way and that way NOT knowing or caring who you are or what dwells within you. Those voices and forces are not concerned that you possess your own uniqueness and have different desires. And that uniqueness comprises a swirling mass of unknowns that you may have yet to grasp.

People, of course, have a choice as to whether to obey. So, why do people comply and conform?

There are those in your world who demand conformity. Relationships with friends and family may be conditional. It can be as subtle as "Now, that's not how we do things, is it?"

This control of your mind may be indirect, yet persistent, and dictates your actions and spills over into how you move in the world.

At the age of fifteen, I had a boyfriend, Michael. He told me that his father had kicked his brother, Uncle John, out of the family for marrying someone of a different faith. Michael disapproved of his father's ousting of his uncle.

When Michael's mother learned I was not of the family's faith, she called me and said that she did not want her son to be with me because I was not a "nice" girl. Within a nanosecond, I said, "But I am a nice girl."

And remember I was fifteen. We were not dating, and we were not going to be marching down the aisle any time soon, so why did she have to make that call?

The dogma of intolerance that she embraced had turned me into a "not nice girl" in her mind. Fortunately, my mind did not agree so it was not acquired, but it could have been.

In the television series, *The Trials of Rosie O'Neill*, Rosie is sharing her life choices. She became an attorney like her father because he had coveted her favor and she complied. She married someone like her father, an attorney. They bought a beautiful home like her parents. It then occurs to her that she was not living her own dreams.

She is asked, "Whose dreams were you living?"

"My parents' dreams. Now it's time for new dreams!"

Rosie allowed her parents' expectations to invade her psyche. She allowed what she heard and observed to influence her choices. By doing so, she was not living the life she was meant to live but the life she was supposed to desire.

To the outside world, it appeared that she had everything and was happy. But she had fooled herself, as she had fooled those around her. When she began to examine her life, she started to ask the tough questions.

So why had Rosie turned her life over to outside forces? A daughter who wants to please her parents might turn her life over to them. A daughter who has been indoctrinated to believe…. might…. And this applies to sons as well.

These expectations include our life choices, behavior, values, and beliefs that we are expected to embrace. In time you may internalize those same expectations, taking ownership of what others desire. The brainwashing by family and society and the media is gradual. So, you may not detect that you are experiencing the death of your own spirit and your soul.

If you go along unwillingly or with reservation, you may lose your self-respect. You may become angry with yourself for not acting or speaking out. You may feel caged, trying to meet someone else's expectations. The abuses and reprimands for not complying may be overwhelming. You can become worn down.

You must be true to yourself in a world that is goading you into a life of other people's version of you. For most of your life, if you allow it to be so, you are in a play, performing with a script and a handful of directors. You must have the courage to toss out the script and fire the directors.

The realization of how you conformed and performed can make you regretful. Anger and regret yield nothing. You may blame those who have controlled your life, but remember you have given permission by acquiescing. Yes, possibly you did this unknowingly, but you did so.

By taking responsibility, you can uncover what you did and did not do. Once you have identified those controlling voices, you are forewarned and can plan your pushback. Then you can forgive yourself for the time you complied and focus on moving on, promising yourself not to fall into those traps again. And if it does happen, hopefully you will remove yourself sooner the next time.

If you have to conform or are silenced, punished if you disagree or diminished when you start to speak, that relationship is conditional.

How many conditional relationships can you have in your lifetime?

What suffering do those relationships place on you?

What are you denying yourself in order to comply?

Why have you given others permission to dictate and control your life?

Have these outside forces led to a lifetime of a false existence because you performed and conformed?

A loving family or friends do not push and pull you in their direction, control your deepest desires. They allow you to think for yourself, make your own choices, and ask what you want. They provide inspiration and guidance, not dictates telling you what you should desire and think.

Unfortunately, there may be only a few people in your life who will not make demands on you. You must cherish friends and family who encourage and support you, who listen without judgment, reach out when you are struggling, accept all your shortcomings, and do not condemn your mistakes.

Society is not so loving. Treasure those people and those times.

Three
Predators of the Mind

"The individual has always had to struggle to keep from being overwhelmed by the tribe. If you try it, you will be lonely often, and sometimes frightened. But no price is too high to pay for the privilege of owning yourself."
Friedrich Nietzsche

I left the publishing company in New York City and eventually landed in San Francisco and started my management consulting and executive coaching company. I was entering a male-dominated profession, and I would be offering a service, not a product.

I believed it would be helpful to speak with someone in marketing to hear another voice. I learned of an organization that provided guidance to small businesses. Their "experts" were retired and would meet with entrepreneurs on a particular topic.

I walked into a room and an older man looked up at me and scowled. "So, you want to start a business?"

I spoke about my plans and expressed the services I would be offering and the challenges I thought I would face. I did so in a calm voice and demeanor. At his urging I told him about my education. Maybe he thought degrees were important or that I was too young to have much of a career or….

He said, "So you got a doctorate?"

I nodded and he responded, "Well, I have found people with Ph.Ds. do not have any business savvy. And you are too quiet and soft spoken. I can't see you making it in the business world you wish to enter. I cannot see you being successful!"

I got up from my chair. "You don't know my business experiences. What right do you have to declare that I won't be successful? You don't have a crystal ball! And aren't you supposed to help me be successful?"

I did not defend myself, listing my accomplishments. I had no need to prove him wrong. I did not care for his good opinion, plus he had a closed mind. He had already decided.

I left his office. By the time I was down the elevator and stepped on to the street, I decided that I was calling the head of the organization and reporting this *expert*. He had not deterred me from moving forward with my plans, but if he said that to another person, a woman, she could become defeated.

In addition to the acquired mind that pushes you this way and that way, there are predators of your mind. And that can be a person, a group, a culture, a cult, a leader with an agenda. And predators exploit and manipulate ruthlessly and eventually crush your spirit and rob you of your soul.

Predators prey on you if you are vulnerable, inexperienced, and naïve, which we all may be to varying degrees, especially when we are young or insecure. They mess with your mind, ultimately stealing your life from you. And often times you are totally unaware or you deny, deny, deny that there is anything amiss.

One day Lea, age eight, was shouting horrible things to her sister, Caroline, age ten. Caroline teared up, and Lea shouted, "You cry to get your way!"

Caroline knew that wasn't true. She would never feign any behavior or lie to get her way, but in that instant, her sister acquired her mind. Caroline promised herself that she would not cry again. And when she started to cry, she scrunched up her face to keep the tears from flowing.

Twenty-five years later when she moved to another city, she started to cry one evening. She cried because she could, allowing to flow all the tears she had never cried. She had finally cut the ties that bound her to denying the sensitivity and tenderness that resided within her.

One day while visiting with her parents, Jenny was sharing with her mother that she was going to start classes for her Master's Degree. Her sister, Meg, yelled out, "When are you going to stop this nonsense and be a wife and mother?"

Meg was telling Jenny the path she had chosen was flawed. She was to make another choice—that of wife and mother. In this instance, Jenny's mind was not acquired, and she got her Master's degree.

When Pat's daughter, Jamie, did not want to have a graduation party, Pat said to her sister, Wendy, "It's bad enough that Jamie looked like you when she was born, she had to grow up to be like you!"

Predators and robbers do not always come from the adults in our lives. Messages can come at a young age from siblings, teachers, and classmates as well, and if the voices are not stopped, they continue into adulthood.

If vulnerable, your mind is fair game, and comments that target your mind can bury themselves deep within and take over. The judgments and criticisms of others are meant to defeat us, ordain how we are to move in the world.

Comments, such as, "Girls are sugar and spice and everything nice," "Women are the fairer sex, the weaker sex, inferior, flighty," are roadblocks on the path to living a life with courage. Destructive comments are also roadblocks to experiencing an authentic life. Little girls are made of insight, compassion, tenacity, courage, and sacrifice. The heck with sugar and spice! The heck with fairer and weaker!

Children and adults are not aware that negative comments and dictates are riddled with agendas. They may be cloaked in the words, "I'm only trying to help." And it is difficult to believe that sometimes prejudice, cruelty, and malice trigger these comments, even by those we trust and look to for guidance.

But often the messages are pervasive. In my earlier story about Perry Mason, I wanted to be an attorney, but I heard voices in my head. I did not know they were based on what society had taught me. I decided my future on what I wasn't and what I didn't have. Those voices stopped me from going after that dream. By the time I had met that marketing expert, I wasn't that girl any more.

Kathy, as a young girl grew up poor, with an outhouse for a bathroom. She saw her mother buy day-old bread and sweets and cut coupons. She heard her parents argue over money at the dinner table and was told by her mother, *"You can love a rich man as easily as a poor one."*

She sought a rich man for a husband—not for love but for a gilded carriage. And when she divorced him after he had an affair, she searched for another rich man. After the second divorce, she was older and had more than enough money not to marry.

Jayson is ashamed and embarrassed when he is teased and called a mamma's boy. He chooses to take up wrestling, lift weights, and picks fights with other boys. The caring, compassionate boy he was is now a man who shouts and abuses women, including his mother, and he gets in people's faces over the slightest thing.

Carrie shared with me her desire to be a doctor. She had gone to her father for advice. He told her that if she wanted to marry and have children, it would be difficult to do both.

No words of encouragement to be a doctor, no guidance or support on how to make this desire come true, so she took another path.

I asked her, "Why didn't you ask your mother that question?"

Her reply, "Because my mother wasn't educated."

"What do you mean, not educated?"

"She did not have a college degree."

"But your mother was a mother. And yes, she did not work outside the home, but maybe she would have given you encouragement. Maybe she would have said, 'Don't worry. I will help you,' just like you are helping your daughter who is a doctor raising her two children."

Carrie was silent, so I continued, "Your father saw the situation through his eyes, as a man, a husband, a father. He was a man whose wife was to take care of their five children and did not work. His image of a woman was a wife who waited on him and took care of the family.

"And why did he speak of marriage and not your desire to be a doctor? Your mother might have said, 'Make sure you marry someone who will help with the chores and the children. Not someone who is going to expect you to be his maid, while bringing in the money.'"

Carrie realized she had put her life in her father's hands because he had a degree and she regarded him as better able to help her. She believed he had wisdom that her mother did not because she had been manipulated by a world that had weaned her on "father knows best," and that degrees gave him the right to determine her entire life. Also, although subtle, her father was telling her that she was expected to be a wife and mother, no matter what her other choices.

In my 30's I was teaching, enrolled in a doctorate program, a member of several organizations, president of one, and managing a local political campaign. I was at an event and met a woman with energy and spirit. She shared she had a teaching degree and was a stay-at-home wife and mother of three children.

She called her husband to join us, introduced me, and briefly told him about my activities. With a big smile on her face, she said, "When the kids get older, I want to do what she is doing!"

Her husband glared at her and declared, "When the children are in their teens, they will need you home more than they do now!"

That was the end of her dreams. Robbers can be subtle or as blatant as that husband who insinuated quite clearly in that instant that the children were her responsibility, not his, and she would not be a good mother if she were not home 24/7.

Sometimes those closest to us do the most harm. Now, they may not see it that way, convinced that they are being helpful. Or in the case of the husband, he believed he had a right to dictate to his wife what choice she had to make.

There are parents who want their daughter to have that grandbaby, but she is not ready. Parents may want a daughter to play a sport like her siblings or maybe because her parents had done so, but the daughter prefers playing the piano or is interested in her studies.

There is the husband who says to his wife, "Oh no, you cannot do that. You don't have what it takes." And if she does embark upon a career or gets a degree, the husband makes her life miserable, does not help with the children or chores, and complains and pouts.

The responses when faced with these situations may be: "Oh, my mother would only want the best for me." "My father is only…." "My parents think I am good at…." "My husband loves me. He wouldn't hurt me. That's not him."

So, we must be continually mindful that these forces are often disguised, even with the words, "I am only trying to help."

In the film, *The Heiress*, Catherine, the daughter of a man who lost his wife giving birth to her, never has a kind word for her. Not only does the father fault her for his wife's death, he tells her what to do, what to think, and criticizes her for whatever he deems an indiscretion. She never goes through any initiation, like a first date, a dance, an outing with girlfriends…. She never has a chance to step out into the world and experience any events or any predators. At the same time, he was a slayer of any dream she had for a life.

When she meets Morris, who flatters and pays attention to her, she is attracted to him, believing he is different from her father. He is not. In time she learns that he is just a younger predator with different tactics and motives.

The tactics of predators and robbers can be more damaging than the collective because their words are not limited to "should." They send messages of disappointment by criticizing your actions or inactions or withholding praise and approval, robbing you of your self-confidence.

Eventually, you may bend to their wishes and make choices you would not otherwise make. At the same time, they rob you of the life you wish to live. Your self-esteem may be damaged, and you may come to believe you are inferior, unworthy, incapable.

Words can become assassins of your soul and spirit and life force by taking up residence in your psyche. Just like the acquired mind, they affect how you regard yourself and your choices.

Robbers of your soul can overturn your knowing, the feelings or hunches you have, your instincts and intuition, what you want to do or what you are drawn to do. And these forces at their most fanatical and pervasive will cause you to confront your total annihilation, leaving a puddle of dreams and hopes and most importantly abilities and life force on the floor.

These predators, to be successful, must find someone who is gullible, inexperienced, hurting, and seeking answers, and wishing to be rescued. But most importantly, a woman or man must be seeking approval so she or he will easily comply.

You cannot be wrapped up in cotton. So, it is imperative that you step out into the world at a young age again and again throughout your childhood, adolescence, and adult life. Learn to recognize the forces around you that will harm you and those that can guide you. Reach for the opportunities to be challenged, and do not allow fear to overwhelm you. Ask yourself: What is the worst that can happen?

And please note that age does not determine whether you are at the mercy of the predators and robbers. A woman who has left her father's home and now resides in her husband's home and never had an opportunity to learn about the predators and robbers is vulnerable. Anyone who has been given everything her heart desires, without ever facing challenges and difficulties, or has been rescued again and again is susceptible. And even the experienced can fall prey to slayers and robbers because of loss of focus or vulnerability.

Your task is to recognize those who are trying to take over your life and protect yourself or know when and how to escape. And doing it sooner rather than later will help you avoid the difficulty of extracting yourself from those forces in your life that are trying to deny you your life.

Plato said, "People are like dirt. They can either nourish you and help you grow as a person or they can stunt your growth and make you wilt and die."

For your own well-being, stop letting people define you and start defining yourself. Difficult you might be thinking. Hmmm. More difficult to continue to be fair game!

So, how do you push back? Courage! Courage to say NO to those who are pushing and poking. You must take responsibility for orchestrating the life you want. It is also helpful to have someone in your life who supports and inspires you without dictates or criticism. You need opportunities and experiences to learn and recognize the subtleties of manipulation and exploitation so they cannot take hold.

You must heed that voice inside telling you that something isn't right. Jung says, *"The unconscious mind sees correctly even when the conscious reasoning is blind and impotent."* Trust your unconscious mind—that voice inside of you—when it speaks to you. And bring forth the courage that resides within you.

You can start saying yes to your desires. Realize you are the one who knows what you need, and begin to value your gifts and silence the predators. All this will soon become a habit, and you will not stop to think about it.

Your true self will also begin to emerge because you have started to cut the ties that have chained you to someone else's version of you. Remember you are not taking this journey of reflection and discovery to blame yourself, feel guilty, and live with remorse. Instead, you will experience freedom, and you will be inspired.

In the film, *The Help,* Abelene, the maid, says to Elizabeth's little girl, "You is kind, you is smart, you is important!"

So, I say to you that inside your very being you are courageous, determined, a recalcitrant force. You have an unequaled knowing. Stop denying those truths! Purge those predators from your mind. And I know for those of you who have been beaten down, it is difficult to extract yourself from those outside forces. So, you must rally every ounce of spirit and soul you have within you to recapture your essence and focus on how to turn the page.

Blessings on that journey. And remember Maya Angelou's words, "But, still, like air, I rise."

Four
The Masks You Wear

"The world will ask you who you are, and if you cannot answer, it will tell you."
Carl Jung

Somehow you may have learned from the collective, friends and family, that if you present your true self to the world, you will not be regarded positively or you will be rejected. You may want to speak, but you feel shackled. Those imaginings that you will be viewed negatively if you state a different position or take a different path will force you to stay silent and acquiesce.

If you are not sure how to present a different position so it is accepted or at least heard, you may say what you believe will be acceptable or you stay silent. If you wish to protect a relationship, you may choose to perform or bend.

In time, you mask who you really are to protect yourself from disapproval and punishment. Psychologist Carl Jung called the masks people wear the *persona*. By buying into the dictates of the collective, which you do consciously, your *persona* is molded and affirmed. And often you are unaware because like other methods, they are clandestine and subtle.

This public veneer is believed to mask what you do not like about yourself or believe others will reject. The face you present may make you feel confident in your relationships. You may believe disguising what you believe is offensive will garner acceptance, and you will avoid disagreement and awkwardness in relationships.

But there are two major problems to wearing a mask! First, denying your true self can be painful at times. Second, the mask you choose to wear may get you acceptance into a certain club, but it may keep you out of another. That "other club" may be a better fit—one you can embrace and be yourself. And because you are hiding and denying your true self, those others will be lost to you, and you will have to keep wearing those masks.

If you have a high need for approval or acceptance or a desire to fit in, you may wear many masks. If there is a strong drive to avoid conflict, please others, or the relationship is important, the more masks you may wear.

My mother, who would be considered a force to be taken seriously, did one thing I decided to address. She would say, "I'm Mrs. Paul Rodenz."

I was about twelve years old when I said to her, "Mom, your name isn't Paul. It's Caroline."

Oh, it's subtle, and you may argue it was tradition, but society had given her a mask to wear that minimized her and dismissed her identity by taking away her name. But what I realized later in life was that as a young girl I did not question taking a husband's last name until I did.

Below are a few lines from the poem by Jenny Joseph:

"When I am an old woman, I shall wear purple with a red hat which doesn't go, and doesn't suit me.

And I shall spend my pension on brandy and summer gloves
and satin sandals, and say we've no money for butter.

I shall sit down on the pavement when I'm tired

And gobble up samples in shops and press alarm bells

And run my stick along the public railing

And make up for the sobriety of my youth.

I shall go out in my slippers in the rain

and pick flowers in other people's gardens

And learn to spit...."

WHY WAIT? The time is NOW!

Five

The Ego-Run-Amuck

"The very young, the uninitiated, the hungry, and the wounded have values that revolve around the finding and the winning of trophies."
Clarissa Pinkola Estés

The word ego is tossed about as though the concept is simplistic in nature, but it is not! In workshops and classes, I show a picture of a kitty looking into the mirror and seeing a lion, demonstrating that who you believe you are is not always accurate or what others see.

An understanding of the EGO gives insight into what you are observing in friends and family, co-workers, management, and leaders throughout the world. And most definitely, your EGO affects how you move in the world.

The term EGO traces its origins back to ancient Greek philosophy, specifically to Plato and Aristotle. In Greek, the word "ego" translates to "I" or "self." However, the concept of the EGO took on new dimensions with the introduction of psychoanalysis in the late 19th and early 20th centuries.

Psychologist Carl Jung stated that the EGO is largely responsible for how you regard yourself. The EGO drives your consciousness, so you may make conscious choices to keep your EGO intact—choices that make you think well of yourself. The masks you choose to wear serve the ego, and it is a constant struggle to monitor whether your ego is dictating your choices or not.

There are three levels of the EGO: The *weak ego, the unhealthy ego* (my term is *ego-run-amuck*), and *the healthy ego.*

A *weak ego* is fragile, so you may feel insecure and lack self-confidence. You feel unworthy and believe you are never good enough. You care about what others think of you and are constantly trying to please. You may make degrading comments about yourself, such as your attractiveness, personality, abilities, and so on. You may apologize, just to apologize. You may stay silent, afraid to speak for fear of offending or being judged negatively. You may try to mask what you have deemed to be your inadequacies. You are easy prey for exploitation and manipulation.

And the behaviors of a *weak ego* can diminish you. For instance, if you jokingly say, "Oh my, I am so clueless," the receiver of that information will now respond to you as though you are clueless or watch for how clueless you are. That not only affects what you say and how you say it but how it is received and the response. If you apologize again and again, especially for no reason, you could appear insecure.

So, pause and reflect and ask yourself why are you doing so? Who diminished you? Why did you accept any negative judgment of yourself, remembering you have given them permission to influence your view of yourself?

How have negative comments affected your confidence and the choices you have made? Then, begin by silencing those voices and focusing on the gifts you have been given. And yes, you have gifts, some you have yet to identify.

An *unhealthy ego* makes living an authentic, ethical life impossible. Imagine a hollowed-out tree trunk. The hollowness represents a person's unhealthy ego. He starts to fill that hollow with leaves, but the leaves keep falling out, never filling the emptiness. The *unhealthy ego* is like that hollowed tree trunk. It will never be satiated.

Another image of an *unhealthy ego* is that of a well with no bottom. No matter how much water rushes into that well, the ego will always be thirsty, wanting more and more and more, and doing anything it can to fill the emptiness.

If you have an *unhealthy ego,* you seek endless approval and applause. The EGO needs constant reinforcement because you know you are lacking in whatever is valued by others. It can also drive you to hide those aspects that would harm your image. You may inflate your accomplishments and your successes. If you know you are lacking in substance and have struggled with success, you may use bravado, exaggerations, and puffery to cover up that deficit or may lie and fake it because you cannot admit to a mistake or flaws.

You are not content or confident because you are lacking in ability and intelligence, and so on. Your inability to achieve or your failures contribute to feeling ineffective and nullified, without anything to sustain a positive image of yourself. If you are insecure, afraid to be found out, you may deflect and scapegoat others. Instead of apologizing, like those with a *weak ego,* you use bluster and boasting, and you humiliate and denigrate others to elevate yourself and take the focus off you and your inadequacies.

You could be vengeful and assault and punish others who do not agree with you. You grab and harm anything and anyone in sight. You live in fear of never acquiring enough or in fear of losing what you have acquired. Greed is a result of an *ego-run-amuck* because it can never be satisfied. So, one begins to acquire trappings in an effort to fill up that hollow that says, "Look at me! I'm successful!"

But it is false in every way and is not lasting. You will have to try continually to fill the hollow in that tree, just like the thirst that will never be quenched until the unhealthy EGO no longer controls your life. And if your agenda is wrapped in greed, the EGO can drive your soul underground and your needs will have heightened importance.

If you have a *healthy ego*, your EGO does not dictate and control your life. You become independent of other people's beliefs and values and dictates. You are unwilling to conform in the face of society's pressures. And most importantly, your choices are not self-serving. Your decisions are not based on what benefits you alone, but what benefits others and what is not going to harm another.

Instead, SELF is your inner guiding force. And for SELF to be your guiding star, you need to set aside EGO, put it in its proper place, and always question if your response is ego-based—about you and what you desire.

When SELF drives the psyche, your ego no longer determines your action. SELF acknowledges your gifts and flaws and does not diminish them, like the *weak, fragile ego* or dismiss them like the unhealthy ego. And although the EGO is part of SELF, the EGO does not dominate the psyche.

For example, the EGO is threatened by anything that could cause you to think negatively of yourself, so you will dismiss anything that suggests flaws or mistakes. But the SELF desires to know.

So, how do you ensure that SELF is your guide?

You have confidence in yourself—no bravado—and you are in touch with reality of your worth.

You focus on what you do have, and you use your gifts to help others.

You do not overstate your abilities, experiences…. No inflation, no puffery.

You set boundaries about what you will accept and not accept, and you do not violate them. That definitely means you do not allow others to diminish and assault you, and you do not allow someone to make you feel unworthy.

You speak out and are honest and are not afraid of repercussions for that honesty.

You do not blame others. You are not a victim. You take responsibility for your choices and what happens to you.

When you admit to a mistake and do not make excuses, others will respect you. The words can be as simple as "I made a mistake." And if necessary, apologize and tag on words, "Next time, I will…." OR "I realize that…."

You embrace your warts and all your wondrous gifts.

You do not pretend to be something you are not or change into someone else's version of you. No masks; no conforming and acquiescing when your whole being is saying NO.

You are content with who you are. You do not need to attach yourself to others, namedrop…. to feel worthy.

You do not scapegoat another or have to degrade others to elevate yourself.

You are willing to listen to another's point of view, even if it is in strong contrast to yours. At the same time, that does not mean you force yourself to listen to name-calling, lies, assaults, fabrications, and comments without substance.

You are not envious of another. Instead, you inspire others and celebrate their successes.

You do not need to compete.

You do not need to belittle or diminish others so you will not be found out for what is lacking in you.

You are not obsessed with acquiring trappings that give the appearance of success.

You are not envious of another's appearance or personality traits. Being envious of someone who is more accomplished, beautiful, intelligent… will not make you more accomplished…. so instead celebrate the gifts and beauty within you.

You realize you do not need to do everything on your own to prove yourself to others.

A *healthy ego* paves the way to living an authentic life. It allows you to accept, embrace, and appreciate your true self.

Clarissa Pinkola Estés' quote at the beginning of this chapter is worth exploring.

The very young, those who are uninitiated—meaning those who are naïve, vulnerable, and inexperienced; those who have not had challenges and struggles and have not learned the necessary lessons (and that is not limited to the young).

Those who are hungry—meaning those who feel hollow, whose egos are hungry, seeking approval and applause....

Those who are wounded—meaning those who have been injured by disapproval and punishments have yet to heal.

Have values that revolve around the finding and winning of trophies—meaning they desire something that is proof of their worth. Trophies are trappings in the form of money and titles and tangibles--THINGS.

If you are being true to yourself, your ego is healthy and not a hollow shell. Applause and praise and trappings are not your driving force. Although it is always good to experience approval, you do not need others to approve of you. You must approve of yourself.

At its bare bones, being true to yourself, not allowing the ego to dictate your life, gives you a sense of freedom. You will no longer be driven to do what you do not wish. You become your own guiding force.

Mahatma Ghandi said, *"When the ego dies, the soul awakes."*

<h1 style="text-align:center">Six
Tabla Rasa</h1>

"The soul of man is like an ancient tree, whose roots stretch far into the past."
Carl Jung

Not understanding each other, why we are different, makes unity impossible. And unity is impossible to achieve for those who wish to control or desire conformity. Therefore, it is helpful to explore why we are different and why we have different desires and make different choices.

Psychologist, Carl Jung, rejected the idea that the human mind at birth is a tabla rasa, a blank slate, to be written upon by experiences. Instead, EVERY human mind is somehow connected to the past. Translated: You are born hardwired, programmed with certain inborn patterns that influence your behavior and your life choices. That part of the psyche fascinates and astounds me, and maybe you will experience the same.

Jung called this connectiveness to the past the **collective unconscious**. It is that part of the mind that is not yours alone but is universal—shared by all of us. The collective unconscious is instinctual. It is NOT what we have learned or acquired nor has it been influenced by your personal experiences.

Knowing that at times what I say and do stems from the unconscious realm of my psyche explains so many events in my life. It explains times when I felt someone guiding me. I just knew what to do and say, with no premeditation or agenda.

Within that collective unconscious reside archetypes. Archetypes are *potential* patterns of behaviors in the psyche of all men and women. They are considered *potential* because they must be activated by circumstances and events in one's life. If they are not activated, they will not appear.

For example, we identify certain behaviors with the archetype "mother," a woman who is nurturing, who takes care of her children and enjoys doing so. Consider a young woman who has never spoken of wanting children or showed any signs of nurturing or caring. When she has a child, certain nurturing behaviors of a mother archetype may surface, or they may not.

The *Father's Daughter Archetype* presented earlier is a feminine archetype often committed to achieving professional success. Although she desires to aspire just like men, she may not support that for other women. Maybe knowing that will help women understand why this particular archetype may make them bristle when they are expecting support and not getting it.

Another feminine archetype does not desire marriage and children, while another is focused on being a wife. Another seeks a safe haven, someone to take care of her, and so on.

In workshops and classes when I list traits of various archetypes, I will hear from participants, "Well, I can claim this one, this one, but not that one...." People believe they have to possess all of the behaviors attached to a particular archetype. It is not about possessing them; it is about whether they are activated by an event or words spoken or....

Also, when energized, two or more archetypes may appear and combine, so no single archetype will always play out in pure form. They may overlap, influencing certain behaviors of those archetypes. It is like mixing two or more colors together. Once stirred, the colors change again and again the more you stir. So, within you, there may be bits and pieces of different archetypes blended together.

By becoming aware of the different archetypes, you can begin to unravel how they play out in behaviors you may not have understood previously. Once you are aware of these patterns, you can identify those behaviors that were activated in the past, those that have emerged more recently, and those which are inactive. But most importantly, it explains why all women are not the same; why all men are not the same.

So, where is the evidence that Carl Jung is right? I am giving evidence as I share my memories and my stories of others. Evidence of archetypes is everywhere, and you will begin to recognize them once you are aware of their existence

.

Seven
Feminine and Masculine

"Women, if the soul of the nation is to be saved, I believe you must become its soul."
Coretta Scott King

What a tangled web has been created by dividing the behaviors of men and women into two different camps! Evidence abounds that assigning specific behaviors to men and others to women has caused turmoil, confusion, and conflict.

This is a conundrum that will take many reiterations and years to resolve unless we start to think of behaviors commonly identified as masculine or feminine as a spectrum—a range of behaviors assigned to no one gender in particular. Instead of separate and distinct, segregated behaviors, view them as a variety of choices available to all of us and which reside in all of us.

By viewing the behaviors as a spectrum, we can reject the idea that men and women possess distinct behaviors because of one's gender.

To complicate matters further, behaviors are influenced by external forces—do this, not that, and the behaviors assigned to both genders are judged and given positive and negative value.

Women are the weaker sex; men possess strength

Women are emotional and flighty; men are logical and practical

Why are masculine attributes viewed as favorable, while the feminine are not? Yet, whenever women exhibit masculine behaviors, they are criticized as well. The message a woman receives is that whatever her behavior, a negative connotation will be assigned to her by someone in some way, and she may be discounted and diminished. And if a man exhibits what have been deemed as feminine traits, they may also be discounted and diminished.

Gender is often linked to traits in an effort to explain why men and women exhibit different behaviors. If that is accurate and the entire story, then why do some women exhibit what have been labeled masculine traits, such as directness, rationality, courage, and action? Why do we observe feminine traits, such as compassion and caring in a man? It puts into question the strongly-held belief that gender is the contributing factor of what has been observed and deemed as male and female behaviors.

It also forces the question: Are men and women as different as we are told? That leads back to my earlier statement to view all behaviors as a spectrum, instead of dividing the behaviors into masculine and feminine; thereby eliminating gender as a reason.

Psychologist Carl Jung addressed the reason we observed the feminine in men and the masculine in women. He stated that both the masculine and feminine archetypes reside in each of us, so both energies may be observed in both genders. This claim validates viewing the behaviors as a spectrum, not separate and distinct according to gender. And our observations of men and women confirm his belief. Then why are different and distinct behaviors assigned to each gender, even by Jung?

There are a myriad of reasons. One reason, and maybe the most critical, is the roles assigned or dictated to men and women. The activities and work men and women engage in trigger certain behaviors and leave others dormant.

If a woman becomes an attorney, her logic, courage, directness, and assertiveness, often associated with the masculine, have the potential to appear. They do not appear because she is masculine but because her work activates those behaviors. And feminine traits, such as compassion or nurturing, may not appear unless triggered by some event.

A woman who is a first-grade school teacher may exhibit caring and nurturing, associated with the feminine; yet a father who is raising two toddlers alone may also exhibit similar behaviors.

If a woman is restricted to the home raising children, caring and nurturing may be observed, and when would she have an opportunity to use logic, strength, directness—traits associated with the masculine? And, if she is told or expected to be fragile and emotional, she may internalize those beliefs or play along. If a man is never home, never participating in everyday family life, when would caring and nurturing be observed or activated?

Riane Eisler, author of the book, *The Chalice and the Blade*, gives some insight as to how roles influence behavior. She contrasted the peaceful, nurturing, partnership-oriented matrifocal societies and the violent, dominator-oriented patrifocal cultures, illustrative of domination and violence, which she believes structures our current world and influences our future.

Eisler stated matrifocal societies were more contented and joyful, and society was absent of conflict and wars. The partnership model consisted of a democratic and egalitarian structure in both the family and state or tribe. Authority and power were shared. People aspired to whatever they wish to be, rather than being subjugated. There were also gender partnerships and a low degree of abuse and violence because top-down rankings did not need to be maintained. Imagine!

In patrifocal societies, the domination model ranked man over man, man over woman, race over race, and religion vs. religion, resulting in the differences associated with superiority or inferiority. An authoritarian structure in both family and state or tribe existed, with rigid male dominance and a high degree of abuse and violence. Sound familiar?

Eisler reported that societies once revered the feminine and the nurturing aspects of life, reminiscent of the chalice, which are signs of life-giving and nurturing qualities. In cultures where men and women shared power equally, defense against hostile forces was minimal. Agricultural societies thrived and emphasized community and interdependence, rather than competition and battles and war.

These harmonious societies were significantly altered with the invasion of nomadic, Indo-European groups. These intruders brought a ruthless ideology and a warlike mentality, which transformed cultures across Europe and beyond. Matrifocal societies collapsed from the cruelty of the dominator model that fostered hierarchies and coercion. That dominator model has promoted the plundering and pummeling that has occurred throughout much of human history.

Eisler claimed that the enormity of the after-effects of the dominator model resonated throughout generations and prejudiced and dictated societal norms and gender roles.

So, I am intrigued by the possibility that this indicates in a matrifocal society men and women exhibited the entire spectrum of what has been divided into feminine and masculine behaviors in order to bring about a harmonious egalitarian society. But the plundering and aggression that was a feature of the patrifocal societies forced a change in male and female roles and thus behaviors.

The inevitable would be the suppression of certain traits or no opportunity for them to be activated. That suppression and inability to function as before caused confusion and conflict and the dark side of individuals to emerge. In time, divisiveness between the genders was the result. And that divisiveness is magnified today by the rhetoric that is spewing out of the mouths of men who want to dominate with might and right and greed and want women to be subservient to them.

The influence of the collective is another reason why we observe distinct behaviors between the genders. The collective says, "Little girls are…." "Little boys are…." That is compounded by the toys they are given, how they are treated, what they are and are not allowed to do.

It must be noted that history provides evidence that not everyone will comply to the dictates of a patrifocal society, and not everyone will fall in line with their prescribed gender roles. But if praise is desired and punishment avoided, those behaviors that were dictated by external forces and praised may be repeated and eventually become internalized. Those actions that are rejected or criticized or are being denied and hidden for fear of reprisal may become submerged in one's psyche, but they are never lost.

Because of these external forces, behaviors that are repeated are divided into two camps, and they become prescribed behaviors, not necessarily of one's choosing. That separation of traits is often used to disparage the other gender. But considering these traits as a continuum, not exclusive to any one gender, can begin to eliminate the belief that they are separate and distinct. In time viewing behaviors as a spectrum that reside in all of us, we may begin to eliminate the conflict and derogatory remarks made about each gender.

Although assigning behaviors to the masculine and feminine is prescriptive, discussing the feminine and masculine as separate entities is still helpful for an understanding of what has been declared feminine and masculine traits.

To represent the *feminine archetype,* Jung assigned the word *anima,* which literally means **soul**. Soulfulness speaks to the heart, the feeling, and the warmth and compassion that resonates deep within. Two of the main qualities of the feminine include building harmonious relationships and mediation, both within herself and with others. Therefore, a woman with anima traits reflects internally on her own thoughts and actions, and she does the same with her encounters with others. The same would apply to men.

If a woman is secure and possesses a healthy ego, she may reflect with candor and sense of purpose on relationships and encounters with others. She will not excuse her behavior, even if it creates conflict within her. If she has a weak ego, she may take on too much responsibility for the encounter. She may blame herself if there is conflict and wants to apologize to smooth things over.

If she has an unhealthy ego, she might fault the other person for the conflict or misunderstanding, lash out, demean, and even assault and not see her role in it. So, it is important that she enter into this internal dialogue with a healthy ego.

Besides fostering relationships, the feminine also includes closeness, kindness, curiosity, openness, warmth, comfort, compassion, empathy, intuition, and creativity. These qualities contribute to relating emotionally to others and creating relationships. And because these behaviors are part of a complete spectrum, a man may exhibit these traits as well if he embraces connection and intimacy and is not bowing to the collective's call to be a "man" and all that implies.

There are those who claim that the traits assigned to the feminine make women appear inferior or weak, and thereby would make a man inferior or weak. Why are these traits considered inferior? Because the collective has made it so.

What is considered feminine traits are laudable and must be valued, praised, elevated, and acknowledged and not purged or denied. Any woman, anyone, who exhibits what has been deemed as feminine behaviors does not need to deny them, accept any negativity assigned to that trait, nor should she apologize or demean those behaviors.

Jung claimed that anima's "soulful" internal activity is centered on **nourishing inner and outer relationships to preserve the species.** So, intimacy, connections, community, validation, and belonging are fostered and valued, which can eliminate the feelings of isolation.

People who feel validated and are contributing are valued. And as part of a tribe, they have heightened self-esteem and the ability to act for themselves. No entitlement and no rescuing needed. No feelings of insecurity.

And if the desire is to preserve the species, would we allow others to struggle, would we create sorrow and hurt? Would we wage war on people, kill another without cause, or harm another?

The main qualities of the *animus*, the *masculine archetype*, which relates to one's spirit, take place in the external world. They include reason and analysis, logic, intellect, rationality, directness, courage, and physical strength.

Animus' "spiritual" external activity is focused on **doing what is necessary to preserve oneself.** In some ways it appears automatically insular. WIIFM—what's in it for me. And that can create a life of aggression, loneliness, and competition. And if someone is fixated on his own well-being, might he harm another without any feeling of remorse or culpability?

Don't we want to preserve the species, while preserving the individual, sacrificing neither? And **preserving the individual** is NOT about doing what is best for that one person but preserving the uniqueness within each of us, being able to lead the life you desire, not one that is dictated by the collective.

Can you provide evidence that what men in particular are doing and dictating in the world will preserve the species? And unfortunately, every day we have evidence that there are those who are only interested in serving the few and not interested in preserving the species.

The only thing that some men are doing to preserve the species is ensuring women marry and have those babies. But preserving the species includes fostering and preserving relationships and not plundering and killing another.

The traits claimed as masculine contribute to the assertion that men should have careers because those traits are more important than feminine traits. This would also imply that women who display masculine traits should be able to claim their place at the table. But that is not always reality because not everyone in the collective accepts those traits within women as natural.

The collective does not recognize that we all have the entire spectrum of behaviors and are free to allow those behaviors to appear. By keeping the separation of masculine and feminine behaviors, men can continually claim that women are inferior and that there is something wrong with women who exhibit what is erroneously considered masculine.

People do the work, and so an organizational model that fosters relationships, harmony, community, and compassion can benefit. And do not forget creativity, curiosity, and intuition, which is often dismissed as "that thing women do."

In most men, traits such as feelings, kindness, tenderness, curiosity, fostering relationships, creativity, and intuition have been demeaned and are not welcome. The collective says, "Man-up!" "Don't cry!" "Don't show emotion!" A man is called a "sissy" if he is tender and caring.

An article in *Harvard Business Review*, October 8, 2018, *How Men Get Penalized for Straying from Masculine Norms* by David M. Mayer reported that men face adverse outcomes for displaying what are termed feminine *norms* rather than masculine *norms* in the workplace.

The feminine *norms* listed in that article were similar to Jung's list: empathy (compassion), being agreeable (harmony and relationship-oriented), showing sadness (emotion), and being humble (lack of ego-run-amuck, which includes not boasting).

According to this report, biases about how men are to be and behave in the world can determine their worth and how they are regarded. Men associated with feminine *norms* may face criticism and are often viewed as less competent and less suitable for managerial roles. They are viewed as weaker, less likeable, and less deserving. They also experience career derailment and receive lower performance evaluations—more so than their female counterparts.

Are young boys and men who are choosing to be compassionate and caring saying NO to the fathers' dictates and refusing to embrace prescribed masculine traits? Are they rejecting aggression and patriarchal behaviors and dogma? Do they believe they will live a more contented life if it is filled with connections and intimate relationships and tenderness and benevolence?

This may be one clue as to why there are those calling for "masculinity" to solve the perceived "problems" that young men are said to be facing. And that must be a concern for all of us. We must ask who has decided that a lack of masculinity is a problem and why? What evidence is there that young boys and men are not masculine? Why are people embracing this belief?

The psychological effects of the call for masculinity have to be acknowledged and considered. Are men hearing that they are not masculine enough? Are boys and men hearing they are broken and lacking in some way and have to be fixed? Are young men asking why are they being singled out and women are not?

And how is masculinity being translated into behavior? How does one discern if someone is masculine or not? Who decides what it is and what it is not? What are the ills of society that have created the perceived need for masculinity? Why do they have to reclaim their masculinity? Where did it go and why? Do young men agree that they need to become more masculine?

Or are young men being declared as not masculine enough because the "fathers" have agendas and desires that young men are not fulfilling, and they want to make young men in their image?

And when young boys and men hear masculinity, do they equate that to strength and aggression? Three in four boys report feeling pressure to be strong, and two in five believe society expects them to resolve anger with aggression, according to the Oberlin High School Men's Work Project in Oberlin, Ohio.

And movies and television series and real-life events, such as the assault on the United States Capitol and the killing and battering of people by ICE, have done a stellar job of convincing them that aggression is OK, and they won't be held accountable.

Conformity is the opposite of free will and requires a person to be what the collective is dictating, denying who a man is deep within. Problems arise when young boys and men are pummeled with the call to be masculine, especially if it becomes internalized. The stress of conformity can lead to insecurity and a lack of confidence because they are not comfortable with the role they are to play and the masks they are to wear. They will doubt who they are and question whether they have any value.

This is especially difficult for those young men and boys who are struggling to find their identity. They are easily gaslighted at a young age, and unfortunately, young boys and men may translate the need to be more masculine into aggressive behavior, assaulting women and others in word and deed.

External forces can lead to an unhealthy identity or a lack of one instead of one that is wrapped in self-rule and authentic behavior—being true to who they are. That stress can force them to seek validation from the "fathers" in their lives, and if pressure for unhealthy masculinity permeates their lives, it could play out in aggressive behavior.

Women also face issues about what are acceptable behaviors. When women first entered management in numbers during the 70s and 80s, many of them exhibited what was considered masculine behaviors and that was unacceptable. They were not considered kind and understanding, and they lacked compassion.

Men had promoted them, and many did so because those women dispensed with issues in similar ways, either by choice or because of pressure to do so. Some staff responded negatively to these female managers. Their management style was demonized and called disparaging names, and they had difficulty being effective.

The female manager insisted on accountability and disregarded employees' personal lives. Some female staff assumed that a female manager would understand their childcare needs and the struggles of working and managing a household. And maybe a woman manager would be someone they could confide in and with whom they could have a personal connection.

When they discovered that SHE was not any different from a male manager, this was an unexpected turn of events. Once again, biases about how a woman should be in this world affected her ability to function in a management position.

But prescribed masculine qualities do not have to come at the expense of prescribed feminine qualities. And prescribed feminine qualities do not have to come at the expense of prescribed masculine qualities. They do not have to be in opposition, but it benefits patriarchal men to keep the division, and thereby the divisiveness.

The designated masculine qualities, when activated, provide a woman with spirituality and the ability to question and think logically. She possesses more focused awareness, concentration, and rational reasoning.

The process of feminine development in a male is about opening up to tender feelings and welcoming a consciousness, maybe which has been denied or not yet experienced. That would include intuitive processes, creativity, imagination, compassion, and kindness.

Most importantly, these behaviors do not have to be learned. They reside within all of us, so it is important to acknowledge the benefits of allowing those behaviors to flourish. When they are triggered, brought to the surface, let them flow. Do not deny them or try to purge them.

The masculine, according to Jung, whether observed in women or men, is not relationship oriented, so there is the possibility that those who do not embrace fostering relationships will always be isolated to some degree—from intimacy, connection, community, and from feelings and emotions.

The Good Men's Project of 2009 highlighted that men do not have connections with others—the one and only confidant being their wife, which can lead to isolation. So, since this article is dated 2009, this phenomenon of isolation is not recent. Isolation, to varying degrees, has been a struggle for men, probably for centuries.

Those who are relationship-oriented are aware how beneficial close connections are. Those who are not relationship-oriented are often clueless as to how not having intimate ties to other people has harmed them.

They are also clueless as to why they often have to resort to coercion or criticism or punishment to get someone to deliver. Lacking in relationships of intimacy and connection, their contributions in organizations, in the world, may be limited or lost.

Wouldn't it benefit anyone's well-being to have heartwarming relationships with whom to share joys and sorrows or see the sun setting in the West?

And the isolation that is being experienced by young men has increased due to technology. One solution would be to realize that connections, intimacy, and feelings should be valued.

Also, men can cast aside the dictates of opting for masculine behaviors alone and not fear the assaults that try to purge the compassion, caring, and tenderness that reside within them. And men may welcome the freedom to embrace what has been relegated to the feminine without fear of being chastised.

A man who combines strength of purpose, logic, reasoning, and a sense of calm with tenderness, caring, and compassion is an enticing combination for many women. And fostering intimate relationships, helpfulness, and concern for others is laudable and would be welcomed in any society that is not patriarchal.

And the logic, directness, and courage in women could be embraced, rather than assaulted and regarded as a liability. By embracing both the masculine and feminine, looking at those traits as a range of choices, their differences would not be part of the equation and would not continue to fuel divisiveness.

In the book, *Lying with the Heavenly Woman*, Jungian Robert A. Johnson writes: *"Almost all of a man's sense of value, worth, safety, joy, contentment, belongingness, and happiness derive from his inner feminine nature… Men, in their arrogance, generally think it is their strength, possessions, and dominations that bring them happiness. But it is not so. Happiness is feminine in a man, a feeling quality and generally mysterious to him."*

And do not confuse the "call for masculinity," which has many versions, with masculine traits as defined by Jung. In reality, both masculine and feminine traits are value neutral, and not one advocated over the other. There are no dictates of how a man or woman should be. They are observations of different traits that reside within and that we can all embrace if we see the wisdom in doing so.

It is the judgment that people put upon them that makes any behavior good or bad. It is the expectation of what a woman should be or what a man should be that has contributed to the divide between the genders and how they are viewed.

Jung's work on the feminine and masculine has come under some scrutiny because of the patriarchal influence of the time. I have chosen to use his work as a stepping stone to analyze the masculine and feminine from a variety of perspectives. It is also beneficial to frame them by acknowledging the need to preserve the species and the individual.

But I do not agree that they should be viewed as two distinct and separate entities. And there is wisdom in Jung theorizing that to live an authentic life, to be contented, to be in balance, and to be more effective, all men and women will benefit by allowing the spectrum of behaviors to thrive within each of us.

There is no prescription—no one way for any of us to be.

Eight
The Devil Made Me Do It!

"Unfortunately, there can be no doubt that man, on the whole, is less good than he imagines himself or wants to be. Everyone carries a shadow; the less it is embodied in the individual's conscious life, the blacker and denser it is."

Carl Jung

The *shadow archetype* resides within the realm of the unconscious and is part of the psyche of every human being. The *shadow* is made up of negative emotions and is often summed up with the saying, "The devil made me do it!"

The *shadow* represents the *unknown* dark side of a person and plays out in harmful, negative behavior. And knowing that there is a dark side provides understanding but does not give a pass on that behavior.

"A scorpion wants to cross a river but cannot swim, so it asks a frog to carry it across. The frog hesitates, afraid that the scorpion might sting it, but the scorpion promises not to, pointing out that it would drown if it killed the frog in the middle of the river. The frog considers this argument sensible and agrees to transport the scorpion. Midway across the river, the scorpion stings the frog anyway, dooming them both. The dying frog asks the scorpion why it stung despite knowing the consequence, to which the scorpion replies: "I am sorry, but I couldn't resist the urge. It's in my nature."

And the dark side is within everyone's nature. Whatever you learn that is deemed inferior or evil and whatever you reject in yourself becomes part of your shadow. For example, a woman who exhibits only masculine behavior may have learned that it is undesirable to exhibit feminine behaviors. So, she not only sublimates her feminine behaviors, she rejects women who display them. She may accuse them of being weak or too emotional, not strong enough, too nice…., just like a man might do!

Rob's father emigrated to the United States from a country that is denigrated and slandered, and its people viewed as inferior. By the time he was ten, he was ashamed of his father and his heritage. As an adult, he speaks against that country and its people every chance he gets.

The dark side is also triggered by events in someone's life. For example, a *mother archetype* exhibits nurturing behaviors and is kind and compassionate to her child. If her relationship with that child is threatened, the shadow side may appear in a possessive obsession that does not allow her child any freedom. She keeps her caged, comments negatively about her friends, aunts, grandmother so her daughter stays close to her and no other.

Since the ego cannot accept anything that paints you in a negative light, it battles against the dark side — the *shadow*. The shadow appears, but the ego may deny its appearance. It may blame the response on someone or something else. But denying the existence of the shadow does not mean it does not exist. And you can only know your true self by embracing, rather than denying your shadow.

Ponder and think about those people you know, those who capture the headlines, sometimes daily, and ask yourself: Who are being driven by their ego, what is self-serving? Who are not? Who are wearing masks, saying what they do not believe to get applause and approval? Who is not? Who are displaying their shadows? Who are not?

Nine
The Fathers in Her Life

"Two thousand years ago we lived in the world of Gods and Goddesses. Today we live solely in a world of Gods. Women in most cultures have been stripped of their spiritual power."

Dan Brown

For thirty years, Olivia struggled in a business world that did not accept her—a male dominated world and a world of youth. And she became more of an outlier in that world as she aged in the workplace.

Olivia was convinced that if she worked long hours and supported her male manager, he would embrace her, give her adequate raises and bonuses, and champion her efforts. Yet for years, a series of managers disappointed her again and again, denying what she believed were appropriate pay increases, bonuses, and promotions.

She begged and fussed and fumed when she did not get her "just desserts." She was convinced her managers did not like her and her style of operating. This drama was repeated again and again, year after year, always asking for more, pleading her case, and getting denied. Yes, a few crumbs were thrown her way, but it was never enough.

Her one option was to quit her job, but her identity was her job. Her vice president title, passed out like candy in her industry, represented a testimony to her success and was used to keep her quiet. She also believed she could not make the high salary anywhere else. And her salary, although not enough to please her, was also testimony to her perceived success as well.

When reminded of how she was disregarded and what she had done to survive, it was as though she had amnesia. Her defense of her bosses, "It wasn't that bad." She could not bring herself to remember all those years of turmoil and begging and pleading. Often denial is a way of justifying and excusing bad behavior—yours and others.

By justifying and excusing, Olivia would not have to take responsibility for allowing the situation to continue year after year. She would not have to feel guilty for accepting tiny pieces of the pie that were dished out to her. She would not appear foolish for begging the fathers in her life all those years or admit that she did not have the courage to make another choice. These statements are not to condemn her but to explain her behavior and why she made the choices she did.

The men in Olivia's life had always pulled her strings. Her father had cast a wide net over her destiny. He told her when she divorced that she would never earn enough money to take care of herself. Her father's comment took hold of her psyche, and Olivia was going to make sure he was wrong about her.

Olivia is like other women and men who conform and perform and bend because they desire what is being offered. They believe they have no other way of getting what they crave. Some do it consciously, well aware of the deal they have made, although often unconscious of what they are denying themselves. Others are unconscious on all levels, unaware of the details of the contract, unaware of the psychological impact it has made upon them, and oblivious to what they have sacrificed.

When I decided to leave the corporate world and start my own management consulting and executive coaching company, Olivia told me to quit such silliness and get a real job. I asked her what she meant by a real job.

"One where you get a salary and benefits."

For her, that translated into perceived security. So, I responded, "Does that guarantee you happiness? Contentment? For years, you have fought to get what your male colleagues are getting. You have been turned away again and again.

"Every day you wonder whether you will have a job the next day. Every year you are denied the raise and bonus you deserve. I'm putting my destiny in my hands. I'm betting on me."

Besides embracing the fathers in her life, Olivia was putting her fears on to me—fears that she lived with for years. I wasn't having it. But that did not silence her. She did not relent in telling me to get a "real" job." Every time she called, she inquired if I had made any progress on getting clients. It got to the point that I did not want to pick up the telephone.

When I did speak to Olivia, I was positive. I never shared any concerns because I wasn't concerned. It appeared that Olivia wanted proof sooner rather than later that I had made the wrong decision. Fortunately, I was patient with myself, but I knew Olivia would never be.

Another long-time friend, Marilyn, was once my colleague in the corporate world. There was no doubt Marilyn was concerned about my decision to start my own business. But instead of telling me to get a real job, Marilyn supported me and connected me with some contacts, concerned that I had no immediate income. Those contacts gave me a few projects that I could do until I got my business established. That is the type of support needed when women decide to swing on a limb.

After several months of "get a real job" urgings, Olivia called me and said she ran into someone I knew quite well in the business world. Olivia had only met Luke a few times and briefly. He asked about me, and Olivia told him that I had started my own business. "Well, good for her. She should never be working for someone else. She's got a lot of business savvy and creativity…."

As she told me of this encounter, her voice was light and positive. It was obvious she was now on board with my decision. Was it because she thought Luke knew better? If he declared it was the right thing to do, then it must be so? Whatever the reason, she never mentioned my getting a *real job* again.

If something went wrong, she declared she was unlucky. The *god of unlucky* got blamed again and again. Admitting to a mistake may be too devastating, changes in behavior may be too daunting, so blame it on the *god of unlucky*. No effort required, and she did not have to do anything differently the next time.

She continues to believe she did everything right. And if she admitted that she had made a mistake, she would have to admit that wisdom does not reside within her. She would have to admit that she has to make other choices—choices that may put her out on that limb by herself. She would also have to admit that coveting the fathers in her life may not have served her career—a career being the driving force in her life.

Also, Olivia was against women on her staff having time off when they had a baby. It disrupted the workplace and her department's ability to be successful. That mindset led her to hire a man as her assistant, and ultimately, he betrayed her.

Olivia does not support women's rights. Admitting to inequality signifies that she had attached her dream of success to the coattails of the fathers in her life—fathers who will never admit her into *their boys' club*.

If I would point out to Olivia an instance of inequality that a female experienced from a male manager, she would say something like, "Well, maybe she did not perform as well as she thought," even though she had experienced a similar situation. Or, "Well, men have the same problem." Yes, but why does that negate a particular woman's situation? And in every instance, she did not have the particulars of that woman nor did she ask. She was too quick to exonerate the man, and there was also no basis for her comment.

She never saw the hypocrisy of those statements when she herself had the same experiences. She never once said, "I guess I didn't perform as well as I thought." Although she said time and time again that her male counterparts were getting larger bonuses, it was always because her manager did not like her.

Admitting to bias and inequality would force her to admit that she could not climb the ladder of success. She believed she could and would because, possibly unconsciously, she thought she was the exception. She was not like other women, so inequality did not apply to her.

Have you guessed that Olivia is a *Father's Daughter Archetype*?

In one of my favorite feel-good movies, *Baby Boom*, J.C. Wyatt is the Tiger Lady in the business world, expected to soon make partner. When she becomes the guardian of her cousin's baby after he and his wife are killed, her life is turned upside down. She embraces her role as a mother, somewhat shedding her *Father's Daughter Archetype*—the persona of the Tiger Lady.

An account is taken away from her because she is viewed as losing focus. It is given to the young man she had mentored. Mortified, she chooses to leave and move out of New York City into the country.

Soon she establishes her own business selling baby food. When her former boss brings her an opportunity to sell her company, she is at first ecstatic. She would be back in the game. Then she realizes what she will have to give up, and she declines the offer, saying that "The rat race is going to have to live with one less rat!"

If she accepted the offer, she would be putting her life and career into someone else's hands once again. She would have to perform and conform, possibly limiting her possibilities, wanting and waiting. She told them that she could do what they could do.

She was still a businesswoman, an entrepreneur, a formidable force, but she was doing it on her own terms and in a different way. She no longer had to bow to the *fathers* in her life.

Remember all archetypes reside within you. The path you choose is your decision alone. You have choices, and those choices make you who you are.

Ten
The Sister Archetype

"You can tell who the strong women are. They are the ones building another woman up, rather than tearing each other down."

Unknown

Why do some women support and inspire each other, while others do not? Why do some women choose to dictate how another woman should live her life because they believe they are right? Why does a woman who rises to the top of the ladder pull it up behind her? Why....? Understanding the various feminine archetypes can provide insight into why women have different desires and travel different paths.

The *Sister Archetype* is at the other end of the continuum to the *Father's Daughter*. She does not covet the fathers in her life, nor does she embrace dictates or dogma. She is more interested in contributing and being involved in a cause that speaks to her, such as equality, cruelty to animals and children, and supporting women and those who are disenfranchised. She may fight against the injustices and suffering of others, without concern for her own well-being.

She epitomizes the type of sister and friend some women might wish to have in their lives, and most definitely if she herself is a *Sister Archetype*.

Elizabeth Bennett in Jane Austen's *Pride and Prejudice* cheers her sister Jane's love affair with a suitor, never saying to herself, "Oh my. I don't have a man, and she does." And even though she is not seeking a spouse, she supports Jane's desire to love Bingley and marry him. She rejoices in Jane's joy, praises her kind demeanor and beauty, and cares for Jane when she becomes ill. She then turns down a marriage proposal from Mr. Darcy when she learns that he has spoken against Bingley's affection for Jane.

Elizabeth tries to help her sister, Lydia, who she believes is going astray and will get herself into some kind of trouble. As a *Sister Archetype*, she is seeking to help Lydia, not wanting her to fall in a chasm vast and deep and wide, even though she may consider her silly and ridiculous.

Elizabeth never joins in on her mother's drama and never expresses any inclination to marry, which vexes her mother indeed. She refuses to marry Mr. Collins, to the horror of her mother, but to the delight of her father. But neither her parents' approval or disapproval would cause her to marry. As a *Sister Archetype*, Elizabeth says that only the greatest love will cause her to marry.

Elizabeth experiences upset and embarrassment by the behavior of her mother and her younger sisters. Yet, she never lashes out at them. She only attempts to intervene, trying to rescue her family again and again. But her father does not heed her warning. Her mother cannot be silenced. And Lydia cannot be stopped.

In all instances, Elizabeth was supportive of her family, and she was trying to ensure their happiness. Her concern for Lydia and Jane was genuine. She did not want to see either of them harmed. And throughout the novel, she stays true to her archetype.

The *Sister* Archetype balances both the full spectrum of traits attributed to the feminine and masculine. Elizabeth says about her interactions with Darcy, "There is a stubbornness about me that never can bear to be frightened by the will of others. My courage always rises at every attempt to intimidate me." Yet, she is caring and has strong connections to Jane, her friend Charlotte, and her father.

Although Darcy has position and money, Elizabeth spars with him, continually calls him out on his inappropriate behavior, and refuses his marriage proposal. In doing so, she says to him, "Do you think that any consideration would tempt me to accept the man who has been the means of ruining, perhaps forever, the happiness of a most beloved sister?"

Of all of Elizabeth's objections to Darcy, the harm to her sister is paramount. This is true of a *Sister Archetype,* who protects and supports women, who rages at injustice.

Although marriage would secure her future and the future of her family, Elizabeth cannot be forced into marriage. Although she realizes that she loves Darcy, she only says yes to his proposal after learning that he saved Lydia's reputation and removed his objections to Bingley's proposal to her sister Jane.

Elizabeth's support of Jane and her railing against Darcy for his unfair treatment of women are telling of her archetype. Jane Austen may not have had the advantage of studying archetypes, but she was a student of human behavior, as are many writers of literature.

Lady Sybil in *Downton Abbey* had no difficulty expressing her opinions, without remorse and could not be silenced. Her speaking out again and again, especially on women's rights, is a signal to everyone that she does not wish to be agreeable or acquiesce to anyone.

Lady Sybil steps out into the world, becomes a nurse, and helps a maid secure employment as a secretary at a time when a woman did not leave service. The maid was to stay in her lane. Sybil falls in love and decides to marry the family chauffeur. She does not change her mind when her father shouts and threatens that she will receive no money from him. And of course, she will lose her title LADY Sybil, but as she says to her father, "Nobody cares about that stuff!" But it is she who doesn't care about that stuff.

A *Sister Archetype* does not get her identity from the fathers in her life. The status, title, employment, money, prestige, or lack of these trappings of her father or husband are not important to her. Elizabeth in *Pride and Prejudice* could have agreed to marry Darcy if his position and titles were what was important to her, but they were not. The only identity important to a *Sister Archetype* is hers.

There are many examples of this feminine archetype in history and literature, and now that you are aware, you may begin to recognize them.

The *Sister Archetype* has no doubt she is equal to men. No one will convince her otherwise. She is a patriarch's nemesis. She is quick to cry out, *"That's not fair,"* when a boy or man is allowed to do something that has been denied her. She often has no hesitancy in taking action when she feels she is being treated as "second best."

And most importantly, she fights for equality for all—the rights of both men and women because men are also demeaned and assaulted by the patriarchy. Unlike a woman who covets the patriarchy, the *Sister Archetype* challenges them and tries not to suffer at their hands, nor will she do the patriarch's bidding.

Both genders may find a *Sister Archetype's* determination, confidence, courage, and unwillingness to bow to the dictates of a patriarchal society welcoming and noteworthy. But just like all women who chart a different path than what is expected, she has challenges. And those challenges are magnified in a patriarchal and matriarchal society. So, others may find her troublesome—someone who must be silenced, punished, painted negatively, eliminated. She can be maligned by men and rejected by other women, but she perseveres.

Unlike a woman vested in her own well-being, contentment, and security, she is motivated by getting behind a cause she feels deeply about. She isn't deterred by how she will be regarded and the punishments that may be delivered upon her.

There are and have been women who care more about issues than their own safety. Dian Fossey lived in the outdoors and studied gorillas for eighteen years. She fell in love but would not leave her gorillas. She was passionate in her fight to save them from poaching and smuggling. Dian was killed in her hut; her skull cracked open. Her killer was never identified. It was reported that she was naming high government officials for crimes of smuggling and poaching.

Suffragettes marched and were beaten and jailed, went on hunger strikes, and were force fed. English suffragette, Emily Wilding Davison, fought for the vote for women in Britain in the early twentieth century. She was called a militant fighter and was arrested on nine occasions, went on hunger strikes seven times, and was force-fed forty-nine times. To draw attention to the suffragette movement, she threw herself in front of King George VI's horse at the 1914 Derby, resulting in her death.

Some might see the profile of this archetype as a feminist. But her contributions often extend beyond the fight for equality for both men and women. She may call out men on patriarchal behaviors, but she is just as quick to call out women who harm other women. She is also the protector of those who cannot fight for themselves — animals, children…., and she believes in equality for anyone who is denied. If she sees someone drowning in abuse or diminished, animals being harmed, people in peril…., she will be quick to speak out about the injustice.

Like all archetypes, the *Sister Archetype* has a dark side. Her rage at injustice is swift. For example, it has been recorded that Dian Fossey tried to force an exchange by taking hostage the small daughter of a Rwanda woman who she accused of abducting a baby gorilla.

The *Sister Archetype* can be a woman of fury, especially if she or others have been violated, or in the case of Dian Fossey, her gorillas. Unlike the *Father's Daughter Archetype*, who does not expect to be betrayed by men—mainly because she covets them—the *Sister Archetype* is not surprised at a man's betrayal. But she may be devastated by a woman's betrayal, especially if she has inspired and supported her.

Just like all feminine archetypes, she may be a mother and a wife, but if true to her archetype, her main focus will not be marriage. Her relationship with her husband will be one of equality. She will have as much say in any matter as he does, and if he tries to push her aside, depending on her situation, she will most likely speak out. As a mother, she will treat her sons and daughters equally.

The *Sister Archetype* is not only in fiction but all around us as well. Have you noticed these archetypal behaviors in yourself or one of your friends or maybe your mother, grandmother, aunt?

Eleven
The Matriarch Archetype

*"How wrong is it for a woman to expect the man to
build the world she wants, rather than create it herself?"*
Anaïs Nin

Any woman who desires to be a wife above anything
else, often spending her nights and days finding that perfect
someone to marry, is displaying one of the traits of a
Matriarch Archetype, also known as a *Wife Archetype*.

She is seeking a relationship in which her husband or
partner will provide for her and her children. She will
receive the gifts bestowed upon her—the Mrs. title, and
maybe a house, a car, a credit card, children, and maybe a
fairy tale life. She has an unspoken and unwritten contract
that dictates in return she will take care of him, support him,
and not go against him.

But note that **not** all women who are wives are
Matriarchs. And if a woman is not a *Matriarch Archetype*, she
most likely will not fit into the patriarchy's idea of a wife
unless that archetype is activated or she conforms.

A *Matriarch Archetype* gets her identity from her
husband, possibly bragging rights, protection, and
essentials from his work and reputation, so she will do
whatever is necessary to make her husband successful. And
because her identity is tied to her husband and the successes
of her children, they will often be a topic of conversation.

Although times supposedly have changed, she still may
introduce herself as Mrs. John Smith, not Cindy Smith,
especially if her husband's name would be recognized. She

may speak of her husband's work. She might even say, "My husband says….," instead of giving her own opinion.

In the film, *Mona Lisa Smile*, set in the 1950s, there is a course at a prestigious women's college on how to entertain your husband's boss to make him successful. Yet, many of those women could have had their own careers, but it was her husband's career that she was to ensure was successful. And that way of thinking has been passed on.

Since she gets her identity from her husband, a *Matriarch* fears losing him to another woman. Who would she be without him? Allowing a single, attractive friend to get close to her husband is avoided. Couples are friends with couples, believing a married woman is safe.

She may blame the other woman for her husband's dalliance. A husband of hers would only stray if tempted. And if the shadow appears, she will bring a reign of terror upon him and the other woman if she is removed from her throne. You might remember the story of Betty Broderick who killed her former husband and second wife.

The *Matriarch* is a take-charge-woman who will do everything for her husband and children because they are a reflection of her. She expects them to value her, and she expects her children to obey and be guided by her. And she will often covet her son over her daughter, supporting him and his efforts and praising him.

Where it can get messy is when she becomes dogmatic about how her children should live their lives. She can become angry, even outraged (the dark side) if a child has smeared the family reputation, which she tries to protect.

Think of the young girls who were put in homes, some asylums, when they got pregnant, their child taken away. Think of young men tossed out of a family who are on drugs or a gad-about, not delivering what is expected of them.

When Allison's husband died at an early age, she looked for a second husband. When she discovered her second husband wanted to spend her money and misrepresented himself, she divorced him and started looking for a third husband. When the third husband was diagnosed with dementia, she divorced him.

When I met her at the age of eighty-two, she was looking for her fourth husband. When I asked her why she was seeking a husband, she was surprised at the question. Her reply, "Women should be married! I've been trying to convince my divorced daughter of that for years."

Claire, a neurologist, and her husband, a neurosurgeon, had moved to a wealthy, posh part of suburbia. One day she met several of her female neighbors who were stay-at-home wives. After introductions, the first question from one of the women, "What does your husband do?"

They did not ask her if she had a career, which upset her. In the minds of her neighbors, her husband's career gave her an identity, maybe a criterion for her to be welcomed into their club.

One night I was asked by a colleague, Janet, to join her and her friend, Linda, in the city (New York) at an upscale nightclub on Park Avenue. Hmmm! Not my scene.

At the same time, I was free and wanted to get out and about, so I said yes. At the end of the evening, Janet had to get the train to Long Island, leaving Linda upset about an encounter with another woman. Concerned for her, I said, "Let's go for a cup of coffee." I did not want to send her home feeling bad about herself.

We found a coffee shop and sat there talking for a while. About what I do not remember, but what I do remember is that at one point she glared at me and shouted, "You're the reason I'm not getting a husband. All I want is to be a wife and mother, but men don't want me. They want women like you. Women who have careers; women who are interesting."

I never thought of myself as competing with other women because I never thought of other women as competition. I didn't want to be with a man who was attracted to another woman, and if it occurred, that was between the two of them, not me.

Here I was doing what a friend of mine would call a good deed, and I was being assaulted. Was she trying to make me regret my choices, my life? What was I supposed to do? Turn myself into someone else to make her happy? What would the next woman want me to do?

The issues were hers, not mine. But she was trying to hand them off to me so she would not have to do anything different—just keep insisting the reason she was not married was because of women like me.

I mentioned that it was not too late to find a husband and that maybe she needed to be patient with herself. I also suggested she join an organization or volunteer where she might meet men who are liked-minded. Bar hopping, searching for a husband, was a waste of an evening.

Also, she was wrong. It was not easy for me either. I too had difficulty because at the other end of the continuum, women who have careers and degrees are not what many men desire. I did not mention that to her. Would she care? And she already had made up her mind about me and dubbed women like me the problem.

In the film, *The Help*, Abeline states, "Miss Hilly was the first of the babies to have a baby, and it must have come out of her like the eleventh commandment because everyone at the bridge table had to have one too."

Miss Hilly was in charge of her friends and treated them as children, needing her guidance and telling them what to do and what to think. These women were afraid of her wrath. So much so that Elizabeth, one of her charges, forced her husband to put a toilet outside for "the help" and made sure Hilly's deviled eggs were prepared the way she liked them.

One of Hilly's missions was to find a husband for a former classmate, Skeeter, and was happy to introduce her to a prospective husband. She made fun of Skeeter's education and her work life. If Skeeter marries, it is testimony to Hilly's choice of marriage over a career, invalidating Skeeter's choice. Skeeter would join the ranks of married women, a holy state.

Nancy Reagan is an example of the shadow of the *Matriarch Archetype*. A biography, *The Triumph of Nancy Reagan*, by Washington *Post* writer Karen Tumulty, stated that the Reagan's relationship often interfered with their connections to their children. Their allegiances to one another and to his legacy as a politician often overshadowed their responsibilities to their kids.

"When she was displeased about something, they all knew it, and those who were not in her good graces tended not to last for long, "Tumulty wrote.

Stu Spencer, President Reagan's chief political strategist from early on in his career, described the couple as "an inseparable team politically and personally. He would never have been governor without her. He would never have been president without her."

All of Ronald Reagan's titles and positions bestowed upon Mrs. Reagan an identity—those she would not have without him. She was not going to let her husband fail. So, when he was not capable, she took over and was happy to do so without public acknowledgment. She wanted to preserve her husband's good name, his legacy that reflected upon her. And Mrs. Reagan's support of her husband and dismissal of her children are testimony that a *Matriarch Archetype* will choose her husband over her children.

In television series and films, there are many examples of the *Matriarch Archetype*. They are often the happy housewives who please their husbands and take care of their children and do so with grace and charm.

The *Matriarch Archetype* fears never getting married, and when married, she will keep her marriage intact, no matter what. To help her overcome her fears, she might consider learning how to live on her own and doing for herself as much as she commits to doing for her husband. And most importantly, she must consider that attaching herself to someone else may not bring her contentment and happiness. She may lose herself, and in time may not recognize the person she has become.

Like all archetypes, the *Matriarch* has positive aspects, and at the same time she can overstep her in-charge stance. She may get pushed back if her children are not willing to comply with her dictates. So, there is wisdom in looking at what is at stake when she becomes dogmatic, such as what harm she might do to a relationship with her children and others in her life.

Attaching herself to someone else for happiness may only bring her disappointment, and although she may struggle alone and unmarried, they will be her struggles. And the day she chooses a partner, she will do so with wisdom, courage, confidence, and the knowledge she does not NEED the relationship; she desires it!

To step out on her own, a woman can ask herself why this archetype is so dominant within herself?

Did she want to be a wife or believe she had to be?

Were the virtues of marriage and children extolled, and she believed she had no other choice and would be chastised and embarrassed for not marrying and delivering that baby?

Was she ever encouraged to step out into the world on her own?

Do you recognize this archetype in others, in yourself? Think of your mother, grandmother, aunt, or a friend. And yes, you can have a sister or friend who is a *Matriarch Archetype.*

Any archetype can be a sister, friend, aunt, grandmother, mother, manager, and their archetypes and your archetype will influence the relationship.

Twelve
Mother, Maiden, Sage

"If they don't give you a seat at the table, bring a folding chair."

Shirley Chisholm

Reflecting on the *Father's Daughter, Sister, and Matriarch Archetypes*, imagine how their patterns of behavior influence their relationships with other women and men as well. Understanding archetypes is helpful when we try to sort out why a woman is different from other women and why women have different desires.

Even a discussion of a few of these archetypes gives insight about the relationships between women, whether they are a mother, friend, sister, aunt, grandmother, co-worker. It also gives a myriad of explanations of a woman's relationship with the men in her life because there is no doubt men gravitate to women who are different. Their choices, like all choices, reveal who they are.

For example, a man may find a *Matriarch* just what he wants in a woman—someone who wants to be married, will take care of the home and children, and support him in his work life. Another man may desire a woman who is out in the world shaking the trees, such as a *Sister Archetype*. Another may....

Besides the *Sister*, *Matriarch*, and *Father's Daughter Archetypes*, there are three other feminine archetypes—*Mother, Maiden*, and *Sage*—that you might find interesting and noteworthy.

Like the *Sister Archetype*, these three are in contrast to the *Matriarch* and *Father's Daughter Archetypes*.

The *Mother Archetype* desires to be a mother. And when she does have children, they become her life's work. If she does not have children, she will seek opportunities to nurture, possibly become a teacher of young children or mother those with whom she works.

In the office she may be the one bringing in the donuts in the morning, listening to her colleagues' problems, offering to… Her calling is to help and nurture others. Her identity is wrapped up in her children and others she nurtures. She may tend to those she doesn't know and for the sick, and she is concerned to keep everyone happy, even sacrificing her own happiness and well-being.

Unlike the *Matriarch Archetype*, who may support her husband over her children, the *Mother Archetype* will protect and support her children over her husband, her employees over her boss. And yes, she may be punished for that choice by a *patriarchal father*.

On the dark side, she can become overcontrolling, a helicopter mom, over-protective of her children. If her children toss her aside or abandon her for a relationship with someone else, she may lash out. She may become jealous, fearing she will lose that relationship to another, and that other will pay dearly. She may also use guilt to command others to serve her desires.

Jackie in the film, *Stepmom,* is a most exacting example of a *Mother Archetype*, showing the light and dark side. Her life is wrapped up in her children, and she believes no one can care for them as she can. After divorcing, her former husband, Luke, becomes involved with another woman, Isabel, a career woman. Jackie comes to resent Isabel's relationship with her children, so much so that her son, sensing her animosity, says to her, "If you want us to hate her, we will."

Jackie is told she has cancer and has to turn to Isabel to take care of her children, all the time poking and prodding her inabilities and faulting her again and again. Realizing she is going to die and Isabel will be their mother, she decides to include Isabel as part of the family.

One of the most telling scenes of the transformation in their relationship is when Jackie asks Isabel, a professional photographer, to take pictures of the children so she can make them their last Christmas gift. Another is when she tells Isabel of envisioning her daughter on her wedding day and her daughter not missing her. Isabel in response says she fears the young bride saying, "I wish my mom were here!"

Jackie had given up her animosity and gifted to her children her acceptance of Isabel, and in the final scene includes her in the family photo. She had purged the dark side of the mother archetype and gave her children the greatest gift she could upon her death.

With her innocent and almost childlike qualities, the *Maiden Archetype*, also known as the *Daughter Archetype*, desires to live a charmed life, unconcerned with life's mundane chores and difficulties. Stress and worries do not affect her, and her self-confidence can be contagious.

A *Maiden Archetype* desires a loving relationship with her mother in which she pleases and is compliant. She is often called "Mommy's little girl," but that most likely occurs if her mother is a *Mother Archetype*. However, a *Maiden Archetype* may not welcome her brother receiving the same attention.

With her "take-care-of-me," attitude, the *Maiden* looks to someone else for her every need. It removes her from taking any responsibility for her life, for any decisions that are to be made. Safety and security motivate her to establish relationships that will serve her. But if she experiences a situation where she will lose that safety and security, she has the potential to become independent.

A *Maiden* is comfortable with other females who are like her and may form a clique that may ostracize others. She doesn't understand the consequences of her actions because she is being served.

If the *Maiden Archetype* does marry and has children, the mothering instinct may appear, but there is a possibility that someone else will take care of her children. She will play with them and want to be their friend and join in with her children's friends, but she may not provide the nurturing they need.

An image of this archetype is Blanche in *Golden* Girls. Although some may deem her a femme fatale, her desire to retain her youth, her need to have other women around her—a clique in many ways—signals her maiden-like qualities. Lucy in *I Love Lucy* is always cajoling Ethel to be part of her schemes, getting her into one difficulty after another. And because it is a comedy, we may overlook how she is tied archetypally to Ethel.

On the dark side, the *Maiden* can be a troubled teen and rejects all rules and authority. She is vulnerable to cults and may believe she is above the law. Think of Patti Hearst who was abducted by the Symbionese Liberation Army and later joined her captors in a 1974 San Francisco bank robbery that earned her a prison sentence.

Men may see a *Maiden Archetype* as inexperienced and clueless, sexy, and childlike—someone who needs to be rescued, so she may attract domineering men. Others may be attracted to her innocence and want to take care of her — a man who needs a purpose and wants to be a provider and protector. But he may become dictatorial and controlling , and one day she may awaken and realize she wants to take back her life. She may be the perfect, younger second wife because she makes a man feel younger, and she is grateful for the protection and safety he provides.

Within her resides the capacity to stand on her own two feet, to support herself, and make commitments. To do so, she needs to assess her abilities and strengths, which she does possess.

Her sensitivity may be intense, so she can be sympathetic and compassionate, feeling the thoughts and emotions of others. She can be very strong if pushed and can be a friend to others—helping them through their struggles and pain.

And a *Maiden Archetype*, like the other archetypes, may want to explore why this archetype is dominant, especially if other archetypes have not emerged as she ages. Maybe she was spoiled by her parents, especially her mother, so she played the role expected of her. Maybe her mother was overprotective and over-possessive. Whatever the reason, she can choose to retain what qualities serve her well and purge what choices are causing her to struggle.

The *Sage Archetype*, also known as the *Mystic Archetype*, is one of mysticism and contentment. She may seek a sense of order, and at the same time a sense of being in the world—connected to something greater than herself.

Being alone with her own thoughts is her best company, and she finds bliss in solitude. Her calmness, her quiet manner, and her unique way of viewing events create a mystifying world. She may step into another realm and often she says and sees things others do not grasp. If her observations are expressed, she may leave them wondering if she is "all there," flighty, but she is not.

Her internal world is rich with thoughts and others' feelings. She is usually quiet, composed, and does not want her privacy invaded, desiring a space to be creative. Yet, she takes pleasure in gathering people around her table.

The *Mystic* Archetype is not focused on marrying, but if she does marry, it may be because she has no other choice. One example of how this archetype copes with marriage is Charlotte in *Pride and Prejudice.* She marries because she MUST. There were not many choices for women at that time in history. Once married, she created a home where she was comfortable and ensured that her husband, Mr. Collins, did not invade it often.

One of the struggles of a *Sage* is she tries to keep the peace and struggles with becoming more assertive and direct. On the dark side, she can become too insular, and can think of herself, excluding others.

She has patience and could be seen as naïve and easy prey. But underneath is an understanding woman with wisdom who will listen to another's problems.

In many ways, the archetypes of *Mother, Maiden,* and *Sage* do what is necessary to make their way in the world. And whether they are involved in the desire for equality and covet the patriarchy will depend upon many variables.

When we explore the six archetypes described—*Father's Daughter, Sister, Matriarch, Mother, Sage,* and *Maiden,* it is evident that we cannot expect the same behaviors of all women. Remember the lines in my poem earlier in the book, *"Women are like colors in a box of crayons. Lumping them together, fool hardy, done for eons."*

It is also important to note that you may observe more than one archetype in yourself and in other women.

Different combinations of archetypes affect women's relationships, and not only the mother/daughter relationship but sisters, friends, co-workers…., and, of course, men. Something to ponder when you have a moment.

Archetypes are a way to understand differences among women and help answer the question, "Why do women…."

I have not delved into all the nuances of all archetypes. My intent was to expose you to why women are different and why you may have strong ties with some women. And why other relationships among women may be riddled with upset and conflict.

There are many resources that explain these archetypes and others in depth. Jean Shinoda Bolen's book, *Goddesses in Every Woman*, has been my most important resource on feminine archetypes, and a must-read if you wish to explore these archetypes further. And *Gods in Every Man*, also written by Bolens, delves into the masculine archetypes.

If you want to pursue your understanding of archetypes and apply that knowledge, watch your favorite television series or a movie. Can you discern the archetypes of any of the characters? In *Little Women* Jo is a *Sister Archetype*, Amy is a *Maiden*. Meg is? Elizabeth is?

Every so often, I gather a group together. We watch movies and then have a lively discussion, trying to figure out the archetypes of the characters. And you too can gather a group of women or women and men together and watch movies and have a lively discussion. And, of course, use Bolen's books for more insight and clarification.

Enjoy the challenge and the journey.

Thirteen
Act Like a Man

*"Do you really want to look back on your life and see
how wonderful it could have been had you not been afraid
to live it?"*

Caroline Myss

Despite checking off the to-do list of achievements, a woman, who is climbing to the top of the mountain, chipping away at the glass ceiling, may feel trapped in a life that looks complete, envied by others.

Yet, inside there may be frustration and discontentment, plagued by the nagging feeling that something is missing. She may feel guilty for selling her soul for her success. She may deny her suffering. She may realize she is working too hard for too little. She may numb her sufferings and disappointments. She may pretend, try harder, and become satisfied with the trappings of success. She may explain her problems away by justifying and making excuses, but the discontentment, even anger and possibly rage, could still persist.

Along the way, a woman who is trying to succeed may purge her prescribed feminine traits and embrace the prescribed masculine. That traps her—she is betwixt and between—confused and pretending.

Two women, Patty and Karen, shared with me their fathers' advice, "If you want to succeed in a man's world, you have to become more like a man." And that is word for word from both!

Patty asked me what I thought of her father's words. Before I could speak, she said, "Oh, please don't tell me my father was wrong!" So, why did Patty ask me? She did not want to know my thoughts. She wanted confirmation from me that he was right, that she had taken the right path.

Of course, that advice the fathers gave both women was riddled with problems. And the words those two fathers had spoken had taken over the minds of Patty and Karen at a young age. Like the ugly duckling who believed she was a duck, women are sent messages about who they must be.

Both Karen and Patty had been told to take on masculine behaviors in order to succeed in a man's world. Often upon hearing those words, a woman may believe that she has to eradicate the feminine traits that reside within her and become masculine. And her role model is often her father.

Patty was sure to let everyone know she was once with the FBI, although not an agent, and that she was always "packing." The first time I met Patty she attempted to bully me. I was about to tell a dog rescue story around the dinner table when she announced in a loud voice that I was not allowed to tell my story. She believed it was going to be upsetting. When I did not bow to her wishes and continued my story, she walked out of the room; yet she had no idea what I was going to say.

I guess she thought showing her displeasure would silence me. It did not. She later returned after realizing my story was not what she had expected.

Later that evening we connected on something we both embraced—our common interest in rescuing animals. I explained to her that I told the story to encourage people to rescue. She nodded in agreement.

During another gathering Patty found one of the few men present and spent the entire evening speaking with him. When she was leaving, I said to her, "I hope you enjoyed meeting my women friends. They are lovely." She looked toward the women sitting around her and shrugged.

Patty's husband once thanked me for inviting them to a gathering at our home, sharing that the neighbors did not extend invitations and found her difficult. I did not find her so. To me, she was caught between two worlds—who she really was and who she thought she should be.

Karen had an in-your-face style and used a loud voice that often had an edge. During the first session of the workshop, she talked over everyone, got in everyone's face and was argumentative, grabbing the floor when another woman spoke. Her looks could be fierce, her voice strident, and she interrupted everyone, including me.

Karen often commented that women did not like her and insisted that other women were envious of her. Yet, none of the examples she gave rang true. What did ring true was she wanted to wield superiority over them, and they had not given her permission to do so.

Karen and Patty resisted warmth, compassion, and a personal connection with other women. They dismissed women who were kind to them.

Both women embraced their fathers' words and acted accordingly because they wished to curry the favor of the "fathers" in their lives. And those behaviors were now fixed, even though the father was absent.

Like the young daughter in Rumpelstiltskin, Patty and Karen were willing to acquiesce to the father. But more importantly, the words of their fathers created an invisible prison that charted the course of their lives and kept them from stepping into the full power of their authentic self.

But Patty and Karen can make other choices. All of us can choose another path, another way.

Fourteen
An Unexamined Life

"We cannot change anything until we accept it. Condemnation does not liberate, it oppresses."
Carl Jung

Frederich Nichter wrote: *What if a demon crept after you one day or night in your loneliest solitude and said to you. "What if this life, as you live it now and have lived it, you will have to live again and again, times without number, and there will be nothing new in it, but every pain and every joy and every thought and sign and all the unspeakably small and great in your life must return to you, and everything in the same series and sequences— and in the same way this spider and this moonlight among the trees, and in the same way this moment and I myself."*

An image that appears when I read Nietzsche's parable is a person spinning in a circle—traveling the same path again and again. Spinning in that circle, connection to your inner guidance is lost—the forces that are saying, "This way, not that way."

The spinning force is so great it keeps you fixed in that place, repeating the same patterns again and again. Eventually, you may spin out of control. That is how some people experience **this ONE life**, often repeating the same behaviors, making the same choices, over and over and wondering why nothing is different.

Psychologist Carl Jung states this quite vividly, *"It is often tragic to see how blatantly a man bungles his own life and the lives of others yet remains totally incapable of seeing how much the whole tragedy originates in himself, and how he continually feeds it and keeps it going."*

Spinning in that vortex yields no forward movement and causes frustration and discontentment, possibly resulting with anger and disappointment in yourself. But it also can trigger the blame game—making someone else responsible.

Neischtze said, "what if," so you have choices. An obvious question then is how do you keep from being whisked around and around in the same place, spinning ad infinitum?

Evidently, you must take a different path, but you cannot do so if you keep saying, "NEXT, NEXT" without reflecting and assessing.

Socrates said, *"An unexamined life is not worth living."* I disagree! *"An unexamined life is difficult to live."* An unexamined life leaves us wanting and discontent, which is harmful to one's sense of self. Unless we take this journey of reflection to examine our lives, often we may stay on the same path, repeating the same suffering, pain, and struggles and never experiencing joy and contentment.

To follow a different path, you must reveal the truth about your choices and actions. Difficult you say! Definitely, I say! But it's not without rewards.

Instead of a circle, imagine a spiral. You start your journey, something happens, and then you stop and reflect, often answering some tough questions. What did I do to contribute to what just happened? What would I do differently next time? What would I say? And so on. Instead of repeating the same path, you make an adjustment, make a difference choice, take a different path. And you do the reflecting and questioning again and again. So, the journey resembles a spiral, each time moving forward instead of spinning in that one place. And yes, that different choices may also bring you difficulties, so by reflecting again, you eradicate one more thing that is causing you problems.

This journey of exploration and discovery requires honesty as you begin to reflect on your choices and your actions. Examining your life is a never-ending journey with many twists and turns, but if you take this journey, you can come to know and accept your whole self as you truly are, with all your gifts, fears, and flaws.

But it is not a journey of condemnation. If you condemn yourself, you cannot be free of the chains that keep you planted in one place. And you cannot free yourself if you insist on being a victim and do not take any responsibility for your actions.

Revealing your fears and your flaws does not mean you take a bat to your head. There is no need to feel guilty if you did not act honestly or did something you later regretted. You cannot change anything until you reveal it. Then accept your role, setting your ego aside, and promise yourself you will not travel that path again. We are all flawed; we all make mistakes. If you accept that in yourself, maybe you can begin to accept that in others.

Examining your life's journey also affirms and assists in sustaining in you the best, which is encouraging and inspiring. And most satisfying, it is the process by which you have the opportunity to become more fully yourself, not someone else's version of you.

By reflecting and examining your life's choices and acting with intent, you can begin to chart and change your tomorrows.

Part Three

Emancipation from the Chains that Bind

Unknown Sorrow

When we spoke of suffering
You spoke of losing your job.
For me, suffering conjures up images of being trapped
Trapped in an unfulfilled existence
Caged in a life that others mapped out

Not worrying about losing the one you love
Or missing the woman you never knew
Never allowing her to be who she was
Visions of her unlived life haunting you
Sorrow is not personal to you

I envision not being useful
Not experiencing the life I am meant to live
Afraid of dying while I am still alive
Allowing someone to pull the strings
And that is personal to me

When we spoke of fear
You spoke of being found out
Of others realizing you hide behind a mask.
I spoke of those relegated to the shadows, no identity, insignificant
Helpless, stripped of the freedom to choose

Fear permeates society
Manifesting itself in prejudice and injustice
Squashing another's potentials
Crushing people's dreams
Making the lives of others a hell

Fear—such a tiny word, just four letters
It pours out from the veins of those who deny others
Cutting to the quick those who reach for a better life and justice
Using misleading claims to justify their depraved actions
Rewriting laws and perverting history, jeopardizing democracy

Fear denies workers, keeping them downtrodden and powerless
Demeaning and diminishing those asking for a fair wage
Enslaving people with no remorse for their suffering
Wielding power like a sledgehammer
Patting themselves on the back for the sorrow they cause

Judging people negatively by skin color, gender, age, religion
Never discovering who they are and what they can be
Eliminating them as competition in the workplace, in life
Denouncing them — they're only women, laborers, immigrants, lazy,
*   uneducated*
No need for equal pay, opportunities, a way to feed their family

Fear disguised in the form of rules and laws
Exposing weaknesses and hatred and scorching one's soul
Exploiting those who cannot reason — easy targets, ripe for big lies
Fear, uncertainty, and doubt — the marketer's mantra of sorrow
Preying on people's appetites and frailties and hatred

The humiliation I feel for our people, for this country, overwhelms
Sorrow suffocates as I walk around saying, "No, this cannot be."
Yet, deep within I know injustice grounded in fear is winning too
*   often*
There must come a time when justice, tolerance, compassion will win
People will rise up, say enough, no more sorrow

No more bloodshed, no reason for guns
A place for everyone at the table
Prejudice and hatred and injustice and sorrow a faint memory
Those marginalized no longer hungry and cold and dismissed
No need to strike down another to be whole and content

Fear is a tragedy of this day in which we live
Fear makes people irrational and causes others sorrow
Fear forces the fearful to justify their actions with make-believe
If fear continues to permeate our society, we will perish and joy will
*   be a faint memory*
And if we survive, our shallow lives will not be worth living

To the Reader .... A Few Words

"My mission should I choose to accept it is to find peace with exactly who I am. To take pride in my thoughts, my appearance, my talents, my flaws and to stop this incessant worry that I can't be loved as I am."
Anais Nin

The critical issues swirling around us cannot be deliberated in isolation, focusing on one issue while ignoring the entire landscape. And although there are many bits and pieces of issues that seem disconnected, they are all intertwined. There is no straight line, no resolution of one issue that will make a significant difference and move us into the light, leaving behind the plundering, vitriol, evil, hubris, greed, and suffering.

We have to rummage through the rubble and call out those who have put all of us in turmoil and peril and begin to reveal the blatant and clandestine ways they do so. We must expose and call out those who continue to cause people to struggle and suffer and endanger our world, and we must not only impeach them, we must emasculate them.

Needed change cannot happen until people are awakened out of their slumber or in some instances from their catatonic state. No worthwhile strides can be made if people are unaware of the many nuances of the issues, are in denial, cannot admit to their role, and are unwilling to take action. No worthwhile strides can be made unless we reveal the divisiveness permeating our country and our world. And yes, truth is elusive, but truth is a light that can take us out of the darkness.

There are those who are struggling to use their gifts and abilities and are being denied. And that includes men who want to be free of the chains that bind them to an existence not of their choosing. They may feel hollow and inadequate, never believing they have delivered the expectations that have been dropped upon them by the collective.

There are those who yearn for opportunity and are no longer content to be relegated to the shadows, dismissed as unworthy, demeaned, and silenced.

There are those who have been deprived access to what the minority have been privileged to have.

There are those who are plundering and pummeling the majority.

If you want to live in a country, in a world, free of oppression, assaults, and sorrow, we all must be willing to say what is not popular to say and do what we are afraid to do.

People and societies claim their humanity again and again. But what is the basis of our humanity?

Should it be who we support and inspire or who we make suffer?

Should it be who we include or who we exclude?

One
The Sorrow Eaters

"The world is a dangerous place to live; not because of the people who are evil, but because of the people who don't do anything about it."
Albert Einstein

The *Sorrow Eater*, one of the characters in Kelly Barnhill's book, *The Girl Who Drank the Moon,* awakened me and brought me into a new light. As a young girl, the *Sorrow Eater* locked away her heart. She was void of kindness and compassion and empathy. At the same time, she wanted to control everyone and everything around her so she could orchestrate events to create sorrow. That sorrow was her source of sustenance and fed the emptiness within her.

In the quiet of the night, I realized that those who are orchestrating suffering are *Sorrow Eaters.* The evidence has been there all along, but these two words—*Sorrow Eater*—coalesced into a stark epiphany! A *Sorrow Eater* has locked away his heart. Feelings have become frozen; no benevolence or empathy. That death of his heart makes it possible for him to plunder, assault, and rape the spirit and soul of another without guilt or regret. Then he can feast on the sorrow he created, congratulating himself for his efforts.

A *Sorrow Eater* could have been wounded as a child and that wound has never healed. A wound could be a comment that hurt so deeply it cannot be forgotten, such as, "You will never amount to anything." A wound could be failures—not achieving what is expected. Some wounds are minor; some are so destructive, they hang around ad infinitum.

A *Sorrow Eater* could have feelings of inadequacy—the knowledge he is lacking in abilities and intelligence. That combined with an *ego* that is struggling with confidence and competence can be overwhelming. Buried within such words as, "I can never get it right" "Will my father ever think I'm a success?" "Why can't I….?" could be constant.

Maybe a man fears being found out for his shortcomings. His inability to acquire the brass ring is all-consuming. And if he does acquire it, he becomes afraid of losing it or it is still not enough. He is unaware that he is thrashing about trying to face the tragedy of his life.

A child who has never felt loved may doubt that someone will love him or will approve of him. That may result in his always looking for proof of adoration—gifts, applause, praise, and he will transact for that love and approval. He takes that unloved feeling and feelings of inadequacy into the world, and he can become a man without a moral compass.

It is difficult to spend years wondering if you are thriving, rather than just surviving. Surviving cannot define a person. So, the wounded may feign success. He may inflict suffering on others, thinking, "Maybe if I harm someone else, I won't hurt!" "Maybe if I degrade someone, no one will notice that I am lacking."

A *Sorrow Eater* ends up alienated from his feelings. No intimacy, compassion, or community. No regard for the struggles and misery of others. And within the wounded person, the fury, vengeance, and cruelty that erupts is pervasive and destructive. And the history written of this time may claim that the emptiness and corrosion of the soul in *Sorrow Eaters* are more than in any other time in history.

Those causing the sorrow not only feast on the suffering and heartaches of others, they are happy to contribute and then celebrate. And there are those who collude in the assault on others by their unwillingness to recognize the clandestine agendas of those who, instead of lifting up and inspiring people, are plundering and assaulting them.

And although the *Sorrow Eaters* and their followers appear to be of one mind, coalesced into a cohesive group, they are estranged from each other and from themselves. They do not realize they have sold their souls for a few fleeting moments now and again, but they will never feel satiated, always empty.

Sorrow Eaters have no defense nor would they see anything wrong with their actions. No remorse! It's like the scorpion who bit the spider; it's what they do!

And the history of the world is riddled with suffering that was orchestrated by the *Sorrow Eaters.* This lethal club is a destructive collective in its most oppressive and tyrannical state, and if one is honest and brave enough to look at history, that may be too kind.

And now in the United States health care has been denied! Women have no control over their bodies! Freedom of speech is punished and in peril! Honest elections are in jeopardy! Companies and institutions are intimidated, held for ransom! People are threatened, arrested, and clubbed. Homes are broken into, children and citizens harassed and dragged away! Cities are invaded by military—reminiscent of another time in history! And people's lives are in jeopardy around the world.

Young men, who are being told repeatedly they are not delivering what is expected, are suffering. But what is expected of them? Are they expected to continue the legacy of the patriarchy rather than choosing their own path?

Women, clinging to the ideal of equality and continually denied, are suffering.

Immigrants and minorities who are seeking a better life and contributing to society in positive ways are maligned and deemed inferior. They are suffering.

And there is no doubt the world is suffering!

It is disheartening that so many, unaware of the agendas, are carrying the water for the *Sorrow Eaters.* All the while the *Sorrow Eaters* reap the rewards and feast on the suffering.

Sorrow Eaters relegate women to the shadows and chastise men who wish the freedom to make their own choices—choices that are different from what is expected.

Sorrow Eaters are content to enjoy their spoils at the expense of the lives of the majority.

Sorrow Eaters allow families, especially children, to starve by not paying men and women enough money to support a family.

A *Sorrow Eater* denies child support for his children and punishes the woman who is raising them. He can harass her, threaten her, while he feasts on her sorrow.

Sorrow Eaters wage wars, causing millions of deaths and feel no culpability or remorse at the suffering.

Sorrow Eaters have taken away hard-fought rights from women and are threatening others. They are not only doing so to make women suffer, they are saying to women, we have control over you. We can take away from you anything we want, and some women are helping them to do so.

Mahatma Ghandhi said, "There is enough in the world for everyone's need, but not enough in the world for people's greed." When we look at the riches in the world, no one should go hungry, no one should suffer. There are ways to relieve that suffering, and we definitely should not be causing more. But *Sorrow Eaters* would rather feast on the suffering of others than do anything to ease their struggles. And they do so without shame or any responsibility.

Where is the moral compass of those who are impervious to the sorrows, struggles, and hardship of others? Are their hearts blackened by the fire of hatred and fear that burns within? And no words of scripture can change that!

Sometimes the most perilous and tragic place to be is inside one's heart that is broken and fragile and can no longer feel. The obliteration and blackening of soul is so profound in the *Sorrow Eater* that a hollowness resides deep within.

Civilization has been floundering in needless warfare and plundering and competition throughout the centuries. Once again, deranged, irrational ruling *Sorrow Eaters* are warping cultures, corrupting democracy, causing sorrow, and spewing hatred in countries around the world, threatening our existence. We cannot deny or dismiss the fear they have instilled in people, the rights they have taken away, and the suffering they are causing.

This collective loss of soul of those *Sorrow Eaters* has plunged us into darkness. Wounded people are not only wounding others; they are wounding our country, our world. Our society, indeed the world, must undergo a transformational journey in order to heal. And that journey begins by impeaching the *Sorrow Eaters*, calling them out for the suffering they are causing, and then denying them.

So, when people celebrate and praise the *Sorrow Eaters*—applauding their coercion and oppression and the violence they bring down on the heads of others—remember they are *Sorrow Eaters.* And it could be your sorrow they wish to feast on next.

Two
Sorting Through the Patriarchy

"Male domination is so rooted in our collective unconscious that we no longer even see it."
Pierre Bourdieu

A patriarch is regarded as the man in charge of a family, and his family acquiesces to his wishes. They have learned that is what is expected. Or they comply because they believe they must. They are afraid of the consequences if they do not and hopeful for praise and approval. Think of the fathers in movies and television series who are looked to for guidance, and often dictate to their children the choices they are to make about their careers and marriage.

Tevye in *Fiddler on the Roof* and Gus in *My Big Fat Greek Wedding* are both fathers who believed it was their right to tell their daughters how to live their lives and who they should marry. Although the stories appear to be benign, and each father may be seen as a "nice guy," these fathers believed they could dictate the choices their daughters were to make. And those dictates caused the daughters to suffer by denying them the right to choose or punishing them for their choices. Also, think of the fathers who insist their sons go to college, carry on the family business, enter into a particular profession; no other choice being an option.

The patriarchy is transactional. Transactions, along with reciprocity, permeate cultures. "I will marry you, provide for you, protect you, give you children, and for that privilege, in return you will…." "I will hire you for this job and give you raises and promotions but only if you…." "I will ask you out, pay for your dinner, but you will…." "You will go to college, and I will pay for it but only if you...." Written and unwritten transactional contracts will take over our lives if we allow them.

Inherent in those transactions is the belief that someone has the right to dictate what others should do and want. No connection and no meeting of the minds. The patriarch is not vested in another's desires; only dogmatic rule.

It has been said that patriarchs dominate, oppress, and exploit women, but they also dominate, oppress, and exploit men. A man who attempts to pull the strings of anyone is a patriarch. But this puppeteering extends beyond the social structure into the political and economic structures as well, into government and institutions.

Ruling patriarchs participate in the governing institutions of a country, a state, a city...., and they institute rules and policies, often to control. The ruling patriarchs have an economic power dynamic that they use to ensure that their agendas are served. They can provide or they can deny and take away.

As we have observed on the world stage, the ruling patriarchs do NOT always perform their duties with finesse or wisdom but in a commanding way. They use dogma and a know-it-all, bullying demeanor. They have no inherent, sustaining power so they have to transact and use coercion.

Out-of-control patriarchal rule is responsible for wars, domination, plundering, punishment, vengeance, violence, and vindictiveness. And the hungry, unhealthy ego of these patriarchs manifests itself in greed, hubris, prejudice, and power grabs. They may be called bullies, narcissist, and tyrannical. All may be accurate but name calling fails to reveal what they will do to retain control, the havoc their behavior causes, and how that plays out in suffering!

Unfortunately, and with sadness, some people follow these patriarchs because they desire and believe what is promised. I use the word "sadness" because they believe they are unable to do for themselves and that is disheartening. And if the promises are not fulfilled and results never materialize, they keep hanging on, wanting and waiting and hoping because they feel helpless.

The ruling patriarch, which I refer to as *Father Archetype #1* or the *King Archetype,* rules with might and right. And there are several methods used by patriarchs who want to ensure he gets control and stays in control.

- Ensure others feel victimized by finding scapegoats, such as women and immigrants, to make them believe that someone else is responsible for their problems and struggles and their inability to succeed.
- Use the marketing mantra—FUD. Instill FEAR, Uncertainty, and Doubt. Make them fear that something will be taken away from them; something they believe they deserve but have not earned.
- Convince them you can save them; you have the right answers.
- Make them fear retribution so they are silent, not because they agree but because they are afraid of the consequences of not agreeing.

Unfortunately, their victims want done for them what they believe they do not have the ability to do for themselves. I say "victim" because many have been manipulated and exploited and follow blindly.

But an effective leader would lift people up and support their efforts so they have the confidence to do for themselves. Instead, the *Sorrow Eater* continues to keep them down by focusing on their victim status. He wants them to believe they are victims who need him.

Their followers can also be vengeful and resentful, just like their leaders. They want to punish those who are different, who they believe are threatening or taking something away from them that they believe they should have. And if they believe they have been deprived, they can feel justified in hurting others and causing suffering.

Instead of looking at their own lives, the choices they have made, and what they have not achieved, these followers lash out and harm others. Instead of taking responsibility, they accuse others for their difficulties, and hatred and vitriol sustain them.

Unfortunately, today there are too many people who support the ruling patriarchs because they are wounded or are reaping rewards or believe they will. And consider that, just like the ruling patriarchs, these followers are also *Sorrow Eaters*, although they may be unconscious of that fact.

It must be reiterated again and again that not ALL MEN are patriarchal, although it is often heard as such. And not all of those who are in ruling positions are patriarchal or *Sorrow Eaters*. By knowing they exist and some of the methods they use, you can begin to recognize them and push back and deny them.

Institutional patriarchs, who are also the *Father Archetype #1*, are on the boards of corporations and the upper tiers of management. It is impressed upon us that management is put in place to ensure employees perform and succeed. Hmmm?

In reality, management's role is to mold you into what is desired by the company, laced with economic power. Managers may hold and attend meetings, make some decisions, and push papers, but the majority are mainly in charge of controlling a person's work life—what they can and cannot do. They can limit or expand an employee's challenges and career trajectory. They can diminish those who do not deliver and throw out crumbs to keep employees in line.

An institutional patriarch's resources are praise, money, the promise or hope of opportunities and promotions, and punishment to get employees to conform and perform. They can be authoritarian and create economic and personal sorrow by limiting increases in pay and bonuses and promotions. They do so without remorse or guilt and do so because they can.

Entrepreneur Kevin O'Leary stated, "A salary is a drug they give you when they want you to forget about your dreams. Because it's very easy to stay in that world where someone is mitigating your risk. You just have to perform certain tasks, do them well, for a third of your day, and they will feed you a salary."

And it works for some as long as an employee is getting paid adequately for the work, is inspired, challenged, and given opportunities, and is not held back by a manager. Or they accept being denied and forget their dreams, as O'Leary suggested.

The institutional patriarchs can be bullies! They can be *Sorrow Eaters!* But not all managers are patriarchal or *Sorrow Eaters,* and those who are may not be easy to recognize.

The *Father Archetype # 1* wants to be respected for his title. He fears that someone smarter, younger, stronger will usurp his throne. He wants to be admired and respected for the fear he can instill in others and dismisses those who have a different point of view. On the dark side his *might-and-right* mentality makes him believe he is powerful, but using coercion is not power.

He marries and has children to preserve his legacy and extend his kingdom. The daughters are to marry someone who is accomplished, desire children to preserve his legacy, and bring money to the family. The sons are to marry a woman who want to be a wife and mother and having money and status are a bonus.

The institutional and ruling patriarchs castrate men as well as women. It's been done for thousands of years and continues through economic power and ruling over people's lives in organizations. Tell men and women they can only rise so far, limit their educational and employment opportunities, portray them as not the brightest or the best, and they begin to doubt themselves. They can feel unworthy and helpless and become discouraged, believing they CANNOT…. so, they accept whatever deal they can make.

The traditional patriarch (*Father Archetype #2*) is the head of the household and rules solely in the home, such as Tevye in *Fiddler on the Roof* and Gus in *My Big Fat Greek Wedding* mentioned earlier. He may have been born into privilege, with money and education, but poor or wealthy, educated or not, he does not have the skills to succeed in the world of business, institutions, and government.

An obvious role for him to play out his desires is to rule over his family. And he often rules by what pleases and displeases him and *with* might and right. He can be dogmatic, with fervent emotional outbursts if things do not go his way.

In *Downton Abbey*, the British series, Lord Grantham does not have the acumen to take care of his estate, runs it into bankruptcy, makes bad investments, and tries to dictate to his daughters who they should marry and what they should want. When his daughter, Sybil, wants to train to be a nurse, he rants and tries to deny her. When she wants to marry a chauffeur, he threatens and denies her any money.

When he does not agree with what someone says, he has emotional outbursts. All are efforts to control because he believes it is his right to control everyone and everything.

Like all patriarchs, the traditional patriarch promises to take care of his wife and children. In return the wife is to stay home, perform her duties, support his career, and take care of his every need. A wife can become co-opted by the promise of a life of being provided for and protection.

A traditional patriarch can be a bully! He can create the conditions to harm his wife and children. And just like the ruling and institutional patriarchs, he can be a *Sorrow Eater*.

And the traditional patriarch who rules solely in the home serves and supports the ruling and institutional patriarchies but that does not automatically get him a membership card into the ruling and institutional patriarchies — *the GOBs, the good old boys* (nothing to do with age). The majority of men who support the ruling and institutional patriarchies are often "wannabes" who may never be, although they are definitely unaware of that fact.

A patriarch — ruling, institutional, and traditional — can lock a woman into the nuclear family from which she often cannot escape if she wants. The line in the movie *Mississippi Burning,* said by a man, sums up the struggles of some married women. "Women spend their years in high school dreaming of the man they are going to marry, and then spend the rest of their lives wondering why."

Women stuck in the nuclear family will not be available to challenge men for opportunities and have a voice in the workplace. The wife's efforts on her husband's behalf and not stepping out of place make him respectable — a family man for others to applaud.

And in families where the wife does not work, the economic power dynamic ensures that she does not control the purse. A wife who wants to escape may fear she will not have the money to take care of herself and her children, plus she often lacks the skills to get a job. And if she finally does escape, she could be stalked, challenged in court, threatened, denied her children, causing her more sorrow.

And why doesn't a man experience shame when he has to resort to such drastic measures to keep a woman chained to him? Because he is too busy feasting on her sorrow and believes it is his right to make her suffer.

And the patriarch's many clandestine activities are to keep control. Tell women they are sinners, inferior, and the weaker sex. Deny them opportunities and promotions, pay them less than men for the same work, and punish them for stepping out into the world. Then instill fear in them and assault them.

How many women (men as well) are born into suffering and heartache, stumbling through life, broken by injustice, prejudice, and hubris? Every woman's father, husband, brother, son, uncle, grandfather, manager, male friend…. are her potential patriarchs, and they can be dictators, betrayers, rapists, and persecutors—*Sorrow Eaters*. That is difficult for some women to acknowledge and admit, but for centuries it has and will continue to be a woman's reality unless she has the courage to say NO or walk away.

The patriarchal male is the major nemesis in women's lives, even women who support them and are unaware.

The patriarchal male is also the nemesis of men who are not and do not want to be members of the *boys' club*.

The patriarchy is a nemesis to those men and women who wish to be free of dogma and fear and who wish freedom to live the life they desire.

So, who makes up the patriarchy? In the United States heterosexual, purported Christian white men, but there is no doubt that non-white males are trying to break down the door and become one of them. Why? Maybe they want to be included in the male population that portrays themselves as superior and "in charge." Maybe they do not want to be regarded as women and minorities, as second best and inferior. They are signaling, "I am different."

It's the shadow-effect. "If I align myself with the *haves*, degrade those who are thought to be second and third-rate, I will not be considered one of them. I will be thought of more favorably. Maybe I'll even get a seat at the table." Maybe if these "wannabes" would take notice, they might want to consider that they are being used.

Robert A. Johnson, author of *Femininity Lost and Regained*, stated: *Our Western heroic achievements are the envy of the rest of the world, but they were won at the cost of our capacity for warmth, feeling, contentment, and serenity. We are so rich in things and so poor in feminine values!*

In the story of Oedipus, Haemon, Creon's son, is betrothed to Antigone, Oedipus's daughter, but Creon orders the execution of her and her sister. He summons Haemon to him:

Creon: Son, you have heard, I think, of our final judgment on your late betrothed. No angry words, I hope? Still Friends. In spite of everything, my son?

Haemon: I am your son, sir; by your wise decisions my life is ruled, and them I shall always obey. I cannot value any marriage tie. Above your own good guidance.

Creon: Rightly said. Your Father's will should have your heart's first place. Only for this do fathers pray for sons. Obedient, loyal, ready to strike down their father's foes, and love their father's friends. He whom the State appoints must be obeyed. To the smallest matter, be it right—or wrong.

Johnson claims that Haemon, a weak man, is coerced by masculine authority, and though he knows better (and later he does show his true feelings), he makes no protest when faced with his father's cruelty. And isn't that what young men have experienced in the past and are experiencing today, in this very moment and in every moment? To fit in, to be thought of as "one of them," men must pretend, conform, bend, be a man, be....

In time will men realize they have been co-opted by promises that will never be fulfilled and a life that will never be fulfilling? If they have become aware, will they rise up and declare their independence and begin extricating themselves from the chains that bind?

Haven't men for centuries suffered trying to deliver what the collective desired? Are young men suffering now more than ever because they cannot or do not want to deliver what is required? And maybe it is time for this generation of young men to say, "No more!" Or maybe they are, and no one has noticed or cares.

We all must come together. We all must fight for the rights of all who are left wanting and waiting, not segregating ourselves into factions, believing we have different goals and motivations. We need to come together based on our similarities and common interests—our one desire to cut the strings of the puppeteers who control our lives and cause people to struggle and suffer.

Carl Jung said, *"I am not what happened to me, I am what I choose to become,"* so at this moment in your life, who do you choose to become?

Three
Living Without Courage

"It is unfortunate that society has historically limited women's access to education and opportunities for creativity. By removing these barriers, we can tap into the immense potential that women possess and truly revolutionize the world."

Albert Einstein

Are there people afraid that Einstein was right—that women possess immense potential and that women will revolutionize the world? It definitely needs some changes!

From the dawn of civilization, women have made important contributions to society within the family unit, institutions, government, and the world. But many have been treated as a footnote in history or ignored. And both men and women have contributed to society while being oppressed and struggling for opportunity. But why should they have had to do so? Why would the collective not want their contributions?

Psychologist Carl Jung said, *"Woman is a very, very strong being, magical. That is why I am afraid of women."* Finally, a man who was willing to admit his fear of women.

Yet, Jung experienced this magical force again and again. Instead of rejecting women, he surrounded himself with them. Women had positions at his institute in Switzerland. He wanted to learn from them, to be in the presence of that magic. He saw them as a vital force and embraced them into his world as contributing members. And with those associations, he benefited. And so can all men!

Einstein and Jung, as well as other men throughout history and today, have seen the wonders that reside within women. So, what exists in the minds of men who have relegated women to the shadows for centuries and are still doing so? When everything is considered, one of the answers that surfaces again and again: FEAR.

At their very core there are men, but NOT all men, who fear women! And that fear plays out in anger and hate, determination to harm women, and wanting to control, oppress, and deny them.

Are men afraid of losing what they believe is their divine right—control over everyone and everything?

Do patriarchal men fear the strength, courage, compassion, wisdom, and intelligence that reside in women?

Do men fear women will take their places at the table, participating fully in society, in organizations?

Are they afraid that a woman will be as effective as any man, perhaps outshining men?

Are they afraid they will have to share, and if women get a small piece of the pie, they will get more and more?

Are men afraid that the women and MEN they are denying will contribute in ways that patriarchal men would wish they did not?

Why not come face to face with women and those they have been denying? Why not sit across from them and engage in meaningful discussions and develop rewarding, worthwhile relationships?

Miraculous happenings could benefit everyone. But if men fear women, fear losing their control over anyone and anything, they cannot make that choice.

The fear that men experience manifests itself in many ways and is evident by pondering the questions:

Why is so much time and energy devoted to ensuring women are only a supporting cast in history?

Why is so much effort exhausted trying to keep women out of the workplace, paying them less, denying them childcare in the workplace, and denying them promotions?

Why would they silence women's voices, humiliate, and disrespect them by raping their minds and their bodies?

Why not let women, anyone oppressed, play the game and see how they do? Remember the cry during the Civil Rights Movement: "A mind is a terrible thing to waste." Yes, it is. And that includes a woman's mind as well.

Men who fear women lack the courage to include them. The proof is everywhere, in the past and still today. Now, I'm not making that accusation against all men, but those men determined to deny and punish women do fear them.

Can you state without reservation that women receive adequate and just rewards for their contributions? Can you state without reservation that women are respected, cherished, and supported, even by their loved ones?

And maybe these questions are not asked or answered by women because of fear as well. To do so, a woman would have to admit that the men she desires in her life do not revere and love her as she would wish or are harming her. A woman would have to consider that a man calling her the fairer sex is trying to keep her believing she is fragile, and therefore not capable.

And as the patriarchy oppresses and denies women and disenfranchises men, as they carry on their assaults and abuse, they do so without remorse or guilt because they are impervious to another's suffering and pain. Fear—just four letters, but it has done harm to so many.

President Jimmy Carter stated, *"The abuse of women and girls is the most pervasive human rights violation on earth."*

Four
Patriarchy and Women!

"The role of a writer is not to say what we can all say, but what we are unable to say."

Anais Nin

The stories we do not want to hear are the ones we must hear. The issues we do not want to discuss, because they are too painful or we would feel guilty if we did nothing, must be discussed. The issues we wish to ignore must be faced head on.

A constant refrain I hear from many women is why don't women support other women? And there is no doubt that there are women who covet the patriarchy and support their efforts. Women, like men, assault and put up roadblocks for women who have different desires and wish to travel a different path.

Sue Monk Kidd's must-read novel, *The Invention of Wings*, was set in the South in the 1800s. The main fictional character, Sarah Grimke, wants to be a jurist and is thought by her father and her one brother to have superior abilities. The father also announced that she would be a better jurist than her brothers.

Yet, she is denied that opportunity by that father because she is female. She is to desire marriage and children. Sarah's mother, seeing her daughter's upset, comes to her and says she understands her desires. She intimates that as a young woman, she had similar yearnings. But her desires did not stop her from acquiescing to society's dictates to marry and have children—seven in all—and from encouraging her daughter to do the same.

Sarah was boxed into a life dictated to her, without her consent. She was to deny the life she wished and accept the decrees of a culture into which she was born. Added to her father's edicts and denial of opportunity, she had a mother who asked her daughter to follow the dictates of a society that denied women freedom and opportunities.

Possibly the mother believed her daughter was not strong or courageous enough to handle the punishment society would bring down upon her head. Maybe the mother did not want Sarah's choices to reflect badly on the family. Maybe it was the mother who was not strong enough to take another path. Whatever the reason, in that moment Sarah was trapped in a life she did not want to live. How many times is a similar scenario repeated again and again and not just in novels?

When I pause to focus on women's oppression and struggles and heartbreak, one thing that puzzles me is how a woman cooperates with her jailers and how other women become the jailers. It is a tragedy that some women oppress, assault, and deny women who wish to make a different choice.

Imagine a woman who is ignored, shoved in a corner, hands tied, her voice silent. She is obedient, docile. She has become numb to being diminished, abused, and embarrassed. She dismisses or is unaware of the many ways a man controls her actions and her words. She doesn't realize her vulnerability, fragility, and shallowness—that she fades into the background, that she exists in body only. Unfortunately, there are women who do not have to imagine.

The patriarchy's effectiveness depends upon women nodding approval, going along. It depends on women looking the other way, ignoring, accepting, or making excuses. It depends on women pretending, and they may do so while suffering silently.

A woman may not desire a place at the table in the outside world and that is her choice, but why not support those who do?

There are those sounding alarms because the happy housewife isn't always happy. A young girl has no desire to be sweet. The accolade, "Sugar and spice and everything nice" is no longer embraced as a compliment. Women are no longer waiting for the phone to ring, a text message, a date. Women are no longer marrying in their twenties and having those babies.

They are too busy climbing mountains or tunneling through, slaying dragons, creating the lives they wish. And that frightens many women who support the patriarchy, maybe as much as it frightens patriarchal men.

A woman who desires and chooses to be a wife and mother is not in question, if that is her choice and not one she is pushed into. What cannot be her right is to dictate to another woman that same choice or punish her for choosing a different path.

The woman who pursues a career also needs to respect a woman who wants to make a choice other than a career. A woman should not be dismissed or demeaned and penalized because she decides to have a baby and still work or not work.

The choice to be a wife and mother is appropriate as long as a woman is aware of the contract she has made.

But what happens to a wife and mother when her husband divorces her or dies, loses his job, or becomes ill? How does she pick up the pieces?

Any woman does so first by not giving up her voice. She asks questions and stays involved in her life and the choices that affect her. She plans for all possibilities. She ensures she understands finances, maybe takes classes about something that interests her, volunteers or works part-time so she acquires some skills and abilities as a backup. For her own well-being and security, a woman, no matter what her choice, should never turn over her entire life to anyone.

For too long and still today there are men who expect women to stay on the sidelines, be the cheerleaders, and watch and applaud them, hiding their light under a bushel.

Your choice is your choice! And it is unfortunate that when women were marching to have a place at the table, it was inferred that the choice of being a wife and mother was wrong. It was not! It was different! And no matter your choices, should you punish another woman who makes a different choice?

If you wish to continue to live your life as you have designed it, do not impose that life on other women! Either support them or stand aside and let them be! And whatever a woman's choice, support from other women is a wondrous gift!

If you have finally decided you have been a puppet on a string, if you have become aware of how drip by drip your life has been taken over, if you would have made other choices, it is not too late!

Five
Clandestine Efforts

"The true cost of anything is what we give up in order to have it. It is the path not taken. To take the responsibility of making the choice is crucial and not always easy."

Jean Shinoda Bolen

The most important story we write is our own. But it's not the one we write with words; it's the one we write by the choices we make. Those choices become our story; they become what defines us. And the choices of the collective, any institution, any government defines them.

Woodrow Wilson said that *"Hardship builds character"* as a reason to deny funds to farmers whose crops had been flooded. I disagree. *"Hardship reveals character."*

The choices we make as we struggle reveal our integrity, values, and beliefs—who we are deep within. As we struggle, we can either work and try and try again, or we can choose to whine and blame others for what we have not achieved. We can also choose to live on the dark side and may lie and cheat and harm others to get what we believe should be ours.

The history of the United States and of the world reveals that clandestine methods and not-so-clandestine methods have been used to keep the majority of people wanting and waiting. At the same time those efforts have elevated the minority, resulting in privilege.

Those marginalized and excluded from opportunity for centuries are not limited only to women, although the media and the patriarchy would have us believe that equality is just about "what women want!" If that were true, why did workers form unions? If that were true, why was there the Civil Rights Movement, the fight for LGBTQ rights….? The marginalized includes minorities, the poor, laborers, and immigrants, as well as the older population that some want to toss aside. The disenfranchised include any group that is denied, assaulted, treated unequally, or cast aside.

During the forming of the United States, there were those who were against slavery but decided that forming the country was more important than the choices they made to achieve the goal. It was also more important than the morality of their decisions and more important than ending slavery. And history has proven that the choices made to form the country were not about forming a perfect union but one that served the privileged and those who could afford to bathe in those privileges. And that continues today.

A Civil War had to be fought to eliminate the appearance of slavery. And slavery is a legacy all future generations inherited, and slavery is still wounding and harming and causing suffering generation after generation.

For many years as I delved into the history of the Industrial Age to write a novel, I found myself drowning in the injustices that took place. When workers were needed, capital attracted immigrants to America with promises of opportunity—the land of milk and honey.

There was no curbing of immigration by the government during that time. So, capital sent boats to Eastern Europe to bring back poor, uneducated, non-English speaking men. They were desperate to escape the life under despots, and they could not speak English and make demands of capital. And when workers did protest and went on strike, more men were brought over—scabs—who were unaware they were taking the place of workers.

By more people arriving in America than were needed to work in factories, railroads, mills, coal mines…. wages could be dropped almost to nothing. That, in turn, created the slums that appeared in cities. Laborers often worked twelve to sixteen-hour days, seven days a week, and suffered and struggled and were not paid a fair wage.

There was a hands-off dynamic—the government was not to monitor capital to ensure workers were treated fairly. But the government did pass a law that said to railroad companies and then all industries, you can hire your own police force to curb any worker unrest. So, workers who protested were clubbed and shot. The Coal and Iron Police, the Pinkertons, any private police force hired by capital was given a license to kill.

Birth control was taken away in 1873. That resulted in large families and children who were hungry. But these children could labor in factories and mines. And don't educate them so they will become the laborers of the future, which eliminated the costs or need to bring more immigrants to America.

Without coal, the railways and steel mills could not produce, homes and manufacturing plants could not have been heated, and electricity would have been a dream. And there is an abundance of evidence that the most dangerous job during the Industrial Age was mining the coal.

The Industrial Age was built on coal and the blood of the miners. It was built on people willing to work in steel mills, the railroad, and factories under horrible conditions. It was built on child labor. And many of those workers were paid in scrip—just a piece of paper with the amount they had earned, so they were chained to their employer. Rent for the company house and the items they purchased in the company stores were deducted from that amount. They lived in a cocoon—an insular life. They never had any money in their pockets. No way to escape. No way out.

The laborers during the Industrial Age were abused in word and deed. Men who were prejudiced against the Eastern European immigrants used horrific rhetoric—rhetoric of hate. The newspapers maligned the labor movement, turning people against the workers. In 1884 during the Haymarket Protest, the Chicago Tribune called the labor movement "un-American" and "foreign." A law journal branded the protestors as "long-haired, wild-eyed, bad smelling, atheistic, reckless foreign wretches."

The Chicago newspaper also suggested that the farmers of Illinois treat the tramps that poured out of the great industrial centers as they did other pests, by putting strychnine in the food. Chicago Times called for the public to "whip these Slavic wolves back to the European dens from which they issue."

During arbitration with the anthracite miners in 1902 in Pennsylvania, the attorney for the capital side called the miners "invaders from the Steppes of Hungary," who had come to America to destroy peace and liberty. There were those who believed Eastern Europeans were not "white" or not white enough.

John Baer, president of Philadelphia and Reading Coal and Iron Company, in the anthracite coal district in Pennsylvania said, "These men don't suffer. Why, hell, half of them don't even speak English." He also stated in response to a letter asking for him to address the suffering of the miners, "The rights and interests of the laboring man will be protected and cared for—not by the labor agitators, but by the Christian men of property to whom God has given control of the property rights of the country, and upon the successful management of which so much depends."

America brags about being a melting pot, but history has shouted, "America is a melting pot under protest." Every group of immigrants has faced prejudice, been assigned racial slurs, and discriminated against again and again.

After one of my presentations about the Industrial Era, I was asked, "Do you support unions?"

I responded, "I wish there did not have to be unions. That would mean that workers are respected and paid what they deserve for the work they do. They would not be struggling. Their children would not be hungry. But most importantly, those workers would not have to beg and plead. And that alone is demeaning and demoralizing. What came first—capital who would not pay their workers a fair wage and made their workers toil twelve to sixteen hours a day or the unions?"

Aside from the abuse of laborers and immigrants, the ruling and institutional patriarchs had woven an intricate web of exploitation into many facets of society to support their agendas. It wasn't more apparent than during the Industrial Age. Only two presidents who had the last name of Roosevelt were paying attention, and Teddy was ousted from his party because he supported the labor movement.

One day while trying to find answers to why there was so much injustice, so much greed, why capital was tyrannical and heartless to the workers, it occurred to me that the laborers of the Industrial Age had been left behind in America. The Industrial Age wore many of the immigrants down and left their children uneducated and struggling. They have passed on that legacy and the stories of that time in history, and many have not forgotten the injustices. But the children of immigrants never asked for any help or reparation.

So, not being a squeaky wheel, their cries were seldom heard or ignored. But their anger and "left-behind" legacy have been there all along, and they are now saying not-so-silently, "What about us?" The sadness is that who is there to answer? The one president of this century who supported the workers could not get his party to pay attention.

And no matter how history is being white-washed and tied up in a bow, the ancestors of slaves and immigrant workers who were abused and denied live with that legacy.

I recount this history to make people aware of institutional patriarchs of that time in history and their horrific practices—history that is barely mentioned in history books. Those immigrants, those workers, ensured there was an Industrial Age. It would not have happened without them, but they were used and punished in countless ways because the patriarchs could do so, and they did so without remorse. These immigrants workers have not been forgotten but are remembered, and the ancestors of those immigrants and workers are still harmed by that history.

In an effort to deny and diminish people, another clandestine effort is how the educational system is funded and structured. "We will educate you, but just enough so we can claim we did."

The funding of the educational system is iniquitous. The U.S. Constitution stated that each individual state has the responsibility to educate children. The states, not wanting to be bothered, passed that responsibility to local authorities. Efforts emerged to "apportion the school fund according to the real estate or poll taxes paid by blacks and whites," according to Camille Walsh, a school finance historian at the University of Washington Bothell and the author of "Racial Taxation."

Public schools were funded by local property tax. This legacy created the basis for funding disparities where there was a majority of black or white people, plus immigrants who were in poor areas created by the Industrial Age.

The tax base affects the quality of the education. So, why not change the system? Because it will cost more money, and the system, as designed, supports the "haves." By not doing anything, competition for the few will continue to be limited.

The number of students per class, the pay scale of the teachers, the grading system, what is tested, how students are tested, how a teacher and administration regard students, and their expectations all affect students' achievement. Remember the principal who called me to his office because I was not grading on the Bell Curve, not giving enough C, D, and F grades? That method of evaluation and others are designed to segregate students into becoming "haves" and "have nots."

Not everyone can get high grades in every subject, but it doesn't mean that the system should plan for their failure. Instead of focusing on ensuring all students can achieve at their highest levels if given opportunity and an appropriate environment, the educational system's structure, funding, and grading systems decide at an early age who will succeed and who will not. And often that continues throughout a student's life because they have been labeled and do not have an adequate foundation of the material.

Students get lost in a system that was designed for the few. As long as the government under-educates the majority of people, it's impossible for the majority to compete with the privileged, the advantaged. And as long as they cannot compete, people are trapped. They do not earn enough, so they live in run-down neighborhoods. That means their children go to inferior schools, and they get an inferior education or drop out because the system is not designed to help them succeed.

When they grow up, the cycle repeats itself, guaranteeing ad infinitum a work force that will labor, not being able to compete. And this scenario is repeated generation after generation, ensuring capital will continue to have a laboring workforce.

Another clandestine activity of the ruling patriarchy can be found in the history of the military and draft. During the Viet Nam War, those who attended college were exempt from being drafted until they graduated.

Did those who were not exempt hear the message? "College educated men are better than you. They deserve to live! They have more to offer because they are going to college. You do not!" And then there were those who ran away to Canada or bought their way out by getting a doctor to lie about a health condition.

Then came the call to abolish the draft. Why? Because the privileged, educated, and those who wished to have other choices would continue to be exempt. So, who would do the fighting, risking their lives? Those who wished to be part of the military and volunteered without question. Those whose family legacy was military. Those who wanted an education or skill that the military could provide. Those who wanted to do something they believed mattered, to be of value.

There were also those who joined the military because they were poor and uneducated, and they were hoping for a more tolerable life, needed a home and food, and were suffering. They saw the military as a way of surviving in a world that planned for their hardships and struggles, and yes, it was a way of surviving until they were sent to war.

And do you think Nixon and Congress abolished the draft because they were nice guys? They did it to serve the privileged and their sons and grandsons and....

The end of the draft also paved the way for another entrepreneurial endeavor—private military contractors, which has increased the military budget. And isn't it interesting that their profits are dependent on a war and unrest in the world. Just something to consider!

It would serve all of humanity if rulers did not desire to plunder other countries, if they could solve problems with wisdom. Instead, they choose to cause suffering and sorrow with no feeling of accountability or regret. But should a man, the government, have the right to send a man or a woman to the depths of hell, possibly death because they can? But tyrannical, heartless ruling patriarchs have made it so.

Age is also used to disenfranchise those who have traveled many roads. Their wisdom, experiences, gifts they bring to a situation are discounted because they are "older" or "too old"—whatever that means. Age is abstract and should not be used as a criterion to be included or excluded and that includes youth.

Age as a criterion is frayed with faulty reasoning, as is someone's education and gender. Spirit, experience, wisdom, tenacity, and soulfulness are important assets— maybe more important than a number? But youth is convinced it is their turn. You have to earn your turn! No age or entitlement required!

Betty Friedan said, "Aging is not 'lost youth' but a new stage of opportunity and strength." Shouldn't those who desire an opportunity to contribute be chosen on the basis of ability, wisdom and willingness, not age? And personally, it is my decision when I am done. To those of you who are young, when you are older, won't you want the same regard and respect?

The concept of age is being forced upon older people, and unfortunately, older people have joined the chorus. But then maybe they do not want to contribute or be compared to those who still want to use their wisdom and abilities. Age is not a disease; it does not mean you have to opt out of being a contributing member of society or should be forced out. Older people do matter, and possibly more than some younger people want to admit.

Having courage and taking moral action has resided in people throughout history. Women who marched for the right to vote! The railroad workers who fought for the workers at the Pullman factory in 1874, even though they were not affected by their grievances. Those who marched for civil rights. Now, in 2026, people are coming to the aid of their neighbors and protesting because their community and their country are in turmoil and democracy is jeopardized.

Those who speak out and march about issues are not always the ones suffering. They see the injustices and pick up the gauntlet of justice. And every day there are people advocating and speaking out for others who are assaulted and disenfranchised. But where are the *Sorrow Eaters?*

And women, minorities, laborers, the disenfranchised must call out the perpetrators and not become one of them. Courage resides within each of us, and if you have misplaced it, find it again. We must name the *Sorrow Eaters,* call out their abuse, rip off the crowns, and call out their crimes and stop them!

Six
So…. What is Feminism?

"I myself have never been able to find out precisely what a feminist is. I only know that people call me a feminist whenever I express sentiments that differentiate me from a doormat."

Rebecca West

Wanting to contribute to the community, institutions, the world has lived in the hearts of women for centuries, and they contributed to the degree they could. Of course, it would not have been an issue if women were not shoved into a corner and diminished and dismissed. It would not have been an issue if men who wanted to rule with might and right had not swooped in and taken over.

Over the years, it would have saved the struggles and heartache of women who were denied and abused and assaulted in word and deed. It would have saved a lot of energy debating the merits of gender equality.

And most definitely, for thousands of years the world has been denied the contributions of women because the men in charge decided to renounce and pummel them with claims such as inferiority and fragility. And yes, there were women who achieved and contributed in spite of having to struggle, but imagine what they could have accomplished if a path had been paved for them as it has been for men.

Abigail Adams sent a letter to her husband, John: "If particular care and attention is not paid to the ladies, we are determined to foment a rebellion, and will not hold ourselves bound by any laws in which we have no voice or

191

representation." The "ladies" did not carry out their rebellion. Yet, there was a glimmer of an awakening.

Mary Astell (12 November 1666 – 11 May 1731), a philosopher, is considered "the first English Feminist," at a time when gender equality was denied. She opposed established intellectual authorities from Aristotle to John Locke who regarded women as inferior.

Her words have been noted for her persuasive thoughts. She stated, "If God had not intended that Women shou'd use their Reason, He wou'd not have given them any, 'for He does nothing in vain…. A man ought no more to value himself for being wiser than a woman, if he owes his advantage to a better education, than he ought to boast of his courage for beating a Man when his hands were bound."

Even though the actual word "feminism" did not exist until 1837 when Charles Fourier, a French philosopher, recognized that women were subjugated in a society that favored men. Fourier used the term "feminism" to describe the social and political theory he developed, which advocated for the liberation of women from patriarchal oppression and the establishment of gender equality.

So, what is a feminist? One would think it would not require an explanation, but the concept has been so maligned, especially by so many for decades. And changing the name to gender equality does not change feminism's tainted and maligned history.

The feminist movement of the late 19th and early 20th centuries focused primarily on achieving women's suffrage and legal rights. In the 1960s and 1970s the focus was on reproductive rights, workplace discrimination, and violence against women. Today, feminism advocates for the social, political, and economic equality of men and women.

Those requiring gender equality support a level field for ALL. Specifically, the goal is for opportunity and pay commensurate to that of others doing the same job and that is the goal for men as well. Anything else attached to feminism is wrong-headed. But because it is called feminism, that message has been lost.

Have you asked yourself why would someone support a woman earning less money than a man who does the same work? Why would someone believe that a woman is not worthy to aspire to the highest rungs of the ladder if capable? Why would anyone denounce the quest for equal opportunity and equal pay—one of the goals of feminism?

The obvious answer is that there are those who believe women are not worthy and men are superior. Denouncing feminism serves the agenda of keeping women in the home. And society was misinformed, uninformed, manipulated, and indoctrinated and that has not changed.

There were those who were susceptible, easily brainwashed, unaware or trusting. They listened to the media—a media controlled by men, who projected their own biases onto the movement. And yes, there have been and still are those today who give feminism negative press. And society, and that includes women, do a superior job of convincing women that punishment will be handed down if they do not acquiesce to the dictates of the patriarchy.

The concept of feminism is not the problem. It is how it is interpreted and that it is wrapped in untruths and vitriol.

Feminism is now referred to as *gender equality*. But isn't that what women were asking for—equality? And the only reason why the word feminism was given was because women were the ones denied. In reality, there are men who have been denied as well. But apparently the majority of men did not see inequality as an injustice. It is not their reality, or they believed they already had equality.

But the belief that ALL men have equality is a fallacy. And it is understandable why most men would have difficulty admitting this reality. They would have to admit they are also regarded as inferior and may never have a seat at the table.

By discouraging women from joining the workforce, it would remove them from the playing field, eliminating men's competition. By denying women adequate pay and raises, they could not acquire enough money to make other choices. By keeping the majority inadequately educated, and that includes men, the ruling patriarchs limited their opportunities. And they are given just enough money to keep them tied to the job, while they watch them suffer.

There has been a constant backlash throughout the equality movement. Susan Faludi, author of *Backlash: The Undeclared War against Women*, 1991, stated that women's rights were undermined by the media and corporations. Their rhetoric was to convince women that feminism and not inequality was the source of their frustration. How silly was that argument?

And one of their blatant statements was to call women asking for equality, "men haters" because it deflected from addressing the problems of inequality. Because you bring up the sins of the fathers does not mean you hate men. How many of you have criticized someone in your life? Did you do it because you hated them? Maybe you said something because you were tired of abuse. Maybe because you saw an injustice and wanted it righted.

The public was sent the message that women wanting to work and asking for a fair salary and opportunities equal to men were eroding the family unit. Yet, in many instances it was men's infidelity and the abuse of women, psychologically and physically, that were major contributing factors. Add to that the limited expectations men have of women, a father's lack of parenting and presence in his marriage, and a husband's dogmatic, bullying behavior that negatively impacted the marriage and contributed to the breakup of the family.

There is no doubt that once a woman realizes she has another choice, she might leave the marriage. And because the woman does not leave the marriage does not mean the family unit was intact. It does not mean that the husband and wife were happy in their marriage and that a woman would not leave if she could.

But "blame the woman" once again seems to be more acceptable to some men and women, and even a woman's children might agree.

One of my students became difficult, her grades dropping after her parents divorced. I met with the young girl and her mother. It was evident that the daughter blamed the mother for the divorce; yet, the father had left for another woman.

Her mother had been wronged, but the young girl chose to believe her father had chosen someone else because of her mother. And if that were true, why have an affair? Why not divorce her first? Did he want to ensure he had another woman to take care of his every need, instead of floundering around alone? And children fear that the father didn't want them as well, so blame it on the mother.

This one incident with this young girl doesn't make it so, but it is a reminder of the many films made in which after a divorce, the children miss the father, want to return to the father, degrade and disrespect their mothers who are trying to provide a home for them and put food on the table.

The message to women: Leave the marriage and your children will blame you, maybe hate you. And often the father was absent or left for another woman, but he was the father. He knows best!

And unfortunately, the mother who stayed too long may have contributed in teaching her children that he did know best because she never fought back.

Some of the women who coveted the patriarchy and denounced feminism still benefited from the feminist efforts. There were also women involved in the feminist movement for the benefits they would personally receive, not necessarily interested in benefiting all women. WIIFM, "what's in it for me" was their mindset. It wasn't about equality; it was about opportunity for them.

Even some of the women who joined the movement were unclear as to how to state what they wanted so it could be heard and accepted. The message was either muddled or aggressive, with vitriolic language that maligned and threatened men. And some women advocating equal rights were regarded as angry and hostile and perceived as hating men, mentioned earlier. But it was not all women, but the media would have us believe otherwise.

My comments are not meant to blame and shame because this happens in all movements. People come aboard and are not sure how to proceed. They flounder and may get in people's faces. But if the past mishaps are not acknowledged, we cannot go forward, and we will keep repeating that which was not effective.

The song *"I'm a Woman"* brainwashed many women:
I can wash out forty-four pairs of socks
And have 'em on the line
I can starch and iron two dozen shirts
'Fore you can count from one to nine
I can slip up a great big dip up of lard
From a drippings can
Throw it in the skillet, do my shopping
Be back before it melts in the pan
'Cause I'm a woman   W O M A N

These words were to praise women for all they do, but it also said to women, "This is your job and be proud to do it. And you never, ever have to ask a man to help you because you can do it all!" But why should you have to do it all?

After this song, there were the marketers at Enjoli, a perfume company, that decided a shorter version could promote an eight-hour perfume: "I bring home the bacon, fry it up in the pan and never, never forget he's a man."

That catchy little ditty was tossed about by women with pride, but it said to them you still must do everything even if you work, plus be sexy and available, and that's a good thing because you want to be known as superwomen, right? Men, you are off the hook!

And the efforts to promote a woman's superhuman status gave her a deficit of time. She became overburdened. And the words also said to men, "Anything you can do. I can do better!" Men do not want to hear that.

That created divisiveness between the genders, but the issues swirling around men and women are too complicated to be trivialized to the battle of the sexes. And why would we want to continue to harm those relationships? Hasn't there been enough damage done to male-female relationships?

In society, often the victim is blamed when it comes to abuse, rape, and sexual assault. Countless women, while sharing their story of abuse, state that many men and a shocking number of women blamed it on the woman. "She picked the wrong man." "She should have known better." "Couldn't she tell at the start….?"

So, why not blame women once again? The ills in society are laid at the feet of women because men cannot possibly be the problem!

Blaming her dates back to the beginning of civilization. Eve was the first to sin and blamed for being weak. Jada Pinkett Smith was blamed for Will Smith hitting the comedian, Chris Rock. On his talk show, Bill Maher suggested Will Smith hit Rock because he believed his wife wanted him to do so. Maher claimed she sent a disturbing glare her husband's way and blamed "toxic femininity" for the incident.

Others claimed she was the cause of Smith's downfall. Why blame a woman for a man's actions? Because they can! But doesn't it damn Smith by saying that he cannot think for himself? Doesn't it absolve him of any responsibility and should he be absolved?

Rape and sexual assault victims and mothers alleging sexual abuse on behalf of their children have been faulted because of criminal actions of male perpetrators. Judges and attorneys often still "blame her" instead of the defendant. But no amount of *blaming her* will change the abuse and assault committed by men.

What has changed since Susan Faludi's book? Many would claim the backlash against feminism is worse than it has ever been in our history. And evidence abounds.

Male hate groups against women have surfaced, and some strides in legislation that women achieved over the years have been taken away and others are being threatened. And why? Because men want women to know they are in control, and they can take away, take away, take away!

Seven

The Media as Puppeteers

"Shortly, the public will be unable to reason or think for themselves. They'll only be able to parrot the information they've been given on the previous night's news."

Zbigniew Brzesinski

For years you have watched television and movies. Have you seen young girls and women who look like you?

Do you fit the image of the woman men desire or the mother children want?

Are you pretty enough? Is your weight the ideal?

Have you gotten the gorgeous house with the picket fence? And if you have, has it made you happy?

Has the media portrayed negatively who you are, what you do, and what you desire?

Have the images and stories of wealth kept you hungry and dissatisfied, knowing you could never have that house, that car….?

And how has seeing someone like you portrayed affected your life and your sense of your self-worth?

But most importantly, have the images and stories made you desire something you thought you should want and be? And have you acquired that something? And has it made a positive difference in your life?

I ask similar questions of men as well. Both genders and all ages are brainwashed by the media. The media tells you what will receive praise and what will be punished. It tells young boys and girls what they should desire in "things."

At the same time, it leaves the "have nots" wanting, or the parents struggling to put food on the table, and at the same time they are trying to buy "things."

You are told that women should want to date, expect to marry and have children. Films and television programs bombard women with tales of romance. They have made "love stories" into an art form, convincing young girls and women that they must desire a prince or a facsimile thereof.

Women must have a man to elevate their value in the eyes of society. They get overdosed on the roles of fiancé, wife, and mother, convinced that will make them happy and give them all their hearts desire. And maybe it will? Maybe not?

Reflect on how workers are portrayed in many films, television series, and commercials. Now juxtapose the images portrayed of the blue-collar workers against the images of white-collar workers.

And movies celebrate those who steal. *The Italian Job, Ocean's Eleven, Twelve, Thirteen....* Yes, they were entertaining, but they weren't Robin Hoods—stealing from the rich to give to the poor. Indirectly and unconsciously are people hearing that stealing is OK, as long as you do it with panache and only harm the rich? Oh, it's subtle, but....

We perceive many movies and television programs as entertainment, harmless, taking us away from our everyday lives. And we are conscious of that because we have dubbed them "escapism." But there are inherent messages in the images and words, and they can be imprinted into the mind, sometimes unknowingly and often without questioning. Those images and messages become the lens through which we view ourselves and others, as well as our actions.

Like the collective and the patriarchal fathers, the media shows us what men are to achieve and demeans those who fall short. Men learn the work that is revered and respected and that which is not. Men and boys have to be virile. They have to man-up.

Compassionate men and boys are often poked and joked about. Derogatory names are assigned to those who are not "real" men. Little boys and men who are gentle and sensitive are embarrassed and labeled and chastised and punished.

Society and the media various ways to convince boys and men to deny their soft underbelly, their tenderness and compassion. Men may strive to be what the media tells them women want. They may turn themselves into someone else, pretend and conform just like women have done. If they cannot make themselves desirable, they may become angry and frustrated, lashing out at the women who reject them.

Women are to be attracted to the rich and famous, "doctors, lawyers," James Bond and Indiana Jones clones, and reject those who are not. Women may learn to desire educated men, men with money, men who…. And now, men are complaining because they believe women want them to be accomplished and successful, virile, and courageous. Who taught them that?

But are all women as shallow as films and television series would have us believe? Many women would include on their list men to be present in all ways—spirit, soul, and mind—and respectful and supportive of them but would that make an interesting movie?

The media has tried to convince us that "father knows best." The media has taught us that blonds have more fun and straight hair is sexier. Many years ago, a woman told me, unsolicited, that I was not sophisticated. Yet, I had never expressed that as a desire. She then told me that if I would straighten my hair (it is curly), I would look more sophisticated. I did not heed her advice, but she had acquired a mindset about what hair should be.

Of the one-hundred shows rated at the top that featured a woman in the 1960s, six shows had women at the forefront: *Donna Reed Show* (happy housewife); *Carol Burnett* (comedian)' *The Ghost and Mrs. Muir*; *Ozzie and Harriet* (twin billing with a man); *I Dream of Jeannie* and *Bewitched* (for a woman to gain a top spot, she must have magical powers).

Of course, it was difficult to portray career women because women were not entering professions.

In contrast, for men there was *Perry Mason, Bonanza, FBI, Rat Patrol, McHale's Navy, Mannix....*

In the 1970s, there were more family shows where the women were wives and mothers—no working mothers yet.

A glimmer of programming of minorities appeared. They were comedies—*The Jeffersons* and *Sanford and Sons*— an uppity businessman who has a maid (the norm for Black families?) and a junk dealer. No efforts to reveal the culture or the struggles they encountered, no role models for Black children, and so on.

Laverne and Shirley—two women working in a brewery, *Mary Tyler Moore*—an assistant, and *Charlie's Angels*—eye candy who dabbled in crime.

In the 1980s: *Murder She Wrote*—an older widowed woman who wrote and solved crimes; *Cagney and Lacey*— two policewomen—a show that was canceled three times. The network just didn't know what to do with it.

The Golden Girls--a crotchety old woman, a sexpot, a ditsy woman, and another with a sharp tongue—your typical women of the time and role models for the few? And *Roseanne*—a definite role model for mothers.

The one program in the 1990s that attempted to expose societal issues was *The Trials of Rosie O'Neill*, which lasted only two seasons. Maybe the issues were hitting too close to issues that the collective wished to keep buried.

Although there was a glimmer of programming that portrayed positive images of men and women in the last twenty years, the patterns of past decades have continued. Now in the year 2026, programs such as *Father Knows Best*, are being shown again. Wasn't indoctrinating the boomer generation enough?

The history of this programming is important because it influenced the mothers of that time, who influenced their children, who influenced their children and grandchildren, who…. And it doesn't get any better as the years go by.

The media feeds us continually the behaviors of men who oppress, dominate, and dictate through comedic and dramatic films and television series.

Women who work should be punished—punished by having to run in twenty directions at one time. Women who choose to divorce should and will be punished—no child support, kicked out of the house, stalked, beaten, making their lives a living hell. If the media shows women how they will be punished, will they reconsider divorcing? The *Good Wife* began the series by portraying a betrayed wife as a brilliant attorney, and then for some reason turned her into a female version of her husband.

And once in a while there is a film that shows how a woman survived and won a divorce, but it also shows the price she had to pay, the hell she had to go through. Why? Because there are men who have the resources and desire to make sure the women who want to leave them suffer, and they feast on that sorrow.

I enjoyed watching the film, *Pretty Woman*, possibly you did as well, but when you look under the glitz and glamour, schmaltz, and possibly a happily-ever-after, it is riddled with patriarchal overtones.

We are sent the message that because of her occupation, she needed to be rescued. In reality she was confident, feisty, capable of taking care of herself. But let's make her a prostitute, dress her up, give her a new hairdo, make her into a man's image of what is acceptable, convince the audience she embraces opera (going along with HIS interest), and your prince will fall into your arms. And we never see the dark side of her life. Not every prostitute ends up living a lavish life. Do we need any more fairy tales?

And are we to believe "her prince" has changed from the person he was at the beginning? And if he did change, it was because of her influence. Will she always be the woman behind the man? Will she want to be? And would one day when he got angry, when she got her voice back, wanted to fulfill a desire, would he strike out at her and remind her that he picked her up—she was once a prostitute, and he rescued her? Just some thoughts to ponder!

And not every woman is looking to be rescued. Not every woman is waiting for a man to protect and provide, to give her the life she is supposed to want. So, another choice would be to take his money and run. She can then create her own life, not one he was going to dish out on a platter, and not one where she will have to conform to his life.

I know it's a movie and entertainment, but young girls and women who are vulnerable and naïve and weaned on "someday my prince will come" are impressionable. And often we never see the "ever after." That's another movie.

Women's minds are raped every day in word and deed, at work, in the home, in music and films, in relationships. They are objectified in songs and films. Men congratulating each other for disrespecting a woman permeates our culture.

Women are wrapped in it, trapped, smothered, stifled, imprisoned.... that it has become accepted, normal, so it is ignored or excused: *Boys will be boys!* What does that mean? Are men allowed to do whatever they want?

For decades the media had taught young men and women that bachelors are to be admired, men do not want to marry, women wish to be married, and women must trap men into marriage. If women wished to be married, why has the number of women who have married decreased and why has the majority of women not remarried?

And any woman who has done it all—worked and kept a home, plus possibly raised children, will tell you that men benefit from being married. Most men have never had TO DO IT ALL. Isn't that why some men marry? So, they can replace their mothers and possibly grandmothers and sisters who did everything for them? And now, some men are angry because women do not want to marry and take care of their every desire.

As men watch films where women are raped, punched in the face, kicked and beaten, humiliated and demeaned, do they believe they have to imitate them to be "real men"? Do they feel any outrage when they watch innocent people being assaulted and killed? Do those images trigger any reaction or action? Is the pain and suffering of others felt by those watching? Are men embarrassed by their gender?

Or are men living vicariously through the acts of men who violate women? But more importantly, are men learning that their role is to torment women and then they celebrate and feast on that sorrow?

And when discussing media, social media must be included. Initially, it seemed benign—innocent—a way to stay connected. We have found throughout history that an idea may be value-neutral, but it is people who can trash a good idea. Social media has become the voice of cowardice, hiding behind the screen, buried within that computer or phone.

Hollow people, empty of feeling, use social media as a battering ram. It isn't just about bragging rights and photos of good times and places you visited. That is not the whole story. Conversations that speak to important issues have been replaced by salacious, outlandish comments, and falsehoods are tossed about like confetti.

Because of the interpretation of the First Amendment in the United States, none of these images or words should be censored or creators denied. And one's moral compass also cannot be censored. Instead, we must sensitize ourselves to the games being played by those using the media to harm others and the clandestine methods used, the messages that are sent, and the effects on men and women and children.

And most definitely consider questioning the veracity and validity of what you watch and read, any forms of media. Also, question what you are told. For example, I was told that illegal immigrants do not pay any taxes; yet, they get all kinds of benefits. So, I decided to investigate. According to the Tax Policy Center of Urban Institution and Brookings Institute, "An estimated 22 million immigrants live in the US without authorization. And they pay a considerable amount in taxes. Some estimates suggest undocumented immigrants paid nearly $100 billion in Federal, state, and local taxes in 2022."

The Tax Policy Center stated: "Most people who pay into the tax system also get access to various government programs and tax benefits. However, undocumented immigrants who pay taxes are often not eligible for the same tax benefits as US citizens. Undocumented immigrants are not eligible for Social Security retirement benefits or health insurance through Medicare, although they paid into those programs."

I was told by a female acquaintance that women were now paid the same as men. I questioned this, so she sent me an article in one of her newspaper sources. The wording was suspect and seemed faulty and incomplete. I checked several sources, one was the U.S. Bureau of Labor Statistics, and discovered that the information in the newspaper article was inaccurate. I sent several sources to her. One that showed the disparity between the salary of men and women in the job she once had. The difference was more than some people's salaries. No response.

But most importantly, why would she not investigate that same claim? Because she came to believe that the source was to be trusted or maybe she wanted to believe it.

Will you continue to be gaslighted and manipulated by false messages? Will you allow others to think for you, instead of drawing your own conclusions? Will you question and investigate or are you content to believe false information? Do you want to be like a puppet on a string, being pulled this way and that?

If not, when you watch a movie or television program or listen to the news or read an article or hear sound bites played again and again, pause to think about what messages are being sent and do your due diligence unless you want to be misinformed or share inaccurate information. Ask yourself how you have been influenced and investigate the claims, not listening to other people's opinions but use credible resources.

Eight
Free Speech

"The way of life can be free and beautiful, but we have lost the way. Greed has poisoned men's souls, has barricaded the world with hate, has goose-stepped us into misery and bloodshed. We have developed speed, but we have shut ourselves in. Machinery that gives abundance has left us in want. Our knowledge has made us cynical; our cleverness, hard and unkind. We think too much and feel too little. More than machinery, we need humanity. More than cleverness, we need kindness and gentleness. Without these qualities, life will be violent and all will be lost."

Charlie Chaplin

The damning, vitriolic rhetoric about women has been underground for many years. Yes, snide and belittling comments, hiding behind the words "teasing" or "joking" have been out in the open, but behind-the-scenes, the rhetoric has been vile and the efforts to harm women revolting. And if you are unsure, do some research because I will not embarrass anyone by repeating the comments.

Unfortunately, men have been given permission to be more blatant and outwardly verbal about their attacks of women with the help of technology. The media, especially social media and the internet, are enabling men to light the fire of hatred that is contributing to the carnage.

Are we going back to a time when men are denying and assaulting women, taking away rights, and pushing them back into a corner? And the toxic behavior and rhetoric towards women has always been clandestine in the guise of mocking and pokes and jabs about what women are and are not. Now the social media has given them a cowardice avenue to display misogynistic and homophobic attitudes. And there is also a campaign, often disguised, that is putting the fault of what is happening to men at the feet of women. At the same time that campaign is damaging young men, as well as women.

George Bernard Shaw said, *"Hatred is the coward's revenge for being intimidated."* So, are men using venomous speech that assaults because they are cowards who are intimidated by women? That would give more evidence that men are afraid of women.

And when women were asking for equality and faulting men for inappropriate behavior, they were said to hate men. Then what men are saying about women today goes beyond hate because of the emotional and physical harm it is causing. But who is paying attention?

What is the agenda of those who are spewing the words of hate against women?

What resides within men who would want to hurt young girls and women, to cause suffering and sorrow?

Where did the hate and vitriol originate?

What traumas have these men experienced that has triggered this outpouring of words that assault women?

What will this abhorrent speech accomplish?

Have the words they are streaming changed their lives, improved it? Or is this behavior because they are helpless and feel hollow inside, and hate is like a drug to soothe their pain?

Why are these men afraid and what do they fear? Why aren't they spending time reaching for their life, rather than harming others? Bell Hooks said, *"Sometimes people try to destroy you because they recognize your power."*

Instead of praising women for their accomplishments, let's demean them. Is this language saying that men lack courage, tenacity, and effort? If they were determined and focused on carving out their own lives, would they have to damage those who are doing the same?

Within the manosphere world, women and girls are often presented as emotional, flighty, illogical, scheming, nasty. Men are portrayed as victims at the hands of women. "Oh, woe is me," is signaling a feeling of helplessness—one of victim. Are these men clueless as to what to do? Or do they believe they should not have to do anything; they just want everything handed to them?

And men are juxtaposed against women who are achieving and succeeding—something men could do as well. So, why not encourage men, provide guidance as to how to navigate the challenges they face?

Instead, social media websites share advice on how to harm and abuse women. Online porn contains explicit racism, misogyny, and degrading sexual acts. And there are the movies and television series….

None of this is new, but it has been ignored, excused, cast aside. The *Sorrow Eaters* do not see this as a problem.

If we do not call out this behavior and say NO MORE, our young girls and women, our young boys and men, all men and women will continue to be in peril.

As this hateful rhetoric assaults my very being, I think of my father—a man who would be angry and at the same time in tears at the thought that I would be harmed by this vitriolic language and behavior. And we all know men who would feel the same.

But where are the majority of men? Missing! And where is the legal system in all this hate and harm? Missing! And where is the media? Present and contributing or missing!

Nine
Seriously! Actually!???

"Learn from yesterday, live for today, hope for tomorrow. The most important thing is to never stop questioning."

Albert Einstein

Truth is elusive and often flawed. Analyses are prone to biases! And if we are trying to prove something we already believe, those biases can cause us to dismiss information, especially if it does not align with our forgone conclusions.

It also can compel someone to include information that proves one's already-biased position. It is a slippery slope and complicated. It is more so if the issue has been defined too narrowly, evidence and interpretation of that evidence dubious, and questions are left unanswered.

A magnet kept pulling me into the claims and comments that are surfacing again and again that focus on the difficulties permeating the lives of young men. This rhetoric kept crying out to look deeper into the suppositions and question the implications of the comments and claims.

At first glance, it was evident that the rhetoric was not only diminishing and demeaning young men, it was hurtful to them and casting them as victims. I also became concerned about the fallout of this rhetoric to both men and women now and in the future.

After the 2024 election Warren Farrell wrote an article in a Kansas paper titled, *Trump Won Because Democrats Kept Telling Young Men They're Dangerous and Don't Matter.* Hmmm! Intriguing headline! What was the evidence? Let's follow Einstein's lead and probe further and ask questions!

As evidence, it was reported that in 2020, President Biden won the young men under 30-vote by 15 points. In 2024, Donald Trump won that vote by 13 points. Several instances were cited to support the headline. For example, the Biden Administration had a Gender Policy Council comprised of only women. Because the Council had only women, does that mean *men do not matter?*

Experiencing "not mattering" is not something just young men experience. Male-only Councils, Congress, and courts have made decisions about women for centuries. Did you ever see a headline that said, "Women do not matter?"

And haven't women been told for thousands of years by society and institutions and government that they do not matter by being denied and assaulted?

Aren't women now being told they do not matter by denying them control over their own bodies?

By being paid less than men and denied opportunities, aren't women still being told they do not matter?

And denying older people an opportunity to contribute is telling them they do not matter. They have no relevance.

Attacking and discriminating against immigrants and U.S. citizens whose skin is not white and are working and contributing are being told they do not matter.

No one wants to feel useless and worthless. No one should feel they do not matter. When a young man hears those words, is he upset and angry?! And, of course, no one should suffer. And how do these claims help young men or maybe that is not the intent?

The patriarchy for centuries has dictated to men three duties—provide, protect, and procreate, and all three scream MARRIAGE! The three Ps automatically limit men's sense of worth and their possibilities. Are they not allowed to choose a different path? What if they cannot find someone they wish to marry? Are they to choose anyone and endure an unhappy marriage as women have had to do?

What if they cannot provide because they cannot find work or are not being paid enough? What if they cannot have children? What if….? Are they worthless? Will they become angry if they are unable to fulfill these three duties? Will they become angry because they did? What is the agenda of these dictates?

There are other ways to matter that are not just about HIM! What about intimacy and connection? Where is caring and nurturing? Where is compassion and love? Where is being "present" in the lives of others; not just a body?

To matter, consider contributing to society to make a difference. A man can look around and ask what can I do? Being of value and mattering can manifest itself in standing up for the rights of others. Speaking out on issues of importance. Listening and caring and helping another. Counseling and providing guidance and support. Meaningful conversations with children and friends and family. Inspiring and motivating others. Volunteering! Anything that needs doing!

And a mindset that says, "I need to reach out to others, be present in their lives." And realizing that building relationships is necessary in order to matter and to ensure a person does not continue to live an isolated life.

Another example mentioned was that President Obama sent a letter to universities saying he would withdraw Federal funds if they did not regard a woman's sexual assault charges seriously. And that meant starting with believing her and not dismissing the accusation.

I am not advocating denying Federal funds to get someone to do what is right. It is coercive and transactional and has no lasting effect, but it is a sad commentary that this issue was serious enough to warrant a U.S. President's attention. And focusing on the funding rather than on stopping sexual assaults was telling women they do not matter. Why wasn't the focus on investigating what is happening on campus and showing concern for the safety of women?

Rape, Abuse, and Incest National Network (RAINN) reported in August of 2025 that women ages 18-24 on college campuses are three times more likely than women in general to experience sexual assault. And according to the American Psychological Association: Campus sexual assault makes up the greatest proportion (43%) of total on-campus crimes in the United States, resulting in approximately eight forcible sex offenses per 10,000 students (NCES, 2022).

This is evidence that college campuses are not safe for women. Is anyone asking why? What efforts are being taken to address this issue? Does that make all men dangerous? The number of sexual assaults is evidence that some are, but not all men. And men know deep within whether they are dangerous to women or not. And men who embrace women and support them are harmed by the actions of these men. Are they also considered dangerous because of their gender?

In Farrell's article, ONE college boy claims that all he hears is "the future is female." Are those words suggesting that women are now the preferred gender? Or are women the gender that is achieving and that is unacceptable? And now that women are competition, are young men trying harder or are they experiencing defeat?

It does not benefit young men to be fed this type of rhetoric. It does not benefit them to be rescued, handed opportunity, or let off the hook and not have to recognize and acknowledge the work they need to do if they are to achieve what they are *supposed to achieve*. Or is the agenda of this rhetoric to create divisiveness, to fuel once again a backlash against women because women are achieving?

Are statements such as "the end of men" and "men do not matter" saying to men this is happening to you because women are achieving and receiving support? But maybe it's what the patriarchal society is doing to men, what it has done to men for centuries. Patriarchal men have always been role models for entitlement and being "the man in charge."

Are there parents who are afraid that if women succeed, their sons would be relegated to the shadows? Are those sounding the alarm doing so because if women achieve and men do not achieve to their satisfaction, in the future there will not be enough men for important positions? They will have to choose women!

The future is not about one gender being preferred over another. It is for all of us who wish to participate, and the future depends on all of us.

It matters if comments such as "men do not matter" and "women are the future" are repeated again and again and instill the belief in young boys and young men that they are inadequate, not performing as expected.

It matters if these comments are defeating them, so young men are giving up.

It matters if these comments are resulting in hate language and actions against women.

Repeating negative assertions is harmful to young men and reckless, as it has been for women.

Now on to the headline that *men are dangerous*. Haven't the media, politicians, and the collective been telling Black men and immigrants for eons that they are dangerous and do not matter?

But the facts reveal the following profiles:

Serial killer—White males, 25-34 years.

K-12 shooters in schools—White males.

Place of worship shooters—White males in their 40s.

Shooters at a commercial location (such as a store or restaurant)—White men in their 30s with a violent history and criminal record.

And approximately one out of every five women in the United States has reported rape or attempted rape.

Add to that the number of homicides committed by men, the percentage of men in jail—93 percent.

Haven't men been telling us for years they are dangerous by their actions? What forces are triggering these horrific actions? What is happening in society? Who is concerned about these statistics?

A university professor shared with me this story:

"I had assigned a group project for a public speaking class. One young man -- I will call him Tim -- came to me saying that the young women in his group didn't want to work with him. I asked if he wanted to join another group, but he told me that, actually, all the girls in the class were 'bullying' and 'ostracizing' him. The class had about 30 students and roughly half the class were female.

"I asked the young women in his group what was going on and why they didn't want to work with Tim. The young women said that they were scared of him. Tim was a mixed martial arts fighter (MMA), but more importantly, Tim was always sharing videos of the influencer Andrew Tate…. The message in the videos Tim had shared were that women needed to be subservient to men. I spoke with Tim…. He insisted that Andrew Tate is just misunderstood and is just standing up for traditional values…."

The professor explained, "Universities train instructors on issues like discrimination, harassment, being a mandatory reporter, but they don't offer any guidance on what to do if we see someone *in the process* of being radicalized online."

Unfortunately, besides frightening and assaulting young women with this type of rhetoric, this behavior affects other men. If men value the women in their lives, do not agree, and hold different views, they suffer by association. And what can they do? Challenge them? Call them out? With the aggression that is pervasive in our culture, what can be done? And those who instill fear in others are often not addressed because of fear.

There are many factors that affected the 2024 elections. For example, why not consider the determination and methods the Republicans used to covet the vote of young men since the 2020 election and before? They knew they had to do something to get the under-30 male vote, especially those on college campuses and the minority male vote.

So, what did they do? They beat the drum, made promises, and got articles on the internet that young men frequent. They told them that Democrats were supporting women and twisted bits of information and used any example to speak to those who were unaware, angry, and wanted to deny women. Add to that mix, those who wanted to believe that the Democrats were harming anyone and everyone. Then after the 2024 election, use the loss of the election to sound the battle cry once again.

Men who are angry because women are achieving may desire revenge. Those who are unaware and vulnerable, and parents who are championing their sons who are struggling can be manipulated. And that manipulation can be achieved by saying again and again that women and efforts of the Democrats to support them are the reasons young men are struggling and do not matter. Parents become indoctrinated. Their minds acquired. Gaslighted!

Why would anyone think that a political party could make a difference in young men's lives? Did young men think that the government would rescue them? And have men been rescued? Did young men and parents believe that the landscape and their sons' struggles would be changed without young men having to do anything?

Or did they believe and desire that another political party in charge would deny and punish women, pushing them out of the way so they would not be competition?

And hasn't it been an effective marketing tool of politicians to attract those different segments of the population who are unaware. Convince each faction to buy into promises by focusing on their ONE agenda. Ultimately, all those factions vote for their one agenda, ignoring the others, appearing to make a cohesive group, which it is not. And use the marketing mantra—instilling fear, uncertainty, and doubt in people, and they go along, still unaware.

Could you ever imagine that:

People who state they believe in the sanctity of life would not support laws to curb the purchase of guns, especially assault weapons that kill young children and innocent people? That they would vote for war to plunder and kill, just to acquire land, oil, riches....?

Those who see images of starving children and people or those who have read the story of Jesus and the "five loaves and two fish" would be against assistance to those starving?

Workers whose ancestors suffered because of the greed and abuse of capital by demeaning the laborer would support those decimating the labor movement?

People whose immigrant ancestors suffered and struggled and were abused in deed and word with racial slurs would now be demeaning immigrants?

So much prejudice would be spewed and so much sorrow would be legislated or ignored by those who quote scripture? Could you ever imagine?

In an article in *Psychology Today*, August 29, 2013, Miles Grothe asks: *"Just what prompts a young man to end his young life at a time when his prospects might be expected to be brightest is baffling—unless we consider that they are facing a world that may seem not to have a place for them. And they are keenly aware of this. And they are hurt by it…. They have all read in popular weeklies or on the internet about 'the end of men' or heard the question 'Are men necessary?'"*

So, how these rumors are being spread to young men is answered. As Groth states, "They have all read in popular weeklies or on the internet about…." And because they are hurt by this, their self-worth is damaged. They are being told again and again they have no value, so why repeat these assertions again and again?

The date of the article is 2013, so what has happened in the intervening years, if anything? And if there were efforts, the current rhetoric is saying it didn't have any effect or did not have the desired effect. One thing that has happened is that people have been given permission to be more aggressive, permission to harm others.

And I ask again: What is the agenda? How is this rhetoric helping young men? But most importantly, these issues cannot be addressed appropriately until we know the factors that are triggering what young men are experiencing and to what degree. And who comprises "these young men," such as skin color, socio-economic status, attending college or working….?

The Center for Masculinities and Social Justice *State of American Men 2025 Report* points to "economic insecurity, isolation, and adherence to a rigid masculinity ideology as major drivers of distress for men and boys." The report found "86% of men (and 77% of women) view being a 'provider' as defining manhood…. This expectation is concerning due to *income inequality of men*, wage stagnation, and job insecurity." They also found that men facing financial strain were 16 times more likely to report suicidal thoughts than those who were not, which confirms that expectations put on men are contributing. And where do the expectations come from?

In the film, *Dead Poet's Society*, a young man, who is gentle and caring and would not be considered a manly man by those calling for masculinity, desires an acting career. When the father learns that his son has disobeyed him and is pursuing an acting career, he drags him away, tells him, in an angry, dogmatic voice that he is going to pursue the career his father wishes, not the life he desires.

The son, feeling lost and broken, not knowing what to do, commits suicide with his father's gun that was easily available to him. Not able to consider, yet alone admit, that he contributed to his son's death, the father forced the school to find a scapegoat—the teacher who encouraged his son to be whatever he wished. And the reality was that the teacher freed the son by encouraging him to pursue his desires. He gave him a reason to live, but the father took away that desire by his dictates.

When a young man is prodded into doing what he does not desire, lacking in ability or motivation to meet expectations dictated to him, or desires to take another path, the pressure may become overwhelming and too painful.

But it is difficult for the collective and parents to admit that their rhetoric, their dictates, and their attempts to manipulate both genders are contributing factors to some of the struggles young people experience now, experienced in the past, and will experience into the future.

There are so many unanswered questions. These issues are like trying to carry fog home in a paper bag.

To answer the question of why young men are struggling, why not factor in how young men are raised and what they are taught? What are the values and beliefs of those influencing them? What outside forces are impacting them?

Many men are brought into the world and grow up believing they are entitled. They are the product of "It's a boy" culture. Men have been the chosen gender for thousands of years. That sets up their expectation for being the one in charge, and for the privileged especially, it sets up the expectation of success.

And consider those men who have achieved and held positions and were handed opportunities because there was minimal female competition if any, in the past. And if employers are honest, they have tolerated mediocrity—men who did not perform well in their positions. And added to this mix, there was minimal competition from men who were not privileged and were not expected to achieve.

So, has expectations of entitlement and privilege and the rhetoric swirling around them that they are not achieving weakened young men's resolve and tenacity? And are they in the majority? And what is the collective going to do about it? Who is providing them counsel? And it must be appropriate counsel, not dictating to young men who they should be and what they should desire and not pitting one gender against another! And it must be asked again and again: How is the rhetoric assaulting men helping them?

Some men may no longer be guaranteed a place at the table. They will have to earn it, and possibly lose it to a woman. And being able to choose from numerous qualified candidates will benefit companies. Employers can now choose from the best and brightest, the most qualified, the most tenacious—the one most worthy. And if that candidate happens to be a woman, why deny her? Hiring women also saves companies money because they still are NOT paying women the same as men, so level the playing field for men by paying women the same as men.

When faced with competition from women, young men will need to do what women have had to do—try harder. They cannot accept the status of victim that has been handed to them by the churning rhetoric that keeps them spinning. As we have seen with women, a victim status can keep them stuck, no way out, and is debilitating and demoralizing.

Young boys and men need opportunities to step out into the world and face difficulties and challenges. If not, they can become traumatized when faced with adversity because they never learned to slay dragons.

Mom and Dad should not show up at school when he gets a B, rescuing him and framing him as a victim of the system. That sets up an expectation of always being rescued, and the young man does not have to do anything for himself.

Is the negative rhetoric about young men being fueled by the patriarchy's disappointment in them? Maybe the patriarchy is unhappy that their sons are struggling to compete with women?

Men no longer get a pass on "bad" behavior or mediocrity. And instead of motivating, is this rhetoric defeating them and contributing to their struggles and anger?

Instead of the collective and patriarchy taking responsibility for some of young men's struggles, one of the rescue techniques is to find convenient scapegoats, such as women and those who are supporting them. Then those responsible do not have to be accountable for what is happening to young men. Is it easier to find scapegoats, imagined or not, than look at societal and parental pressures? Man-UP! Get that degree! Find that job! Climb that ladder! Make me proud!

But it would be difficult for those who have contributed to this situation to admit they are culpable. They could no longer live through the successes of their sons. They would no longer have bragging rights. They would not have a legacy of their choosing. And they would have to stop assaulting and blaming women. And that would stall their agenda of sending women back into the home so they would no longer compete with their sons.

And how does a culture that promotes boys over girls, men over women contribute to the struggles of young men? And how does a culture that ensures the few are privileged and determines superiority by skin color contribute to the struggles of those marginalized? Divisiveness, aggression, punishment, hubris, greed, vengeance, and oppression are in full view. How can those images be canceled out?

Instead of looking at how the patriarchy is contributing to a young man's struggles, the hidden message seems to be: Women are a threat! They need to be pushed back into their corner, gagged, and their hands tied once again (subservient to men). Then the problems young men are encountering will go away. Who would want that? Oh yes, the patriarchy, and those who have come to believe they are entitled.

Maybe the patriarchs are the spark lighting the fire and putting women's names on it, and at the same time harming young men? And isn't it a testimony to women's strength and courage that for all the forces that have worked against them for centuries, they have achieved?

History supports the fact that despite the stereotype that boys do better in math and science, girls have made higher grades than boys throughout their school years for nearly a **century**, according to an analysis by the American Psychological Association. But they were not allowed to enter the work force or college in numbers for a part of those hundred years.

Daniel Voyer, Ph.D. and Susan D. Voyer, MASc who conducted a study at the University of New Brunswick are not sounding the alarm about boys. Their study reported in the Psychological Bulletin, April 28, 2014, "Gender Differences in Scholastic Achievement: A Meta-Analysis," revealed that girls' grades have been consistently higher than boys' across several decades with no significant changes in recent years.

"The fact that females generally perform better than their male counterparts throughout what is essentially mandatory schooling in most countries seems to be a well-kept secret, considering how little attention it has received as a global phenomenon," said Susan Voyer.

The significant differences now, compared to decades ago, is that women are attending college and have opportunities in the workplace. They are formidable competition for young men.

Just because a young man does not get the best grades, does not want to go to college, or drops out of college does not mean he is struggling or a reason to sound the alarm. It does not mean he is a failure. He may have realized that he cannot get what he needs from a piece of paper.

Howard Zinn, author and a professor of history, said he learned more about history from reading books in the library. The history textbooks did not include all of history, especially the labor movement. During my 12+8+ years of education, I learned as much, if not more on my own, although there were several teachers who had a positive influence on my life. Most of what I have learned is because I pursued my interests and delved deeply.

I recently spoke with a couple about life on campus. I asked her what she was studying: Political science and English, planning to attend law school. I then asked him. "I dropped out. I couldn't get what I needed sitting in class. I have started my own business doing…. I could figure out what I needed to know on my own…." Maybe other young men are saying the same thing.

There are many factors that contribute to the choices any one of us make, so why are young men not going to college or eventually dropping out? Perhaps they find classes boring, not giving them what they need, and they are unwilling to exchange that for the debt.

Some may want to start their own business, and they may not need a college degree to do that. The job market is changing, with emphasis on vocational training or apprenticeships, giving them something more interesting to do and money more quickly than sitting in a classroom.

The problem for parents is that these choices are not what they wish for their sons. Add to that the fact that laborers are demeaned and often not paid enough. When someone needs a plumber, someone to fix that roof, construct a deck, the workers are expected to work for as little as possible.

Careers, such as nursing, elementary school teachers, administrative assistants…. are discouraged in men. For some parents, a young man not getting a college degree is tantamount to a crime.

Booker T. Washington said, *"No race can prosper till it learns that there is as much dignity in tilling a field as in writing a poem."*

Without the understanding and willingness to investigate what are perceived problems, are the solutions being proposed just band aids? Do something to do something!

The issues also need to be looked at not only from what is happening to men, but what is happening to women, and not just the problems of the few and the privileged. And the issues should not be defined and assessed by what any man needs to be but acknowledge who he is and who he wants to become.

And consider that maybe women are more determined to get better grades and attend college because they must. They have a legacy of being disadvantaged in a society that still considers them the "second" sex so they need all the credentials they can acquire. They are motivated because they are not the chosen and preferred gender.

Many young men are saying they are unwilling to play by the rules and want to chart their own path. And if so, kudos to them. We need to have some faith in young men and young women who do not embrace the dictates leveled at them. We need to guide, support, and inspire them, and even let them fail without being assaulted.

There is no just and right formula for how men should be, what they should aspire to, what they should accomplish. There is no just and right formula for how women should be, what they should NOT aspire to, and what they should NOT accomplish.

Ten
Make Love, Not War

"Women and men have to fight together to change society—and both will benefit.
Muriel Fox

Katharine lived to please her husband, Carl. He was her jailer, provider, and *father*. But he was not her friend or confidant, someone with whom she could express her thoughts without fear of reprisals. She shared and supported his yearnings and his interests. She did everything that he asked of her, and it was always his way.

Then one day Katharine awakened and started a journey of reflection and discovery. She told Carl what she was thinking. It didn't agree with his thinking. He was stunned. She was different! When did that change happen? What does it mean? How would it change his life?

Carl thought the writing in her journal, the volunteer work, the women's groups, and her continual interest in something new kept Katharine busy and out of his way, limiting the demands on his time.

He believed he kept his side of the bargain. He protected and provided for her, gave her children. In return, he expected from her what all women should give—nurturing and the "doing" and never questioning. Now, she wanted something different, and there were conditions—that which he could not deliver, did not want to deliver, believed he should not have to deliver.

She was no longer the quiet, little woman. Katharine had changed, and he never noticed. He lashed out. He got wrapped up in his anger. He could not see her unhappiness.

Just like he didn't notice that she was going through a transformation, he was not seeing her now. He could not see who she had become and the gifts she could bring to the relationship. He thought she was just writing in her journal, attending meetings, and volunteering.

The play, *The Flyer Lovers of Vitebsk,* is the story of Marc Chagall, a man who never saw his wife, Bella, as more than a supporting cast in his own drama. Throughout the play Bella mentions again and again that she is writing. Marc never asked her what she was writing or asked to read it. He takes no interest. She is there to support him, and he is caught up in his own needs, his own achievements.

After she dies, their daughter publishes Bella's writings. In the play Marc is on the phone with his daughter talking about Bella's writing. *"You know, afterwards, when I read her notebooks, I found them so…. vivid! And I was startled somehow that her view was so close to mine, and yet so different to my own. But what a fool! Had it never occurred to me that though we saw the same things, she saw them with her own eyes? And my heart broke again because she had died so hidden—like all those other Yiddish souls, snuffed out before half their life was shed…."*

Marc had never talked to her about her writings, her innermost thoughts. Their life together was about him. He missed knowing the woman she was. At the end of the play, I was in tears—in tears for a life that was denied her, a life she did not get to live.

Can you deny that a relationship can be sabotaged by men who are not present in the lives of their loved ones or want to control the lives of others?

Women are turning away a man who believes a woman is his property to do as he wishes and can tell her how to think and what she is to believe. And there are reports that men fear rejection and accusations of crossing boundaries so they are no longer approaching women. So, instead of a man questioning his behavior and asking what he needs to do differently, he opts out. It is easier because he doesn't have to do a thing. And how is that working for men?

Rejection is something we all experience. Does that mean giving up and not trying? Women experience rejection by being passed over—not the chosen one. Some even by their parents. They wait to be asked on a date, for that promotion, for that proposal....

So, instead of feeling rejected and defeated, there are other responses that might be more beneficial. But these responses are conditional. A man might consider asking himself: Am I interested in a woman as a friend, as someone of value in my life, or is she a conquest? If she is a conquest, and if he feigns behavior, says and does what will get him his prize, he is a charlatan, a sham, someone to be rejected. So, women beware!

If she is a woman to be valued and a man wishes to get to know her, there are some questions and responses he could ask himself with humility: Does he expect a woman to welcome any overture he makes? Did he cross a boundary? If so, why? Could what he said have been offensive? Or he could say to the woman rejecting him, "Have I offended you in anyway? If so, can we talk about that?"

By asking the questions, maybe he can learn something so such an incident does not repeat itself. And yes, he may not like what he hears, but there may be a beneficial lesson. If he expects a woman will fall into his arms just because that is what he desires, he may be in for a lot of disappointments.

And rejection is not only at the beginning of a relationship. It could come a week, a month, or more later. So, during their time together, a man could find out what interests the woman he is pursuing. Yes, he will have to talk to her and listen. He may find she has gifts, knowledge, and wisdom that might not only be interesting but helpful to him in his studies, work, and relationships.

Worthwhile relationships can open up an unknown world and bring wonderous gifts. Joining forces with women, both genders can benefit if they are willing to engage, without judgments and demands.

Myra Brooks Welch wrote "The Touch of the Master's Hand" that tells of an auction at which there was an old, dusty violin offered for sale. The auctioneer didn't expect it would sell for much because of its age and appearance. He started the bidding with a dollar. In time the bidding reached three dollars and was "going once, going twice..." but then....

An elderly man in the back of the room wiped the dust from the violin and picked up the bow and began to play. A lovely sound filled the room. He ended his performance, and the bidding started with one thousand dollars! It finally sold for three thousand dollars! What made the difference? The man looked beyond its appearance, and he made an investment of time.

How many people do you pass by each day that you do not notice or you dismiss as not worthy of your time? How many people do you see struggling and suffering, close to falling apart and decide it's not your problem? How many people do you turn away or ignore because they don't "look right," didn't say something "just right," or aren't from the right side of the street?

Have you considered that maybe you have missed an opportunity? Maybe that someone has a gift for you? Maybe that encounter will give you an opportunity to matter in someone's life? Maybe you will give yourself a gift of a friendship or a loving relationship?

Jung said, "People judge because they cannot think." I believe people judge because it's expedient. No effort required! No investment of time!

I have said many times, "My mother would walk a mile if my father would just walk a foot." I am not suggesting this, but what I had noticed is that my mother was so grateful for words of kindness and consideration and engagement, she would respond with a magnanimous spirit. And it wasn't because my father wasn't a kind and "good" husband in many ways. It was because often he wasn't demonstrative and not paying attention, and he believed his actions were enough. They were not.

And when a woman is speaking to a man, she may have to be direct and matter-of-fact, but she does not have to speak with vitriol and anger, with accusatory language. Other times consider giving him some direction, explaining calmly, having a MOM—meeting of the minds—discussion. Just like a woman cannot read a man's mind, he cannot read hers. And do not assault him with the party line—"men are…." It's inflammatory and may be inaccurate!

Then consider, like a man, doesn't a woman have the right to choose him or not? And in the past, a woman may have felt she had to say "yes" and endure advances, but if she says NO, that does not make her the problem.

And if she accepts a man, that is a greater win for him because that acceptance is not conditional. She welcomes him into her life, not because she is needy or she has no other choice. He won her on his own merits, and he may feel more secure in that relationship.

A man would also have to set the ego aside and not look upon rejection as an affront against him. Rejection is as much about her, as it is him. Maybe she isn't looking! Maybe there is someone else? Maybe…?

Women have had to step up and be what a man wants or just bow and kiss the ring for centuries, ignoring what he wasn't because she could not support herself. Now, a man has to do more than just show up, whisper a few nice words, and do a bit of romancing, if he is even doing that.

The tables have been turned. Some men are angry or have been told to be angry by men who are not welcoming the freedom women are experiencing! And haven't some men feared that once women got economic freedom and their voice, they would have choices, and a man may not be one of them? And isn't that same fear the reason why women have been denied and told again and again NO to their desires and paid less?

If a man is struggling with a relationship, consider that effort is required. A man is not entitled to a job because he appears, and he is not entitled to a woman on his arm just because that is what he wants. And remember, it's the ego that fears rejection, and again maybe there is a lesson to be learned. But to learn a lesson, a man has to be willing to reflect on why he was rejected and not blame rejection on the woman and what she wants. That will yield nothing!

Women are welcomed on campus, achieving, and getting opportunities. They have been thrust into an unknown arena. Their landscape has changed and that requires thoughtful consideration of what that means. Are we to assume they are content, have no struggles, and are not confused?

Men! Do you believe women are to do what you wish? Do you believe they should have the same rights and freedoms as you have? If not, why not?

Women! Do you believe all men are patriarchal? Have you come to realize that sometimes behavior is mimicked and the role models for men are flawed? Are you willing to help him navigate the landmines of the "new" woman?

Another step men might consider is to realize that the landscape of women has changed too and make peace that it has changed forever. No number of assaults and denials and whining about women will take men back to a time when women were chained to them, without opportunity, a time when a woman HAD to have a man. And not returning to those times is a good thing, even for men.

The challenges facing a man today, if he is seeking a fulfilling relationship, suggest he develop a different mindset about women and his expectations of a relationship with a woman. And to do this, it requires him to decide how he wants to be regarded and deep within who he is.

He must reject the belief that women are puppets, and he can pull the strings. He must not listen to those men who believe "all men should…" He must reject the dictates of men who want to turn all men into clones of themselves.

And to reject the dictates invading his mind, a man has to be brave enough to choose his own path. A man has his own desires, interests, values, and beliefs, and he is entitled to act upon them without feeling guilty or being punished.

To do so, he must ask himself if he wants to continue the "all men should" legacy that has been handed to him and mimic the behaviors of the male collective. Or, as I have said to women, should he tear up the script and fire the directors?

In the Farrell article, a young man said, *"Then we are told we're part of the patriarchy that makes rules to benefit men at the expense of women. The conclusion is that 'Men are the oppressors; women are the oppressed…. I can't help being who I am."*

First, does this young man know who he is? That's not always easy when you are young. One's identity is still in flux. So, because he is impressionable, is he following the crowd? He can help who he is by questioning his behavior, his responses. He can also resist the mindset of the gang.

Second, why not pause a minute and acknowledge the reality that men have oppressed others, not only women but MEN for centuries and that is still true today? And consider that how he and other young men are regarded is the legacy of the culture and the actions of their patriarchal fathers.

Third, has he bought into the belief that he is entitled to whatever he desires? He does not have to join his comrades in oppression and assaults. He can join those who understand the issues that the majority of people face—not just women. He can embrace compassion for others and lose any sense of entitlement. And by doing so, he will matter.

A woman cannot expect men to know what she wants and desires. And she won't get what she wants, unless she figures out how to communicate that without assaulting men, especially a man who has potential to be a caring and tender partner or friend.

Instead of accusing a man as part of the patriarchy, which he may not be, a woman might try a different tactic, such as, "If I said that to you, what would you think?" OR "How is what you just said helpful to me?" OR….

There are many questions that can put the onus on a man to explain his behavior or words, and it may be more effective than name calling and understanding may result. And it is true for men too. They can ask questions. Both may benefit, and it might result in an enlightening discussion.

But I also caution that not ALL men should be painted with the same brush. Not all men are oppressors. If that were true, there would not be men trying to lift up women and supporting them. There would not be men who stand beside a successful woman and are proud to do so.

Not all men are patriarchal! Not all men are tyrannical! Maybe, way too many, but not ALL! And if you find a man who is supportive and inspires you, let him know and cherish him.

And yes, some women are angry; women are seeking revenge for centuries of oppression, faulting any misstep. But how has that been working for them?

And yes, there are still ancestors of minorities and immigrants seeking revenge for centuries of oppression, but how has that been working for them?

And men are confused and struggling, and they are angry too. But how has that been working for them?

The young man who complained about being labeled patriarchal said, *"My guy friends. They feel the same. But I'd never tell my girlfriend. She's a feminist. She'd break up with me."*

If asked, could he define feminism accurately? Or would it be tainted by the rhetoric he has heard? Many women are asking to be seen and heard and respected. They are seeking an authentic interest in their desires, and, of course, a woman would expect a man to support equal pay and opportunity for all—goals of feminism.

And yes, it is a possibility that she would leave the relationship if she found out he did not support her. But isn't he being duplicitous, inauthentic, pretending to be someone he is not by his silence or by feigning behavior?

And why should a woman be with someone who does not embrace and support her dreams? Why should she be with someone who doesn't think she should have opportunities and equal pay for equal work?

Problems could arise in the relationship if she realizes that he begrudges who and what she is and what she has accomplished.

And problems will be heightened in the relationship if he blames her success on the fact that she was given something because she was female.

Would he ever be able to acknowledge that she earned her success?

And the difficulties that women face and the issues around equal pay and opportunity exist because they are still being denied by ruling and institutional patriarchs who are content to see women struggle and demeaned by denying them rights and paying them less! But if everything is about him, it is difficult for a man to have compassion and understanding of others.

Women should be more than a supporting cast in a man's drama!

In the same article, Farrell recalls encountering seven guys reuniting at a coffee shop. They were attending different colleges. They were not your average guy on the street, so we are left to wonder what young men not attending college would say. All of them nodded as one guy complained, "If I take a sexual initiative too quickly, I'm labeled a sexual harasser."

When did he make that advance—first date, second date? Within ten minutes of saying hello? And what's the date about? A conquest? And why does he believe spending time with her requires some sort of intimacy? Is he viewing this encounter as a transaction? "I asked you out. You should be thrilled and give me something in return."

He continues, "But if I ask permission to hold her hand, she looks at me like I'm a wimp."

Does she think he's a wimp or does he believe or has he learned that a MAN must be more forceful? Or maybe his move is way too soon, and he knows it. But he is going to try anyway. Or maybe she is just not that interested, and she is signaling that to him by her demeanor.

And why does she have to be interested or willing? Is his frustration because he cannot believe that he is not desirable? Why does he think she should want to engage in intimacy?

He said that one of his friends concurred, *"I feel damned if I do; damned if I don't. … if they're so into equality, why don't they take the sexual initiatives and risk the rejection?"*

Because she would be considered too….? And that is because the collective has decided that any overture is the man's role.

And why is a date about a physical encounter? There are other ways of connecting and experiencing intimacy. Why not allow the relationship to evolve naturally, focusing on the quality of the time spent together and caring about one another?

Worthwhile, meaningful relationships evolve over time. Life is not a movie where you look into each other's eyes across a crowded room, and then seconds later you are ripping off each other's clothes. And do all men want that? Are all women supposed to be willing?

Maybe he might also learn the nonverbal signs that indicate a woman is interested or not. And maybe he is unwilling to accept that it is her right not to be interested, just as it is his! But if a man is determined to conquer, he will not and maybe cannot pay attention to the signs of disinterest.

Or maybe it's that a woman is looking for the right partner—not any partner! Men can no longer count on getting the girlfriend or wife they think they should have, woo a woman into marriage, have someone who provides for their every need.

Today many women are seeking: (and my guess this has also been true for thousands of years)

- Relationships that tap into who they are and their interests and aspirations.
- Relationships that are genuine, intense, and not shallow.

- Relationships that are rooted in trust and compassion and acceptance of their desires, wisdom, intelligence, and courage.

Can anyone argue against any of them? But if a man is absent of feelings and substance, he will become angry because he cannot deliver. And he might blame his lack of availability and capability on the woman. He does not realize that his inability to deliver does not make that woman the problem. But it is expedient to blame her, and he does not have to do a thing.

In reality, there are women who always wanted a complete partner and for other women it may not have mattered until it did.

But in the past the patriarchal culture forced women into marriage, or they had to walk the street, be a nanny or maid, or…. and society is still poking and prodding women today into marriage and children.

Do men have difficulty understanding women's desires because they do not choose their partners based on the same desires? Patriarchal relationships are often transactional. Some men are looking for someone to support their efforts and take care of their every need and desires, arm candy, or a baby maker, and there are women willing to comply.

Fewer women today are willing to make the bargains they had to in the past. And that is not a bad thing! Maybe it is for some men, but not necessarily for society, for the world, for women.

Women come together with other women because they enjoy the conversation, the variety of topics they discuss, the attention they receive—spending time with someone who listens and cares about the other person and what is said…. Can a man say he has interesting conversation and shows an interest in his date and who she is?

So, if men want a relationship, they have to make an effort. They may have to engage women in meaningful conversations. Unfortunately, spending most of the day on the computer or texting does not secure interpersonal and communication skills, which include non-verbal cues.

For many women, engaging some men in conversation is difficult. Sometimes it appears that a man does not want to communicate. Maybe he is uncomfortable, not sure what to say. Women can move that along by being silent and not speaking or asking questions, instead of telling and telling.

Other men regard a conversation as a monologue in which they brag, pontificate, launch as much information as possible about their day, title, position, experiences, exploits, and current interests. And maybe, just maybe, the woman may be allowed to speak.

I was once on a date with a man who talked and talked from the moment he said hello. He then turned to me, and said, "Elizabeth, you are not saying anything!" How could I? Before I responded, he started talking again. Then he said again, "Elizabeth, you are not saying anything." This time I was prepared, and within a nanosecond, I said, "I do not speak on command!" And yes, I did end the evening early!

There are some men who know how to have a conversation. They do not regard any time they are not speaking as an annoyance. They participate in the conversation and do not believe a woman is there to entertain them and do all the talking.

There are men who do not tune out a woman. They listen and are not waiting to speak. They appreciate that a discussion takes two people speaking, asking questions, and actually listening. Both parties are instilled with curiosity and interest. By doing so, the discussion has the potential to benefit each, and they feel heard and valued.

Why should you spend time with someone who is boring and who you do not respect and who does not respect you? And women, before they had choices had to endure their situation. But now that women do have choices, they are able to walk away literally, as men have done for centuries by going to the club, stopping at a bar, playing golf, having an affair….

It is misguided and disrespectful to assume that women should feel grateful for any male attention. It is misguided and disrespectful when a man assumes that all women desire the same thing. It implies that he does not care about who she is and what she desires.

A friend of mine has a son in college who has no conversation. He sulks, takes no interest in family and friends of his parents, and is obsessed with his phone and computer. He laments to his mother that he cannot get a young woman interested in him, and he is angry. And his situation isn't helped by a patriarchal father who keeps nudging him to find that girl.

His mother and I agree! He needs to stop being enthralled with his own importance. He believes he deserves a woman in his life. Until he loses that attitude and belief of entitlement, it is not going to happen unless a young woman is….

My friend has spoken to him about how to engage a young woman with conversation, but he rebukes her. He wants what he wants and doesn't believe he should do anything different. No effort required. But if he continues to do what he has always done, he will continue to get what he has always gotten or not gotten.

And women: Instead of accusing a man of bad behavior, it may be helpful to explain to men what you need, what would be helpful. When I was dating my husband, I mentioned that something he said bothered me. He apologized, which was a good start, but I surprised him when I said, "An apology is fine, but what are you going to do differently next time?"

I explained that apologies are often perfunctory and meaningless if said again and again. And in the future a different response in a similar situation would not necessitate an apology. I knew our relationship was worth taking the risk and the time, and he was willing to listen and have that discussion because he was vested in the relationship as well.

"The ever-evolving societal expectations and pressures are bound to change the dating world," says Tara Lally, Ph.D., a clinical psychologist in the department of psychiatry at Ocean University Medical Center in New Jersey. "Marrying and having children later allows both partners to have established careers and identities, which bring an equal partnership into the relationship."

But do all men agree? Do they all want equality in a relationship? Maybe they would once they give it a chance.

A report from *The Good Men Project*, 2009, states that most women have three or more close friends. Men usually do not have one close friend, and if they do, it is their wife.

So, besides wanting a woman to do the chores, make babies, fulfill all his needs, his wife is to be his sounding board, the person he can share his thoughts. And he knows that she is a good choice because he has seen her willingness to help, listen, offer compassion and understanding. So why not respect and value her? And why not return the favor?

The Good Men's Project also stated: "In 2009, the proportion of American women who were married dropped below 50 percent. In other words, for the first time in American history, single women (those who were never married, widowed, divorced, or separated) outnumbered married women…. At the same time more and more men feel disconnected, disrespected, and angry."

And is it women's fault that men feel disconnected, disrespected? Angry at who? Women? Angry at what? Maybe that their hold over women has eroded, that women no longer desire them or marriage, that women have other choices? Maybe women no longer wish to be subservient?

Many women are confident, aware of their worth, and seek partners who appreciate them, partners who support their desires. Women are asking that men have more substance, are present, communicative, and how do those qualities hurt men?

Men may be surprised to discover that developing communication and interpersonal skills will contribute to connection and intimacy and building relationships that will benefit them in their work life, as well as their personal life. They will have to be more present—not wrapped up in their own lives and their desires.

Women who are not going to settle for less than what they desire are not wrongheaded. Why should they settle? And is finding fault with women who have desires and are successful signaling that these men want women in their place, imprisoned, and helpless? Maybe not, but who is teaching men a different way?

Women who seek relationships built on equality and mutual respect, not gratitude, are not against men. It is about their wants, their desires. The belief that a woman must be interested in a man and marriage and children is an outdated model of the collective. Yet, there are still those who wish women to be needy and are doing everything to keep them or make them that way, so a woman will be grateful for a warm male body.

Yet, there are also young women and men shouting from the rooftops that they don't want to be chained to patriarchal and matriarchal dictates. They will marry when they wish and have children if they wish or not have children. They are marrying across ethnic groups and religions in greater numbers than past generations. Women are having babies and raising those children on their own. And they are doing so without apology or remorse.

Are young men rejecting the traditional model and telling the collective they do not wish to fall in line? The collective for centuries has sent the message to men that they are valued only if they bring home that paycheck. As provider, a man worries about keeping his job and bringing in enough money to provide for his family, plus he has to juggle the needs of both work and family. He may stay in the wrong job because he must. I imagine a man on a tightrope—trying to stay on that high wire. And isn't that also true of single mothers, especially if the man won't pay child support?

Are men and women saying they do not want to be bound to a life they do not desire? And if so, they have a right to do so.

And it is difficult for those making the rules and dictating the expectations to accept that young men and women are saying, "NO thank you! I have other plans."

As a young girl, I heard my mother say again and again, "Marrying is the last thing you should do." At that time I did not realize she was saying, "Go out and find your own life first and do what you want, be who you want. Because when you marry, your life will be different and there will not be the same opportunities. And when you decide to marry, it will not be based on need but on desiring that relationship."

Instead of making the division between the genders wider, men need to consider embracing women's passions and feelings, rather than dismissing them as unimportant or folly, and be tender and caring. And there are no guarantees, but maybe, just maybe, this type of relationship may give men and women greater riches than they could have ever imagined. And there are men who can attest that honoring the women in their lives has given them many gifts.

In the Farrell article, a businessman stated that if a man should assault or demean a woman in any way, human resources would always support the woman. So, human resources is believing her, and is he asking them not to believe her but to believe him? Or is he asking HR not to consider what the man did as an issue and then dismiss it?

His evidence: "If I tease a man, no problem; if I tease a woman, I'll be reported to HR. HR doesn't 'get it' that guys tease people we respect, so if I only tease guys, I'm really discriminating against women." Seriously! Would all men agree? Would all women?

Can he not imagine or admit that maybe, just maybe, his humor could be considered hurtful, inappropriate? Could he imagine his daughter, wife, sister, mother hearing some of the remarks made to women by men who are "just" teasing?

How prevalent is the complaint women make about teasing? What are the subjects and what is said? It's a little abstract for me! But it must be asked: Are men to determine the rules? Are they to keep doing what they have been doing just because they see the situation differently? Are they permitted to deny a woman's point of view, and she does not have a say?

And maybe women might try a different tactic. There is no doubt there may be backlash, labeled as a...., when a woman reports a man of any offense. And sometimes it makes no difference. That is not suggesting that a serious offense not be reported, but in a moment of teasing, why not tease him back and chuckle as you are doing so. Turn the tables. And if it were teasing, then he will not be offended.

If he is offended, the response could be questions, not statement, "So, you are allowed to tease me, and I'm to be silent?" Or "Do you wish to offend me for some reason?" Asking him to explain his comment can be more effective than asking a third person to intervene.

By going to human resources, it's the drama triangle again. A going to C to complain about B, asking to be rescued. Why not rescue yourself? Do not trust that someone will intervene on your behalf and do what needs to be done. Do not allow yourself to be a victim. You are courageous and formidable.

When I was a young woman of nineteen working in a bank, women were fair game in all ways. There was no "C" who would intervene. We were on our own, and I must admit I prefer to handle a situation myself, if possible. I began envisioning a man's head as a balloon, and I was the pin. Try being the pin!

Men and women need to talk to each other, have a meaningful discussion, and leave assaults and vitriolic language out of the discussion and instead listen and seek to understand. Instead of defending your position and make statement after statement, ask questions to learn something.

Maybe women need to lose the entitlement mentality as well in certain situations. Pick your battles wisely. Women are not entitled to have everything their way either. Just as men cannot make all the rules, neither should women.

There are so many agendas swirling around us. It is difficult to identify the clandestine and often blatant methods used to keep women and men battling, rather than coming together.

The tragedy of this time for women and men is heart-wrenching and unacceptable. The divisiveness must be eradicated! And that is dependent on both men and women taking responsibility.

Friendships do not just materialize and the person of your dreams just doesn't appear. A relationship based on being willing to engage and make an effort can be worthwhile and needs to be cherished.

Being buried in concrete up to one's head with a *righteous right* mentality will yield loneliness and struggles.

And shouldn't one of our desires, one of our missions, be to figure out how to have meaningful conversations so we have meaningful relationships? In any relationship, it is about what gifts anyone offers up to a friend, a partner, a spouse, our community, the world.

And if you step back and reflect, when you leave this earth, what will be your most meaningful legacy? Things you have acquired, those you have conquered and plundered, those you have harmed, or those whose lives you have touched in positive ways, those you have supported and inspired, those who you valued, and to whom you showed compassion and warmth and love?

Eleven
Isolation and Community

"When we seek connection, we restore the world to wholeness. Our seemingly separate lives become meaningful as we discover how truly necessary we are to each other."

Margaret J. Wheatley

Maybe young boys and men have always had a degree of isolation because connection and intimacy and building relationships are not high on their priorities. Relationships are usually left to the women, especially in a patriarchal society. Men are taught to make their way through what they know, transactions, and unfortunately coercive action.

Forty years ago, I told my students, enamored with the computer, that the people who would eventually make a difference in the world would be those who could put two sentences together. The rest of them would be blubbering. Back then it was only the computer impacting their lives.

Now, the internet, cell phone, social media…. have disconnected young people from coming together in meaningful endeavors and limited, if not eliminated, meaningful communication.

How can you develop verbal communication skills if you do not speak? How can you develop writing skills when you hunt and peck for a few words? How can you develop interpersonal and communication skills if you have no contact with people? And that includes observing how your communication affects other people. How can you have a meaningful conversation when it is one-sided again and again? How can you articulate an important issue?

One day on campus, I was in an elevator and a young man, his head down, stuck into his phone, pummeled me with his book bag. He did not say, "Excuse me," so I said, "You're excused!" and then added, "You know, there is a whole world out there that you are missing by being attached to that phone."

Of course, he was surprised. He smirked and said, "But there is a whole world in here," holding up his phone.

My reply, "But it is stagnant!" Then I pointed to the phone. "The whole world in there! How sad for you!" I walked out of the elevator. His head was in concrete, but maybe a seed had been planted. He will think about what I said. Maybe?

But then maybe stagnant is safer, and it definitely requires no application, analysis, synthesis—no higher levels of reasoning and thinking. Just data dumping. It also requires no intimacy, no personal connections, no relationships. Again, it is safe.

Conversationally speaking, the technological world has eroded communication and interpersonal skills even though there are more ways to communicate. And by eroding those skills, relationships have been eroded.

Texting, e-mailing, Zoom classes, social media—all these technological advances in communication contribute to many young people entering the workplace without the benefit of having numerous and meaningful one-on-one and group interactions.

Working from home is another disadvantage to developing communication and interpersonal skills. And e-mails and texts have replaced the phone call. All things digital and their increased use have eliminated opportunities to interact daily and often in meaningful ways that are not one sided. There is also no opportunity to hear the tone of voice or read the body language, critical to communication.

Add to that buying online rather than in-store, and chat boxes, rather than one-on-one phone conversations where you hear a person's voice and have two-way communication. And if you do call a company, they do not want to talk with you. You have to press number after number to finally get someone on the phone.

Then after you hang up, you get e-mail messages telling you how to get information on line next time. All this nonsense may save the company money by not hiring employees to communicate, but it costs the rest of us wasted hours and frustration.

Add to that on-line classes and meetings that have replaced in-person classes and meetings. Yes, it's expedient and can serve a purpose within companies, but why does a class have to be on-line? Because it's another revenue stream in some instances. But it is flawed in so many ways for educational purposes. Unfortunately, convenience and the desire for money often win out over what will deliver the best educational experience. The motto: Just get it done and pretend we educated!

A young woman was sharing with me that she was writing a fictional novel. I asked her if she were using the work on archetypes to help develop her characters. She had no idea what I was talking about, so I offered to spend some time with her to explain how to use that information.

She said, "No, thank you. I will look it up on the computer!"

Not the same! It's one-sided information, and she has no opportunity to ask a question, clarify information, have a meaningful discussion, and mine the topic in depth as we could have done together. Plus, there are so many nuances to that topic, such as how the different archetypes relate to each other, which she could not find on the web. But she was convinced all she needed was the computer. She was also assuming the information she would retrieve would be accurate and helpful.

And now people are turning to AI for advice and guidance. Opting for one-way communication is definitely inhibiting the development of critical thinking skills. Interpersonal skills and the art of communication, as well as critical thinking, are endangered, if not already close to being eradicated.

It doesn't take rocket science to link isolation and the inability to communicate to technology, but if suggested and proven, some people's whole world would collapse. They would have to participate in the world in a personal and more meaningful way. That would be terrifying for some, or maybe far too many!

But isn't that what needs to happen? Consider technology as a tool—not an extension of your body and your mind.

And if technology is set aside, how will that change relationships? Will people no longer be indoctrinated and manipulated with comments that are abstract and have no substance? Will they begin to think for themselves? Will they begin to come together in meaningful ways?

There are four universities within two miles of my home, so when I get on the bus, usually ninety percent of those on the bus are students. And, of course, ninety percent or more of them are attached to their phone.

Any building I walk through at the university, there are students stuck into their computers. When I wait at the bus stop to return home, same thing. I seldom observe a conversation taking place. And this occurs in all levels of education, not just in universities, and also in doctors' offices, in restaurants....

One day I walked onto the bus, and there was a toddler in a stroller. He waved hello and started to babble on. I engaged with him the best I could. His mother took the gadget on his lap and handed it to him. I guess he was to entertain himself. He threw it on his lap and started smiling and chatting with me again.

Once again, the mother picked up the gadget and handed it to him. He pushed a few buttons, dropped it, and said hello to the people getting on the bus. This scenario was repeated two more times, with the mother insisting the kid use the gadget, which he refused to do. In that ten-minute ride, she never spoke to him once. But the message was clear. He wanted to communicate with someone, anyone.

Now parents, who are fed up with the screen time of their children, are signing them up for curated digital detox programs at camps. This time away from home for minors, aged 13 to 18, is meant to help children with everything from social anxiety to depression to gaming and social media addiction.

But why can't parents take the devices away? At what age was the child weaned on technology? Why did they give it to a child in the first place? To replace parenting? To keep a child entertained and out of the way?

Why can't parents replace that device with a meaningful conversation, a game, a museum—engage the child or young adult in some significant way? Why can't they help their children to step into the world, contribute, and thrive, not just perform and exist?

If they did not have children to mentor and guide, educate, and engage in meaningful conversations throughout their formative years, why did they have them? To say they did? Because it was expected of them? To live through the child?

Several women and a few men have shared stories with me, giving evidence they had absent parents, even though the mothers did not work. Having a child does not guarantee parenting. Their parents fed and clothed them, but they were not present in their children's lives in word and deed. They could not recount any warm and fuzzy memories, where they felt wrapped in warmth and love and acceptance.

Others tell that they were expected to achieve, browbeaten to perform, and what they delivered was never good enough. They never got it right. And all of them were still struggling to understand the advice given and not given and the caring that was missing in their young lives.

Meaningful parenting involves being present, not just a body who comes in and out of a child's life, dictating what they should desire and punishing non-performance. It is also critical that a parent provide what the child needs, not what the child wants.

There are many books on parenting, but I will sum up parenting as follows. Children need to see a parent's spirit and soul and expressions of love—compassion, engagement, with the child and with the adults and other children in that parent's life. Parents need to have meaningful conversations with their children, create memories together, show an interest in the child's interests, and not force a parent's interests and agendas on the child.... And add to the mix support, guidance, kindness, caring, ethical behavior, and not celebrating the hardships of others and spewing hatred.

During my entire childhood and into adolescence, I only received what would be considered two significant gifts. One was a tricycle for Christmas, and the other was a radio that my father purchased for my sixteenth birthday. Yet, I never felt deprived. I don't ever remember crying out for "something." I never desired anything tangible, except books as a child and a train. And although I never got the train I wanted, I never felt unloved. I felt protected and secure in my parents' love and care.

I did not need monetary trappings for my parents to prove their love for me. My father inspired me by how he engaged me in meaningful conversations about government, history, and politics, and how he regarded and supported me. My mother was also supportive and inspiring because she believed I could do whatever I set my mind to doing and applauded my efforts. They were interested in me and did not diminish me.

And at the same time, they did not have the education and know-how to guide me in my life's work or money to help me make my way. But in time I did that for myself. I did not need someone to rescue me or do for me. And I could do so because of what they instilled in me and their positive regard for me.

I am not trying to give parenting lessons. And some would call me out for that because I never had a child, but I was a child. I know what made me feel loved and valued, and it wasn't THINGS!

What percentage of parents use the television and computers as parenting tools? What percentage replace parenting with sports, clubs, and activities and demand performance? So, maybe when kids feel deprived of attention and do not feel loved for who they are, expected to perform for grades and in the sports arena, THINGS are like a band-aid that covers up the wound until another band-aid is needed and another and another.

Or maybe THINGS are being offered because a parent feels guilty for not being present in their child's life so they bow to the pressures of a child's wants! Or maybe they do not want their child to be the only one without, and so, they give in to the pressure of the "haves" and work hard to provide. And then throw in companies that sell to kids everything and anything, putting more pressure on parents to buy, buy, buy.

Children must go through initiations—opportunities to take flight. The mother and father birds push the young bird out of the nest and teach it to fly and forage for food. They show an interest and teach the baby bird what it needs to know to survive, and then once the bird is out in the world, it is not expected to return to the nest because they do not need to return. They have learned the lessons they needed under the guidance of the parents.

Children must have opportunities that challenge them, and they will and must fail because that will happen throughout life. They cannot expect to be rescued or blame someone else for a mistake or lack of success.

One of my relatives had a young boy who was good at everything and often demeaned his siblings who were not achieving as he was. I said to his mother, "Jake needs to fail at something!" Of course, she was appalled at what I had said. Her "baby" fail, oh my!

I explained that if he fails at the small things when he is young, it won't be so difficult later in life. He will learn how to pick himself up and move forward.

Soon after, he failed his driver's test. Minor, and he could recover. Then he wasn't hired after attending university. Failure! Disappointment! Not fatal! Then, he got hired, but not for the job he wanted. Disappointment! Although his ego was bruised, none of this was fatal, but there were lessons learned.

The manosphere draws young men in because it offers a sense of belonging and validation. That is such a disheartening and damning commentary on parenting, the school system, the workplace—the collective. It is also evidence that the insular world fostered by technology in the home and in schools will continue to fuel isolation.

Instead of computers in the classroom, doing whatever, students could be put in small groups for discussion. Large-classroom discussion only ensures that those who want to talk, are ready to talk, or want to be noticed will speak, so small groups will get more voices heard. The possibilities are endless, but the schools must be willing to acknowledge that the overuse of computers is harming children and young people.

Parents could limit computer and phone time and plan outings, play games, discuss an important topic, listen to sons and daughters.... Workplaces could limit time working from home, meetings on the internet.... The opportunities to reconnect people to society are endless, but it takes effort and willingness.

But we also must ask why aren't the alarms being sounded that women do not have a feeling of not belonging and isolation? Does the collective not care? Have they not noticed the struggles of young women? Do they believe young women have no problems because they are achieving? And is the concern because the only measure of a man, anyone, is achieving? Another sad commentary on the collective!

Or is there something about what women are doing that might benefit men knowing? The most obvious is that women who are relationship oriented and seek out interaction will not feel isolated. Interaction with others, engaging in conversation where someone is listening, there is a sense of validation and belonging, so every opportunity to do so should be part of our society. Instead, efforts over the years have limited those opportunities.

My goal here is not to solve the problems but to present a few thoughts to get parents and schools and the workplace to think about what they could do to prevent the feelings of not belonging and lack of validation. This is not a "man" problem; this is a collective problem!

To answer what is happening to children and young people, there are many questions to consider. And the answers may not be that complicated, but the questions must be asked to begin the journey of responsible parenting.

But most importantly, parents must be vested in their children's welfare and that doesn't mean doing for them and chastising them when they do not deliver. Instead, they must inspire, listen, and support them and set their own agendas aside.

And parents and the collective must be willing to examine the impact of the media and technology on all of us. Just because an idea makes money does not mean it should be embraced.

Twelve
The Legacy of the Father

"The truth is that male religious leaders have had – and still have – an option to interpret holy teachings either to exalt or subjugate women. They have, for their own selfish ends, overwhelmingly chosen the latter. Their continuing choice provides the foundation or justification for much of the pervasive persecution and abuse of women throughout the world."

President James Carter

There are numerous examples of how patriarchal dogma flows throughout society. And there are also historical events that set the stage for what women experience and have experienced for thousands of years. In fact, this chapter title could fill another book, but some of the inexplicable thoughts and nefarious activities that have permeated women's history are worth remembering.

Aristotle described the female body as a male body that hadn't developed properly. However, he never explained how a body that has not developed properly could give birth to another human being.

Maybe because there are men who were troubled by the fact that a woman can do something a man could not and would never be able to do, at least without some miracle or....? Maybe it serves a man's ego and elevates him to a superior position to diminish a woman by claiming her body is inferior, making her inferior?

This imperfect process of the development of a woman led Aristotle to also allege that being inferior biologically, women should occupy a more subordinate position in society. Psychologically, Aristotle viewed women as less capable of rational thought compared to men. Women were more excitable and governed by their emotions, so they could not reason as effectively as men, raising concerns over a woman's rational abilities.

Apparently, Aristotle had never considered that masculinity should not be about suppressing emotions, but healthy ways of expressing them, with passion, a calm voice, and with words drenched in tenderness and understanding.

Aristotle also declared that a woman's capacity for philosophical understanding and logic was less developed than that of a man. But on the world stage, are we currently experiencing decisions made with logic and reason? And add to that being governed by emotion and ego because there is no logic or rationality!

Aristotle believed his claims justified his assertions that there needed to be different levels of authority between genders. Men he asserted were naturally fit for command and women for submission. Seriously! Flabbergasted! Shocked! There is more!

Sigmund Freud stated that a woman who is confident, intelligent, competent, contributing, and expressive is exhibiting a masculinity complex. If she wants a baby, she really wants a penis. The baby is a substitute for her desire for that body part. Also, a woman sexually attracted to men is discovering her mother doesn't have a penis. Seriously! Shocked! Appalled! Flabbergasted!

Aside from any emotion you are experiencing, stop and think about what messages these statements sent to women.

Because you are female, you are lacking. Because you want a career, you want to be a man. But where was the evidence?

During Freud's reign in history and before and beyond, society has been forever sending messages that women are inferior to men. Freud believed that this was a problem that could never be resolved. That is one of the few things he said of which I may or may not agree if I knew more specifically what problem he was addressing—the male ego, the fear within men….?

I present the thoughts of these men to remind you of the extreme measures that men would go to in their efforts to demean women, and it is still happening today. The sadness is that this tyranny and cruelty were pervasive and still are.

Remember there was a BC, so enter religion. Feminist Barbara G. Walters said, "From the pulpit, men were ordered to beat their wives, and wives to kiss the stick that beat them."

Corinthians 14: 34-35 *The women should keep silent in the churches. For they are not permitted to speak, but should be in submission, as the Law also says. If there is anything they desire to learn, let them ask their husbands at home. For it is shameful for a woman to speak in church.*

Timothy 2: 11-14 *Let a woman learn quietly with all submissiveness. I do not permit a woman to teach or to exercise authority over a man; rather, she is to remain quiet. For Adam was formed first, then Eve; and Adam was not deceived, but the woman was deceived and became a transgressor.*

My comments are not to debate the presence of faith in your life. Coming together for any common interest that fosters community, relationships, support, and caring and compassion can be worthwhile. If faith soothes the soul and gives someone peace, who would deny that?

But why do unfathomable stories and dogma have to be attached to religion—dogma that harms women and causes divisiveness? So, my efforts are to question the tales told and call out exploitation and manipulation of people who seem to be unaware.

Not one of us can read the minds of those who wrote the Bible or any religious text, and we cannot discern for certain the intent of the words of a minister, rabbi, priest….and if there is a hidden agenda? We can only surmise what was intended. Yet, the dogmas espoused contain underpinnings of an agenda and a desire to control the lives and minds of others and often to diminish women.

Eve was chosen to be the one who sinned first. Who commits more murders, adultery, theft, and rape? A reminder that in the United States currently, 93 percent of those in prison are men to 7 percent who are women. And we can assume that has been the same for eons, and possibly the percentage for men higher in the past.

So, why was Eve the first sinner? Consciously or unconsciously was the writer sending the message that women are not as pure as men, easily tempted and deceived, inferior, and sinful? And has it been reality? Was it reality in the past? Imagine how a young child hearing that story might regard Eve—a woman who disobeyed God, a woman who sinned. Can he think well of any woman? Can a little girl think well of herself? She is branded, as are all women, and assaulted and diminished by making a woman the first sinner.

And if a man, Adam, sinned because of Eve, it was because a woman made him do so. But isn't that exposing the weakness of men, that men are easily tempted and swayed, feeble, vulnerable?

Then we are told Eve was made from a rib of Adam. Women give birth to baby boys and girls. So, why would someone write a story that God made Eve from Adam's rib?

Oh yes, I know the story is not to be taken literally, but women giving life is an important gift to the world, given to them by our creator. But it must be an irritation to some men. Why else would a woman have to be created from a part of a man? And because man gave her life, does that mean he has control over her life?

Credit could not be given to a woman—Adam being created from Eve. A woman just couldn't do it! And Eve's sin and Adam's rib elevated man and diminished women.

An unmarried friend in her early thirties complained to me that the story of Noah's ark ruined life for single people. It sent the message that male and female must walk through life together. Going it alone, unmarried, was not acceptable. That was over thirty years ago; yet, being unmarried is still unacceptable to some.

And to add to the absurdity, Mary had to be a virgin—pure and chaste—to give birth to Jesus. And why isn't this questioned? Most tragically, because there are no logical, plausible answers. And by asking, once again it might reveal what men would not wish revealed. That many men want a chaste, virgin woman; yet, there are men who do their best to make a woman unchaste and not a virgin.

There is no way to gauge how chaste a man is, and women are not supposed to care. To excuse a man's gad-about ways, women are often told in a whisper, "It's better if he is experienced." Why doesn't the door swing both ways? And why do women not question, rather than accept? Because men make the rules! And maybe because some women believe men do not have to play by the rules.

Of course, the authors of the stories in the Bible and other religious texts had agendas, and it definitely wasn't to ensure women are thought of positively. Yes, there is Cain and Abel and Joseph and his brothers, but sin started with a woman. Tsk! Tsk!

There are parts of the Bible, especially the psalms that are soothing and speak to the heart and soul. There are many heartwarming, uplifting, and lovely passages, but some of the stories and certain passages that are repeated again and again scream faulty reasoning and an agenda to elevate men! And if questioned, we are told, "Well, it's...."

Riane Eisler in her book, *The Chalice and the Blade*, noted, "When we look closely, not only at what Jesus taught but at how he went about disseminating his message, time and again we find that what he was preaching was the gospel of a partnership society—an egalitarian. He rejected the dogma that high-ranking men – in Jesus' day, priests, nobles, rich men, and kings – are the favorites of God.

"He mingled freely with women, thus openly rejecting the male-supremacist norms of his time. And in sharp contrast to the views of later Christian sages, who actually debated whether woman has an immortal soul, Jesus did not preach the ultimate dominator message: that women are spiritually inferior to men."

For Christians: If the way Jesus moved in the world is admired, then why aren't men emulating those ways, rather than plundering, killing, harming others, and streaming hatred?

I state again that these statements are not to question the presence of faith in our lives. They are presented to question the dogma—man-made rules that can create divisiveness among people and continue to harm women.

My comments are to remind us that men wrote the words in the Bible and other religious texts. And because the religious texts were written by men and the reading and interpretation disseminated by men, they have the advantage of teaching and preaching from an agenda.

It is difficult to admit but must be acknowledged that whether words are truthful and inspirational or lies riddled with agendas, prejudice, and hatred, they will find an audience.

My efforts are to wake up sleeping people, those wrapped in religious dogma that is harmful and divisive and has nothing to do with believing and living a compassionate and soulful life.

Faith, no matter what the religion can soothe a tormented soul, provide peace and contentment. Faith gives us community, a sense of belonging, important to so many, but what are the conditions put upon us for that community? What is the price of those relationships?

Faith can keep us shackled to dogma that can manipulate the masses, but it does not have to be that way. Man has made it that way. Men who want to elevate themselves and control others!

We can come together in fellowship, desiring to create a community of support and compassion. We don't need a set of rules to do that.

And a most solemn example within most religions is that women are relegated once again to the shadows, a supporting cast, and not allowed to spread the word of God in certain religions. And why are they excluded? Are they not worthy? Are woman being told that only a man could spread the words of compassion and love?

That is astounding when prescribed feminine qualities include caring and compassion and the desire to connect with others—qualities that would be welcomed by a loving house of worship.

Then there is the hajib. Years ago, walking through a square in Istanbul, I had on a saucy black hat with a bow. I saw a group of men and women in black Muslim garb sitting on benches in the park—the women with hajibs. My eyes locked onto the eyes of one of the women. By the connection I felt with her and the smile revealed in her eyes, something appeared to be brewing inside her. I felt her cheering me on, living vicariously in some way. In that instant, I believed if she could, she would throw off her garb and join me. I had packed other hats, and she could walk with me, free and confident, embracing her very essence.

Maybe she was chained to a life that she wasn't meant to live. There are sources that say the penalty for not wearing a hajib is the wrath of Allah. Yet, the penalties women pay for walking their own path could be monumental. That could result in the loss of family and loved ones, legal penalties, loss of opportunity for education or a career, family stress, and being ostracized.

Ostracizing, like shunning, is a way of keeping the flock under control, often demoralizing to the recipient because they are being shamed and feel abandoned. For those who have a strong pack instinct, leaving their birth pack could be painful.

Then there is the Bracha repeated by Orthodox Jewish men each morning. "Blessed are you O God, King of the Universe, Who has not made me..." and concludes, respectively, "a *goy* [Gentile]," "a slave," and "a woman." So, being Gentile is a bad thing. And where is the compassion for slaves and women, both who are denied and demeaned?

A gabbai at an Orthodox shul in defense of the Bracha prayer stated, *"I say the Bracha.... since it is easier to be a man in today's world. It's an acknowledgement of my own unearned privilege and my hope that my daughters live in a world with less misogyny and entrenched patriarchy. Prayer helps us articulate an ideal world as it reminds us of the imperfections we are charged with fixing."*

Where is the guarantee that those who recite the Bracha embrace his meaning or that they are doing anything to change the situation? And yes, men do enjoy an unearned privilege. And reminding men and boys that women are disadvantaged does not mean they will pick up the gauntlet and work for the rights of women or treat the women in their lives with regard and caring.

What proof does anyone have that the Bracha has a positive effect on the plight of women and that men embrace women's right to take their place in the world?

Are there other prayers that remind us of the imperfections that religion is charged with fixing? And are they recited every morning? And what are these men doing to address the issues women face, but most importantly, how does the Bracha help to do that? A reminder is not action! And if you have to defend it, maybe....

A female editor of a woman's Jewish newspaper stated: *'Feminist that I am—I do not have any problem with every husband, father, brother and son reciting this blessing daily (the Bracha), thanking God for making him immune to some of the less-pleasant experiences that we as women face. As my sons and husband say this blessing, I want them to feel grateful for their mothers, sisters, wives and daughters ... and think about how they as individuals can make the circumstances of the women in their lives better.'"*

"Less-pleasant experiences that women face?" Less pleasant? Has she walked among the women who have it "less pleasant? "And couching her words in *"Feminist as I am,"* are we to assume that she believes in equality, supports women....? And is it a preamble so we won't question her statements?

She says she wants the men in her life, as they say the Bracha, to be grateful for the women in their lives, but where are the guarantees? No one can dictate that or ensure or know that is what the men who say the prayer are thinking and feeling. One can hope and wish, but hoping and wishing does not secure someone's agreement.

And the Bracha is a continual reminder that women are tainted in some ways, as are apparently slaves and Gentiles also mentioned in the prayer. If women are thought of as unworthy, something a man doesn't want to be, can a young boy who repeats the Bracha reason out that women are not inferior, not desirable? Or that a Gentile and slave are not inferior? Can a man?

What prayers are repeated that lift up all people, acknowledge their contributions, and praise and inspire them. And if they cannot, then leave women, slaves, and Gentiles alone.

We are told by the author of the article that men of all faiths regard women negatively and are insensitive. On that we can definitely agree. Then he adds that because other faiths do so, we are not to condemn this particular religious tradition but to see it as an opportunity to focus awareness on an issue of importance. I agree. Pointing out a different point of view is not condemnation. It is bringing this issue into the light.

Women are reminded of their situation in a patriarchal, religious world every day, if not every hour by how they are disrespected and disregarded. Snide comments, sexual assaults, and limited opportunities, to name a few. They do not need any prayer or religion to tell them that.

Yes, one could say that being disadvantaged is a woman's reality, but it's because men have made it so. So, why do men need to state they are grateful they are not women? If they would change their thinking, regard women's gifts positively, give women opportunities and treat them with reverence, speak out on women's issues, they would not have to repeat the prayer.

Especially in a society, culture, or religion where men are considered the chosen gender, it also solidifies the belief that boys are desired over girls and are advantaged because they are superior.

Then came a new country. *"We hold these truths to be self-evident, that all men are created equal, that they are endowed by their Creator with certain unalienable Rights, that among these are Life, Liberty and the pursuit of Happiness."* Why not write "all people"?

In the preamble, it is: *"We the people..."* Maybe because women have been dismissed for centuries and were never considered to have any rights. Dismissing women as a contributor is one of the tragedies of our human history.

Words matter! Although a lofty ideal, those words in the Constitution, *men are created equal*, applied only to those men who had the privilege and means and desire to bathe in those rights.

And there is a difference between *created equal* and how people are regarded by others that cause the inequality. And regard and respect are influenced by background, status, family and professional connections, prejudice, and....

However, there are certain rights that are a necessity and should be attainable, such as the right to vote, equal pay and equal benefits, and equal opportunity. Unfortunately, all are in the hands of others, and those others can deny and take away.

All forms of contraception were legal in the United States throughout most of the 1800s. In the 1870s, a social purity movement, comprised primarily of Protestant moral reformers and middle-class women, viewed contraception as an immoral practice and claimed it promoted prostitution and venereal disease.

As a result, contraception was made illegal in the Comstock Act of 1873, and birth control information was banned. So, they gave women, especially poor women and immigrants, no form of birth control, no way to control the size of their families. Yet, they never ensured those women could feed their families. At that time, America was the only western country to criminalize contraception.

And why wasn't it done earlier in the century—prior to the Industrial Age? Had prostitution increased that much? Or like today, did they want women to have those babies—to be *birthing women* to please the men in their lives, to ensure there were future workers to feed capital's desires, eliminating the need to bring more immigrants into the country?

There is no concrete proof of the agendas, but surely prostitution wasn't that prevalent to deny ALL women a way to control the size of their families.

It is interesting to note that many of the countries who were predominantly Catholic permitted birth control at this time. By the 20th century, Christians in some of the most heavily Catholic countries in the world, such as France and Brazil, were among the most prodigious users of artificial contraception. That lead to a dramatic decline in family size.

During his pronouncement in 1930 on birth control, Pope Pius XI declared that contraception was inherently evil and any spouse practicing any act of contraception "violates the law of God and nature" and was "stained by a great and mortal flaw." Why then and not before?

Condoms, diaphragms, the rhythm method, and even the withdrawal method were forbidden. Only abstinence was permissible to prevent conception. So, all the Catholics prior to this time who used contraception sinned?

Does this make you wonder why the Catholic Church didn't ban contraception before 1930? Maybe because up until that time they did not consider the effects of contraception and then became concerned that a decrease in population also decreased the number of Catholics?

In 1951, the church modified its stance without overturning "Casti Connubii's" prohibition of artificial birth control. Pius XII approved the rhythm method for couples who had "morally valid reasons for avoiding procreation" and defined those situations broadly. And all of these changes were decided by men!

While the birth control pill was approved by the Federal Drug Administration in the United States for "severe menstrual distress" in 1957, it took years before it was approved for family planning. Issues like reproductive freedom and a woman's right to decide when and whether to have children were only just beginning to be openly discussed in the 1960s. And remember there were many countries where birth control was available and never banned.

The pill was approved for use as a contraceptive in 1960. However, it was illegal in some states and could only be prescribed to married women for purposes of family planning. It has been reported that not all pharmacies stocked the pill, and some who opposed birth control said, "oral contraceptives were immoral, promoted prostitution, and were tantamount to abortion."

Soon after the Federal act was passed to approve contraception, twenty-six states enacted their own laws to restrict access to contraception at a state level. Birth control was not approved for use by all women until 1972.

Today the anti-choice movement is based on the desires of certain religions, and as in the past, it is wrapped in politics. And why should religious beliefs, real or not, of politicians and constituents influence choices for women?

And what are the people, who want a woman to have that baby, doing to help her raise that baby? And often it is a baby she cannot afford to have, and they ignore or deny the problems the mother and child will have. They may be handing down a life sentence to that baby of hunger and hardship and struggles. Yet, they do so with no remorse but definitely culpability. Where is their humanity then, their concern for life? Missing! More sorrow!

It would be a blessing if a woman never needed or wanted an abortion. And where is the empathy for anyone who is put in a situation to make that decision—a decision that will be part of a woman's history and psyche all her days? It would be a blessing if a woman got pregnant when she wished, not by happenstance or rape or incest.

But where is it written that any of us has the right to choose another person's path, impose our beliefs on someone else? Where is the pursuit of Life, Liberty, and Happiness? Why is someone's freedom to choose decided by others who are not privileged to that women's life or her circumstances? The correct term is anti-choice—not pro-life because where is the regard for life when a woman's life is put in jeopardy, her healthcare choices eradicated? It is not pro-life when a woman is not paid enough to feed that child.

There was also the nineteenth century law that stated once a widow remarries, all her assets would be under the control of her husband. Did the ruling patriarchs believe a woman was not capable of managing money or because if she acquired money, she would make the choice of not marrying and not serving the patriarchy?

To add more insult, when a woman married, the money left to her was automatically her husband's. A man could marry her, then walk away with all of the money earned by the men in her family or inherited from a former husband.

Another law passed in the United States in the nineteenth century stated the money a woman earned outside the home was her husband's. Why? Fear again that she would walk off and leave him to wash his own socks and cook his own meals?

Isn't that why slaves were denied an education and not allowed to learn to read and write and never had a coin in their pockets? The slave owners were afraid if they could read and write, they could get a job if they escaped; they would have another choice. And corporate owners during the Industrial Age had the same fears. Isn't that why they paid workers in scrip—just a piece of paper? No money; no ability to flee. But why did they not pay them enough to live? Because of greed, and they wanted the workers to know who was in charge, and those in charge could give and they could take away. Chained to slave owners! Chained to capital! Chained to men!

Then came the call for women to get the right to vote. Were women denied the right to vote because they were unable to reason politics or that it put them on an equal footing with men? Or was it that women would run for office, women would vote for those women, and women might support a more compassionate, egalitarian government? Women might show they possess wisdom and courage and…..?

And is that why once again a woman's right to vote is being questioned? Because they are not voting for those *Sorrow Eaters*. And is that why the United States cannot elect a qualified woman as president and more qualified than the man running against her, and why they have elected men who were not qualified?

For centuries, state laws had excluded women from jury service due to the belief that women were too fragile to participate in public life and needed protection from the "indecent" aspects of criminal trials. Yet, a woman could have experienced indecent and horrible aspects of life, sometimes at the hands of the man, but she was not allowed to determine a man's innocence or guilt.

Wyoming first allowed women to fill jury positions in the 1870s, and it was also the first state that passed a law allowing women to vote in December 1869, more than fifty years before the Federal government passed such a law. Wyoming later earned the nickname "Equality State" for being the first to protect women's right to vote.

Women in most states were excluded from jury service until 1919. Utah permitted women to serve on juries in 1898, just three years after women were given the right to vote. Three states, Alabama, Mississippi, and South Carolina, had historically barred women from serving on juries until the 1960s.

The Civil Rights Act of 1957 granted women the right to serve on federal juries, but it wasn't until 1973 that all fifty states passed similar legislation.

The Supreme Court determined in 1975 that excluding women from jury service violates the requirement that a jury be drawn from a fair cross-section of the community. Despite this ruling, lawyers continued to use methods to eliminate women from juries. Then the Supreme Court in 1994 decided that gender-based selections violated the Fourteenth Amendment right to equal protection.

Again, throughout history women were accused of being too fragile. Yet, women throughout the centuries weren't too fragile to be beaten and raped but could not stand in judgment, if indeed charges were brought. Were men afraid women would determine the punishment that men deserved?

Women being paid less than men for the same work always existed—sending another message of inferiority, signifying women are not as valued as men and do not perform as well as men. There is no evidence that women do not perform as well as men. In fact, maybe the opposite.

There are numerous other rights that a woman did not have until the 1970s. One example is having a credit card in her own name. Banks could refuse a woman a credit card until the Equal Credit Opportunity Act of 1974 was signed into law. Prior to that, a bank could refuse to issue a credit card to an unmarried woman, and if a woman was married, her husband was required to cosign.

Prior to my marriage, I had a credit card for over fifteen years in my name. When I married in 2001, I added my husband's name. The card automatically became his credit card—his name was first. I was relegated to second place, and if I wanted to question or discuss that card, the bank required that he be put on the phone to give permission.

Our tax return has his name first. Our house has his name first. I have argued those points, tried to change the name order, but to no avail.

As recent as 1978 a woman did not have protection in the workplace if she got pregnant. Pregnancy Discrimination Act prohibited sexual discrimination on the basis of pregnancy, according to the U.S. Equal Employment Opportunity Commission. It stated that women who are pregnant or have been affected by pregnancy or childbirth must be treated the same for all employment-related purposes. However, they could not legislate how she would be treated in that workplace.

Sexual harassment had been dismissed as a crime until 1977 when a court recognized office sexual harassment as grounds for legal action.

The Civil Rights Act of 1964 created the basis for discrimination cases in its Article VII and established the Equal Employment Opportunity Commission. But it wasn't until 1980 that the EEOC determined that sexual harassment was a form of sex discrimination.

These are just a few of the events that have kept women out of the way and denied and assaulted again and again. When viewing all of these historical events and for those of you who have enjoyed those privileges because of the women who came before, are you surprised at how much women were denied and so recently? And for those who believe these events were long ago, for many women who lived it, it was more like yesterday.

After the many years of asking and pleading, certain women's rights are eroding.

Ruth Bader Ginsburg said, *"All I ask of our brethren is they take their feet off our necks."*

Thirteen
Change has Happened!????

"Tremendous amounts of talent are being lost to our society just because that talent wears a skirt."
Shirley Chisholm

In the television series, *The Bold Type*, a young woman is having an affair with a man in the company. He is fifteen years older and in management; she is an assistant. They hide the affair because of the repercussions to him—sexual harassment. Eventually, they break off the romance because it is too dangerous for him if it is found out.

Miraculously, a solution appears. Both employees can sign a statement saying that the relationship is consensual. He would now be protected from sexual harassment charges. Ecstatic, he signs the statement.

To his surprise, she does not sign the statement. She realized that once the affair was known, she would be accused of dishing out favors for opportunities and promotions. He would come out without a scratch.

Kudos to her! She knew the fallout to her, not him, should she make that decision. And will that ever change?

There are those who claim that today things are different for women, but are they? Some will say, "Well, we gave women...." (no, they earned it!) "There have been changes..." "It's not like it used to be..." "I know someone who got...." So, we are to be thankful?

The Sorrow Eaters are content, maybe congratulating themselves for the heartache and sorrow they cause women. It's not only because they will never have enough; it's that they are envious of women getting anything.

Most importantly, ego-run-amuck and fear have made them deaf, dumb, and blind. They cannot grasp the contributions women can make and how it would minimize and maybe eliminate some of their pain and suffering.

And because certain changes have happened, does that mean women should be silent and not continue to beat the drums? Are women to fall into an abyss of dreams unfulfilled? Focusing on what women or any other disenfranchised groups have accomplished does not negate that there is so much more to do. And just because changes have happened, are women, any disenfranchised group, to settle and become complacent?

During a discussion about the trials and tribulations women still face, one woman said, "But women have made so many strides. There are now women CEOs, women in Congress…. Doesn't that mean something to you?"

Words came flying out, "I'm not sure. How did those women get those positions and how are they functioning?"

My words made me aware that it mattered how women achieved their positions and how they were performing. I do not chalk it up as a win for women just because. If those women are turning themselves into their male counterparts who knowingly pay women less and deny them opportunities, then it is not a win. And for all the claims that "things" are different today for women, implying they are better, there are still women who are wanting and waiting.

For example, on average, in 2024 women were paid 84 percent of what a man was getting paid for the same work. For college graduates, it was estimated that is a difference of over $26,000 a year. For women who are not college educated and earning a few dollars, the difference can be devastating. That number dropped to 83 percent in 2025.

Today there are more women left out of the opportunities the minority of women enjoy. By shouting about how far women have come, the din often shuts out the cries of women who are still struggling for their voice and for opportunities. A handful of women that rise to the top is just that—a handful of women.

There are women still living below the poverty level. Women who cannot get child support and have two jobs! Women who cannot earn a living wage! Women born in a low socio-economic status, and so on!

Laborers, minorities, immigrants, and women are still being denied opportunities and a fair wage.

Malcolm X said, *"You don't stick a knife in a man's back nine inches and then pull it out six inches and say you're making progress."*

There are still many mountains to climb for women. And the women who are shouting from the rooftops and praising women's strides are those who have bragging rights, and kudos to them. We must celebrate them, but where are the majority of women?

Recently, I was expressing my upset about some decisions affecting women in the courts and state governments—hard-fought rights were being taken away. One of the women said to me, "Why are you concerned with that? It doesn't affect you!" And it wouldn't affect her, but it affects millions of women.

I was crushed by her words. Disappointed that her position was based on what was self-serving. I responded, "What happens to women isn't about me. It's what's happening to all women. What is happening in the world to people isn't about me. It's what's happening in the world to all of us."

Fourteen
My Father—a Feminist

"You may shoot me with your words. You may cut me with your eyes. You may kill me with your hatefulness. But, still, like air, I'll rise."
Maya Angelou

My father proved that "an old dog," no offense to dogs, "can learn new tricks." At seventy years of age, Dad began looking at a woman's place in the world differently.

He was a benevolent father, yet insular in the way he moved in the world. He was quiet and thoughtful, possessed wisdom without a formal education, listened attentively, and provided considered guidance. And although we did not always agree, he never penalized me for my push back or denied me my voice.

My dad provided encouragement by the way he spoke with me and the topics we engaged in, such as politics and history starting at the age of six.

I never told Dad that in his 70s, he became a Feminist. I never said anything to him about feminism, although I had talked about equal pay and benefits and the limitations often placed on women. I did not want to muddle his world. Experiencing his change in attitude was all I needed. I did not need to label it for him.

Dad had always fought for the rights of workers—wanting a fair wage. Working in a factory, Dad never had an opportunity to observe women as capable and experienced or observe how women are treated in the workplace.

My career life gave my father insight into what a woman faces in a man's world, and it was a pleasure to be witness to that change.

Dad did NOT know I was determined to transform him. Each time I visited my parents, I would tell him stories about the challenges I faced so he would understand my work and the difficulties that women encounter in the corporate world until it becomes personal.

At the same time, I wanted him to see my strength and conviction. I wanted him to notice the transformation from that young woman whose first boss caused her restless nights into a confident woman.

I once said to him, "Dad, I don't understand why women are regarded as second-class citizens. If a boy is born, he is considered 'first-class,' smart, and able to be in charge. Yet, when the same mother and father have a girl, it is assumed that she didn't get any gifts from her father. But she's part of her father too!"

I knew he would not want to deny that part of me that was him, and although he did not say anything in that moment, I believe it made him think.

Over the years Dad had started to see me in a different light. When I started my business, he surprised me when he expressed his approval and support. He sent me a check to help pay the rent for a few months and buy a plane ticket home for Christmas.

I realized then that my father had never been against me or any woman. He just had never thought about it. He never was exposed to women in business, successful women, and isn't that true of a lot of men?

One of the incidents that triggered Dad's tirade against the men was the Clarence Thomas hearings when he had been nominated for the Supreme Court. Arlin Specter was the senator from Pennsylvania during those hearings.

Specter's interview questions made Dad's stomach churn, mainly when he spoke about the Coke can. In case Dad is looking down as I write, I will not repeat it because that will only make him embarrassed and angry once again.

Dad had not forgiven Congress, and specifically Specter and Thomas. When Specter ran for the Senate for another term, his opponent was a woman. Dad and I were on the phone discussing the election, and Dad said, "I hope she beats the hell out of him. He's not fit for office."

"Dad, you want a woman to win the election?"

He shouted, "Men have made a mess out of things long enough. It's about time they give women a chance."

Dad finally said what women had been saying for years and that was in the 1990's. Yet, many men—young and old—and quite a few women were not listening.

I was proud that Dad could acknowledge that a woman can be just as effective as a man. After all, he had a daughter who was swimming in the world of *GOBs* daily, first in New York City and then from the East Coast to the West Coast.

Dad did not understand my choices. And I am sure that is true of many fathers whose daughters want to climb mountains and slay dragons. My father's experiences were limited. He did not know career women. And although he did not understand my way of living my life, the choices I made, he never said a discouraging word.

For that, I would always be grateful. It's not because I needed his approval. I was not going to be deterred from living the way I wished once I figured it out. I just never wanted any tension between us or his worrying about me out in the world alone.

Part Four

Be a Light Unto Yourself

Rise Up

Once crying out for equality
Then beaten down, silenced
Settling for a few crumbs, co-opted
Becoming what THEY wanted
The deafening sound of silence
A trampled soul crying out
    You must rise up

Rebuff and cast aside the hurtful words
No more pleading and bleeding
For those desires that will never be fulfilled
Raise your voice above a whisper in protest
Stop cutting your sisters and brothers to the quick
Saying, "choose me"
    You must rise up

Patriarchy reigns with an iron fist
Shackled, under that rule
Puppeteers everywhere
Pulling the strings of your life
Do you know who you are?
Do you still care?
    Everyone rise up

Hoping and wishing never made it so
Don't cry out
Don't beg for that one chance
Sever the ties of expectations
Reject the dictates of others
Cut the webs that entangle
    Everyone rise up

Cast aside the fear of punishment
Silence serves up greater abuses
Shout out what is and what must be
With courage, say "enough," and "no more"
Walk away, never look back
Write your own song and live free
> *Everyone—YOU MUST—rise up*

To the Reader .... A Few Words

"A lie doesn't become truth, wrong doesn't become right, and evil doesn't become good, just because it's accepted by a majority."
Booker T. Washington

Many years ago, I was doing a management retreat. A young manager walked up to me during the break. As she was leafing through the materials I had put together, she said, "Elizabeth, where are the formulas?"

"There are no formulas. I will be speaking about techniques and strategies for communicating, making decisions, inspiring.... how you relate to others.

"As a manager, your role is to analyze the situation and the employee and choose from the number of options. Every person is different. There is no *one size fits all.*"

A look of panic came across her face. The answers could not be found in a formula, there was no-quick fix, and she wasn't having it. She left after lunch.

That is one of the roadblocks to working through issues and making decisions—those who do not want to put in the work. They want to click their fingers and everything goes their way. They do take the time to understand another individual, analyze a situation from various angles. They do not want to try a different approach, learn a different language, or want to take the time.

There are no formulas to get your house in order. It takes a willingness to ask questions, investigate, and explore to become aware as to what is happening and why.

And most definitely it takes courage. And once you get your house in order, you can begin to help your country, the world, to denounce and stop the *Sorrow Eaters.*

One
Concretized

*"I believe that there will ultimately be a clash
between the oppressed and those who do the oppressing.
I believe that there will be a clash between those who
want freedom, justice and equality for everyone and
those who want to continue the system of exploitation."*
Malcolm X

Unfortunately, and still today, there are men saying to women, *"You are to walk the road I have decided you should walk, whether you want to or not. You can go in chains, screaming at the top of your lungs and struggling to break free, or you can walk silently. It is your choice, but you will walk that path."*

In 1967 Martin Seligman and his team did a series of experiments that involved the repeated electric shocking of dogs. On one side of a large partitioned wooden box was a "shocking" floor and a normal floor on the other. The partition between the two sides was low so the dogs could jump over. Whenever the dogs experienced an electric shock, they jumped the low partition to escape the shocking.

Next, the partition was raised so the dogs could not jump over after receiving electric shocks. When shocked, the dogs became frantic and tried to escape, but they could not. Finally, the dogs laid down. Some whimpering every time they felt a shock, but they did not even try to get up.

The researchers said these dogs had learned "helplessness." Their brains told them that no matter what they did, they could not stop the shocks. There was no way out. Even when the door was open, the dogs did not escape.

Think of a wife being beaten again and again; yet, she does not escape. Imagine a daughter experiencing sexual abuse from her father; yet, she tells no one. Consider employees who never get the increase in wage or salary they desire, never get that promotion, so they give up, lay down, and accept the pain being inflicted.

A woman, a man, a child may feel helpless to change their circumstances. They do not know how to reach out for help. A woman's family may feel she should stay in the marriage, in the job, no matter the suffering. She fears the repercussions if she tries to escape. She is traumatized and cannot reason how to leave. Or she avoids or denies there is a problem. Or when the relationship is good, it is very good, and she believes it will stay that way. Or she hopes and wishes and prays things will change. But as my mother would say, "God helps those who help themselves!"

When any one of us believes there is no escape from a toxic situation, desperation wrapped in despair intensifies. A woman comes to believe she is trapped, caged, so she does not make any effort to escape her situation, and just like the dogs, her suffering will continue until her last breath.

Unknowingly, she has learned to be helpless. She exhibits the behaviors of an unhealthy ego, so she kowtows to others, maybe apologizes for mistakes she does not make.

With repeated failures, despite her best attempts, she starts to feel her efforts are folly and stops trying. "What can I do" screams in her head. That can lead to a self-defeating cycle of negative thinking and behavior, as well as anxiety and depression, which can reduce motivation and initiative.

This same scenario happens to men. A man gets stuck in a job he hates. He may be fulfilling the desires of his father to ensure his legacy. He may be pushed and prodded to continue a life he does not want. He has to work to feed his family…. He has to…. He has to….

People become "concretized," fixed in place, unable to move when drowning in suffering and sorrow. It doesn't have to stay that way! But the journey is not always easy, but it is a journey that must be taken.

First, you have to be willing to extricate your mind from the chains that bind you and that includes the need to stop believing you deserve the pain that is being inflicted.

Second, you have to release yourself from the shame you feel and reach out to others. There are people who are generous of soul and spirit who will provide support and guidance. You may not have met them yet, but they will appear if you are open and not trying to hide away.

Remember, you have spirit and soul and courage! You may have put them in a box, forgotten them, but they are there. And remember that it is NOT easier to do nothing!

In the tale *The Woman With the Hair of Gold*:

Here lies a woman with golden hair

Murdered and in her grave

Killed by the son of a coal burner

Because she wished to live.

And isn't that what is happening and has happened? A woman's spirit, her soul, her talents and creativity, and her joy are all being killed because she is being denied the life she is meant to live, the life she desires. And that also happens to men of all ages and ethnicity and socio-economic background who are oppressed and denied!

So, let us declare: Bring it on! We have courage and are resilient. We won't go away! We won't bend, conform, perform! We won't die! We wish to live! And we wish to live the way we desire!

Two
The Monkey Vine

"When one door of happiness closes, another opens;
but often we look so long at the closed door that we do not
see the one which has been opened for us."
Helen Keller

The publishing company where I worked announced that the offices were moving from New York City. I decided not to accept the transfer after being asked twice. I was offered a sizable signing bonus—half my yearly salary. My assignment was going to change, and my opportunities and possibilities limited. I said NO a third time.

Then I was offered an opportunity by a manager in the company to be the president of a business he and his partner had bought. I could not accept. Yet, it would have been easy to take that opportunity, but again I would be boxed in. And besides, I had decided to start my own business.

Then I had two more job offers—a chance to return to safety. Or was it safety? I would be putting my destiny into someone else's hands, but I was now ready to fly on my own.

So, after becoming disenchanted with the corporate world, rejecting the opportunities that appeared, and a few challenging missteps, I finally launched my own management consulting and executive coaching firm.

While I waited for that first client, I did some editing for a publishing company. I was also hired by a total concept house to get an economics book published. I was then offered a full-time position with that company. It was tempting, but I said to the two men who made the offer, "I appreciate your confidence in me, but I'm betting on me. I'm going to get my company off the ground."

Within six months, my company took off, and I was doing management consulting and executive coaching. In time I added business consulting, focusing on product development and marketing. I was not soaring yet, but I had taken flight once again.

One of my clients, Jacqueline, told me about an employee, Barbara, who had left the company for a better opportunity, so she believed. A few months later Barbara wanted to return. Jacqueline told her, "You have to live with this failure" and would not hire her back.

Barbara desired to go from one job to another. By denying her the opportunity to return to employment at her former company, Jacqueline had given her once-protégé a gift. Barbara did not know it then.

As a management consultant, I soon coined the term, "The Monkey Vine Syndrome." In my experience, people desire to swing from one vine to another, never dropping to the ground. Having one relationship before breaking off another is thought to be advantageous. Interviewing and having one job to leap to before leaving the one you have. It dictates securing the next chapter in your life before you closed the current chapter. Isn't that what an affair is about?

So, by swinging from one vine and grabbing onto another, people often feel safe. In reality, it often leaves them spinning—into another bad relationship, into a job that does not make them jump out of bed each morning.

So instead, plummet to the ground from that monkey vine, stay there, rest a while, be silent, dust yourself off, and ask yourself: If no one were looking, what would I do next? What would make me look forward to my day? What is my life's purpose? Who is dictating my next move and the next?

I suggest you step outside of the notion that you must have someone to walk beside you to signify you are worthy—worthy of attention, worthy of love.

I suggest you step outside the notion that you must have that job because your self-esteem would suffer without one.

Yes, you must pay the bills. You do not want to wonder when you will get your next paycheck. And a job gives you that paycheck and experiences, but it also defines you and gives you a feeling of worth or NOT.

But if you end up in a job that does not use your skills, is boring, and does not give you the feeling you desire, the life your desire, is it worth the paycheck? Maybe! Maybe not!

Sometimes we suffer in the wrong job because we cannot let others suffer. And yes, you want certainty and stability in your life. You don't want to agonize, wondering when you will again be employed or if the love of your life will walk through that door. And most likely you also do not want to suffer in the wrong job or relationship.

So, always look to the future and begin to carve out a plan for a more worthwhile tomorrow.

Three
Stand Up, Move Around, Own the Room

"A really strong woman accepts the war she went through and is ennobled by her scars."
Carly Simon

I was consulting with a company in Wyoming for two months. I conducted workshops for all levels of management and coached several key individuals in upper management. During my last week with the company, a new president was hired, and he asked to meet with me.

All the upper managers were seated in the room, and the new president was to my left. At his request, I gave him a brief overview of what had been accomplished. He then asked me about the trust level at the company. How fortuitous! I had just completed several trust exercises with the supervisors.

Unfortunately, they learned that trust was non-existent among them. They were competitive, could not work together, and would do whatever they could to get the upper hand at the expense of what was best for the company.

It took at least a full minute before I pulled my thoughts together. I could tell he was anxious and started to tell me what to say. When I answered, I stated that there were trust issues and started to explain what I had discovered and how we started to resolve the issues.

He stood up and started pacing, and he kept interrupting me with comments to convince me that I must be mistaken. He questioned my findings and used a loud voice and in-my-face body language.

Since he was standing up, looking down at me, I decided to also stand up. It's the "my head is higher than yours" dynamic. I began writing on the whiteboard, although I didn't have much to write. Why? To take up space and take command of the room or at least level the field.

Staying seated, your arms are close to your body, and you use minimal movement. When a man is taller than a woman, he can take command more easily. A large frame and loud voice can minimize and diminish a woman, anyone small in stature or soft voice.

If she opens up her arms and uses engaging body language, walks around the room, turns and faces him, and even gets up close, she can upend him and distract him from his message. If she turns her back to him while he is talking and walks in the other direction, the impression she conveys will be one of confidence and that may say silently that she is dismissing what he is saying as being relevant.

Men diminish a woman to the "little woman," by their size, commanding voice, and their movements. (And that is also true if a man is short or shorter or of slight build and not verbose.)

Men may also joke about an idea a woman presents, poke fun. They know those little jabs that are supposed to be funny, but they are actually degrading and disrespecting you. So, jab back! It will surprise them and knock them off their game.

Also, your voice will have impact if you are confident and commanding. Not arrogant with an edge to it but calm and engaging and not higher but lower, throaty, resonating conviction. Your words will also have greater influence if your language is direct, with no hint of wavering.

It is unfortunate that a woman's body language, height, tone of voice may overshadow her powerful words.

Within two minutes of meeting the president, I knew he was an in-your-face, know-it-all president. But he was unaware that those under him in the hierarchy, those men at the table, were formidable, and so was I.

As he tried to convince me to change my mind, I saw smirks on the faces and head shaking of a few of the managers. They had worked with me long enough to know I would not back down without a reason to do so, and I believe they were grateful. The president needed to hear the problems they were encountering.

I did not change my position because there was no good reason to do so. That frustrated the new president because he had no proof otherwise. He only had his loud voice and bombastic demeanor directed at me.

Did the president try to change my mind, intimidate me because I was a woman? That didn't enter my mind. If it had, as in the past, I would have dismissed that thought. First, I believe I had a right to be at the table and to have a different opinion. If I defended myself, citing credentials, etc., again it would have put me on the defense, having to prove I was competent to make such an assessment. That would take us down a road that demeaned me and diminished my findings and analysis.

In instances of confrontation, it is folly to go on the defensive. Stay on the offense by conveying additional findings and analysis and asking direct questions, making the other person responsible for his words. At one point I said: "You asked about trust. What was your reason for focusing on that issue?" Silence! "Did your prior organization have trust issues? Have you heard rumors that trust issues exist here?" Silence.

Those questions surprised him, and he faltered as he said, "I was just curious."

Questions slow down a conversation. They can force someone to be accountable, explain reasons for disagreement, and stop the slings and arrows.

Questions can reveal insights and faulty reasoning and take away control from the person who wants to dominate the conversation. He has to think to formulate his thoughts or he may ramble.

His answers may trigger additional information that he may not have wished to convey because he was not prepared for the questions and was struggling to answer. What is said could also expose support for your point of view. You might also find some points of agreement.

His behavior said more about him than it did about me, and he was revealing himself to upper management. His bullying style had no effect. I would not acquiesce, and maybe that surprised him, and an element of surprise is always an asset.

He also revealed he had an agenda, and it was not to acknowledge at the onset that there were any problems. If the president acknowledged in any way that there were trust issues, he would have learned something. What possibly concerned him more was that if he accepted my findings, he would have to do something.

And yes, I knew I had just completed my last assignment with that company. But as I say again and again, "If I'm not supposed to be there, I'm supposed to be somewhere else."

Four
He Said, She Said

*"I am no longer accepting the things I cannot
change. I am changing the things I cannot accept."*
Angela Davis

To market my consulting and coaching services, I started speaking at organizations such as the Financial Women's Association and the Chamber of Commerce…. I was not a product. I was offering a service, and I believed that if they saw me up close and personal, that might get me in the door. So, I hosted breakfasts for executives and followed it with a short presentation of a few of my workshop offerings and spoke about executive coaching.

The assistant of the Vice President of Operations of a nearby company heard about my workshop entitled, "He Said, She Said," which explored the differences on how men and women communicate. She called and we spoke about the problems in the company, and she asked if I could do this workshop for them. After she spoke with her manager, she scheduled me for a one-hour presentation. She apologized that he would not agree to a workshop.

I walked into a cavernous room with a tiered seating area. A large group, mainly men, had gathered. One man was sitting at the top of the bleachers, hard hat on his head in clear view, (nothing was going to come down on his head) and his arms crossed. He was sending me a clear message that he was not having any of it. He glared at me during the entire presentation. For me, it was like a red cape.

I often looked straight at him when making a point, meeting his stare without trepidation. I welcomed the challenge, and his *rooster-like behavior* did not intimidate me.

I kept the presentation upbeat, using stories and lots of humor. After I concluded my comments, a man about my size (I'm 5'4") raced up to me and got right in my face. He was the vice president of operations—the man I was to convince. He peppered me with question after question. I answered them without hesitation, without hedging, and got straight to the point.

After about twenty minutes, he asked me to do several three-hour workshops that would comprise an equal number of management and staff and men and women.

The morning of my first session, a man approached me, quite agitated, and said, "I don't want to be here, but they made me."

That came as no surprise. I guessed I would have unwilling participants. But why would he express his agitation to me? Did he want to intimidate me? Was he trying to ensure that I did not say anything against men? That would be my best guess. None of this mattered. What did matter was why he believed I would not be mindful of his concern. He expected that a woman would fault men.

His ego was dictating that he should think well of himself, so any comment, valid or not, from a man or a woman, would fall on deaf ears. There would never be a good result.

So, I said, "Why don't you want to be here?"

"Because you're a woman, and you're going to blame men." BINGO! Confirmation!

"Will you do me a favor? If you believe I'm doing that, point it out to me. Can you do that?"

I shut down the debate he might have wanted to have. I did not give him a forum to voice his thoughts to try to upend me, embarrass me, whatever motives he had. I believe he was surprised that I did not defend the workshop or myself. But I knew no words would convince him. Instead, I made him that offer, and instead of spouting off, he nodded.

Three hours later I ended the session. Not once had he interrupted me. He walked up to me and said that he enjoyed the session. "I'd like to do more of this." I respected him for his willingness to share that with me.

The man with the hard hat in my first session, glaring at me, the vice president getting in my face and challenging me, and the comment from the participant could have made me doubt myself or falter or silence me. With the workshop participant, I did not spar with him, trying to defend myself. Instead, I challenged and involved him. In all instances, their behaviors had no effect on me.

I did not let any of them intimidate me nor did I focus on how I was being challenged or regarded. Instead, I used the hard-hat guy's behavior to spur me on. The vice president with question after question I caught and tossed back. No backing down. It was an opportunity to demonstrate my knowledge and ability to communicate.

In all instances, I did not become aggressive. I was direct, without hedging my comments, and was not hesitant. I was not turning myself into someone with a hard edge or a soft-spoken submissive woman to be accepted. I wanted to send the message that across from them was a strong, confident woman who had knowledge to share and was not daunted.

And men in similar situations, who are also denied a place at the table or challenged, might consider similar techniques with management and colleagues. You might also try a similar technique during a discussion when someone's mind is in concrete.

Whether my actions were intuitive or learned is still blurred for me. I do know that I often act intuitively without worrying about the repercussions. I did what my "knowing" told me to do, and I realize now that often until I spoke, I was not aware of what resided deep within.

I acted then with the belief in equality—that a man is not superior to me, does not have more wisdom than I do because of gender, and should not rule the world because he is male.

And I believe that a manager is not always superior in knowledge, wisdom, ideas, creativity…. than an employee. A husband is not…. than a wife. A father is not…. than his son or daughter. A title or lack of one, gender, and age does not disqualify women, employees, wives, sons, and daughters from having a right to an opinion.

Five
I Can Growl with the Best of Them

"Though her soul requires seeing, the culture around her requires sightlessness. Though her soul wishes to speak, she is pressured to be silent."
Clarissa Pinkola Estés

My consulting business had me crisscrossing the country. Each year I received more referrals and had repeat business from past clients. The rewards of owning my own business were numerous.

I could say yes, and I could say no. I was in charge of me. I was heartened by the response to my offerings, and I found the time with clients rewarding.

I received a call from a company to conduct a retreat for top management. A client had referred me. I was to have a phone interview with the president, vice president, and human resources director to assess my qualifications.

After a lengthy discussion about the possible content of the retreat, the director of human resources said, "There are thirty-three of us. Only one is a woman. Last year we had a program that determined our personalities. Some of us were horses, other porpoises…. but most of us were panthers."

As he was talking, I tried not to laugh. Horses, porpoises…. Part of my consulting and coaching endeavors used personality types to explain behavior. It sounded like tiddlywinks compared to Jung's work on psychological types.

There was a pause, and when I did not respond, he said, "Can you handle us?"

I did not miss a beat. "Well, at my university we were called Panthers. So, I'm a Panther, and I can growl with the best of them," and then I chuckled.

That did it. I was hired. On reflection, I made an appropriate response in that quick second. I did not list my credentials or try to prove that I was the right person. Again, I did not beg, defend, or diminish myself by trying to prove I was qualified and worthy.

I also diffused the questionable statement by the human resources director by saying, "I can growl with the best of them." He should have known better than to refer to the possibility that I, a woman, could not handle all those panthers—all those men. My response also did not call him out on an inappropriate question. It would not benefit me to embarrass or criticize him, but it did have the desired effect—a better effect.

Humility is also an issue women struggle with. A man can boast, but women are to possess humility. Humor took the sting out of my comment, rather than a bold statement about my qualifications or statements in defense of them. You also give your power away when you defend yourself and try to validate your worth. You are putting your destiny into someone else's hands.

Six

Play the Game Better

"Madonna Kolbenschlag suggests that if an awakened woman forgoes innocence and denial, if she refuses to make compromises with herself and defect to patriarchy, then her only option becomes deviance. I choose to be a dissident. To dance the dance of dissidence...."
Sue Monk Kidd

Change is thought to be brought about by changing the rules and creating new laws. If that were so, why did it take twenty-four years after Title IX was passed to get a women's NBA? Why after the Equal Pay Act of 1963 are women still not getting paid the same as men? Yes, we can pass policies and laws to protect women and minorities and give them opportunity, but who is minding the store?

I danced the dance of dissidence throughout my life. As a young girl, I picked my times. As a teacher, I often said I was subversive. When I closed my classroom door, I shut out the voices outside that door. As a manager, I walked my own path. When I started my business, I advocated new management practices—practices that inspired staff. I found myself at times swimming against the tide, which was energizing. So, those words above spoke volumes.

Sometimes it is best to rebel and chart your own path quietly; other times we need to speak out or come together like a swarm of bees. And what can be effective, often without a word spoken, is to play the game better.

I was asked to speak at a local bookstore about a literary/historical fiction book I had written, *Josephine: A Woman of Indomitable Spirit*. I was to share the podium with an author who had written a book during a similar historical period and location. He was the great-grandson of a wealthy family in our area. I had only myself to recommend me.

I also wish to note that on the website for the bookstore, my name and details were listed second, and the print with my information was noticeably smaller. Oh well!

Since having the two of us at the podium was an unfamiliar format for me, I asked the events' coordinator how she envisioned the program. She said I could ask him questions. If I had anything to add after he spoke, I could do so. I was to be his moderator. That was not how it was presented to me by the bookstore owner, nor how it was advertised on the bookstore's website.

Flabbergasted! Angry! That was the reaction of my friends when I told them what happened. That I was regarded as second-best was disappointing and disheartening. It is also interesting to note that this was the decision of the bookstore owner and the one in charge of events, and they were both women.

So, what to do? I sent an e-mail to my male counterpart and suggested that we each come up with five questions or discussion topics. Then we could discuss which ones to use. I also suggested that we take turns speaking first on each topic. Since it was apparent he had no ideas, he agreed with my suggestions.

I could have spoken again to the events' person and disagreed with her idea, spurred by the upset of my friends and myself. Asking her for a different venue could come off as whining and pleading, especially if there was a pushback. That would entail weakening myself by saying, "Hey, there. Why am I being relegated to...?" or "I'm no different than he is..."

I was doubtful that asking her to reconsider would get me the desired outcome, and begging was not in my tool kit, so a different plan had to be born.

I made the mistake of asking her about the format initially. I was not going to take the chance a second time. And it worked! Not only did I sell books, but all but one question asked by the audience was directed to me. And the question directed to the other author came from the events' coordinator who interrupted my response to ask it!

My husband, David, and I would play bridge with a friend, Samantha, and her husband, Bobby. Initially, it was a friendly game. David, who was an experienced bridge player, partnered with Samantha because she was new to bridge. Bobby and I, having some bridge experience, played together. After a while, we switched and the men played together and Samanatha and I played together. I suggested this because I realized that Samantha and I were similar in learning styles and spoke a similar language.

After we moved away, we were visiting them in their home for a lengthy stay, and we played bridge every evening. David always sat to my left, so he always bid after me. One night Bobby suggested that he and David switch seats. Bobby now would bid after me. And bid he did! Every time I bid, he upped my bid, even if it meant setting himself.

He did this again and again, never giving me a chance to have the bid and play my hand. He did so while knowing his wife was unsure of her bridge skills and hesitant about bidding over him, so he took advantage of that.

For several nights this scenario played out. Finally, Samantha pulled me aside and told me that she was angry at Bobby for bidding over me every time and had told him so. She was also angry because his behavior had not changed after she spoke with him.

I appreciated that she noticed what her husband was doing, but I knew her calling him on it fueled his desire to do more of the same. He was competitive, and he was willing to do anything to win. It did not matter that he was hurting his relationship with his wife and me.

Asking to change our seats so David would bid directly after me could meet with resistance. Instead, I said to her, "Let's beat Bobby at his own game." It was going to be a challenge, but we were up for it.

I told Samantha that every time I bid, she needed to bid when Bobby bid over me, which she had been hesitant to do. I knew David would not bid just to get the bid. That isn't how he plays bridge, so the bidding would stop with Samantha.

I told her, "If I am bidding, especially more than once, I have a good hand. I trust you to play my cards, even though the better hand would be laid down."

That solved that problem without any more words spoken to Bobby.

One of the mistakes that is often made is calling someone on bad behavior. It may not yield the results you want, and denial, anger, revenge, payback, and backlash may surface. So, instead do one better. Figure out how to take them out of the game by changing the rules without their permission.

And yes, in this book, I am calling out the *Sorrow Eaters* and patriarchy on their "bad" behavior, and I am not being gentle. My goal is to make men and women aware of what is happening so they are forewarned.

We are experiencing **immoral** moments again and again, and silence and doing nothing are not options! Do not be afraid! Do not hide in the shadows! Play the game better—and doing so subversively is just fine!

When I left the corporate world and started my own business, I was frustrated with mediocrity, and I was rejecting its values and lack of values. It became too difficult for me to be in a position where those who were making the decisions and telling me what I could and could not do had limited knowledge of what my work entailed. But most importantly those in charge were limiting my opportunities.

Yet, those in management never did anything to help me be successful. Yes, I was supported by one male manager, but he could not help me do my work. I was successful because of my abilities, tenacity, experiences....

So, if you have been denied opportunity, trapped in an existence not of your own choosing, you can also choose not to play the game. Instead, you can jump ship. It can be more rewarding to start your own business—run your own show.

Do not wait for anyone to hand down approval, opportunity, praise, or a promotion, or that bonus or increase in salary. Bet on yourself—be in charge of your own choices, of your life.

Many women who make the choice of stepping out on their own want to utilize the skills and have experiences they will cherish, with the added opportunity to expand their challenges without being denied.

Personally, I also wanted to do work that aligned with my values and passions, what I believed was important. I did not want to continue to have to function in a world that limited me and told me what to value.

I was liberated when I started my own company. I was no longer working for an employer who had dubbed himself in charge of my life.

And if you make the choice to step out on your own, you will be released from having to perform and conform to others' expectations. You will no longer have to hide your light under a bushel. You will not have to be silent, be less than who you are so others, and that includes both men and women, would accept you.

The workplace design and cultures do not support all women and all men, especially those who do not function and embrace the expectations of management. There are women and men who want to do work that inspires them, fills them with joy and contentment.

If you are being held back, not doing what you wish, feel empty and frustrated, do not spend your time wishing and hoping, waiting and pleading that things will change. Consider opting out of organizations that are unsupportive and strike out on your own, no matter what your education, ethnicity, age, or background.

And before putting roadblocks in your way, such as where do I get the money and what should I name my business, you need one more thing. You have to give yourself permission to get started as a successful entrepreneur.

Start by saying to yourself: I MUST do this! I MUST do this! I MUST do this! (Three is a magic number). That mindset can bolster your courage, courage that resides within you, to put aside any fears so you can spend your time planning your tomorrows.

Stop waiting for someone to say, "Yes, you should do it!" Have courage! And don't let your mindset about what you cannot do be your single biggest barrier. Once you say "yes" to your desires, then you can use the wasted energy that you used fussing and wondering and focus on all the decisions that follow.

There is information and organizations and others entrepreneurs to assist you. There are articles that praise women that have started their own businesses, and there are many resources.

But it must be noted there may be those who are trying to discourage women entrepreneurs. I recently read an article in which the journalist questions and denounces women starting their own business because it is time-consuming. Isn't that also true of women who are employed and wives and mothers—working long hours, jumping hoops, to prove they are worthy?

Is that article another tactic to keep women out of the entrepreneurial world? Tell them how difficult it will be, as if women are not up for the challenges. But if you have a good idea, speak with like-minded people who are enthusiastic, tenacious, and so on, who knows where your journey will take you!

Imagine if just three to five percent of the female workers in one year, whether they are in the business world or at home, decided to start their own companies. Five to ten percent would be better and would make a monumental difference in women's work life. Then the following year another three to five percent and then another and another....

The possibilities are endless. And an increase in entrepreneurs could change the landscape of how businesses are managed and function for generations. It would put more wealth and property into women's hands, and it could also put wealth and property into the hands of those men who are struggling in a world that has no place for them.

It would begin to level the playing field. But more importantly, you would not have to play the game using rules dictated by those who are vested only in their own success and not yours.

But one caveat: The women (and men) who start their own businesses must not turn themselves into patriarchal clones. There is no place in the business world for a woman or man who is into controlling others or vested only in their own success. There is no place for mediocrity, although we have accepted mediocrity in men.

These new companies must approach doing business differently. They must be egalitarian, inspiring, rich with opportunity, and value and respect their employees, which includes paying a fair wage and ensuring opportunity.

No one is saying it is easy, but is being a "lady in waiting" any easier? And you may struggle in the short-term but what about the long-term? And you do not have to do it alone. It may be wise to have a partner who has different skills or a group of women and men can also come together and form a company or rent space and share the space for different businesses. The possibilities are endless.

Only you can decide whether to bet on yourself or stay where you are. If you choose not to strike out on your own, increase your courage. Don't back down! Take your place at the table, and always be willing to jump ship!

According to Anais Nin, *"Life shrinks or expands according to one's courage."* If we keep retreating every time we are afraid, our world becomes smaller, our opportunities decrease.

Blaming men for a woman's struggles, even though there is an abundance of evidence to validate that claim, often yields little, if anything. It's a defeatist, minority mentality. Purge it! And STOP ASKING and PLEADING! Focus on what you NEED to DO on your own or in concert. By doing, I mean action with intent to change your situation.

We cannot expect changes from those who want to keep the majority of us in the shadows. We cannot expect the patriarchy to give up their control of the rest of us. Women and men who want a better life, a better world, must do it. They must be the ones who turn the page. One way is to play the game better, and another is not to play the game at all by striking out on your own.

Also, use the power, which makes you unique, and do not let yourself be diminished. You cannot expect another to give you what you desire. You cannot expect another to support you and lift you up. You have to create the life you are meant to live. And women and men who have supported those who rule and pull the strings, your day may come when you will see the wisdom of making another choice or find you have to do so.

Embrace your desires and have the courage to chart your own destiny on your own terms. And men, look around, what rewards have you achieved by your allegiance to the patriarchy? Consider how they have been dictating to you and limiting your opportunities as well.

And women, I appeal to you: Stop being competitive with other women. Instead, bond together, inspire and support each other, making your voices louder and ensuring all of your efforts have more of an impact. There is nothing like a fifty-foot wave to knock down the obstacles in one's path, and men, you can choose to be part of the wave. You will be inspired by it, enriched by it, and so will the wave.

Seven
The Blame Game

Ours is not the task of fixing the entire world all at once, but of stretching out to mend the part of the world that is within our reach... One of the most calming and powerful actions you can do to intervene in a stormy world is to stand up and show your soul. Soul on deck shines like gold in dark times. The light of the soul throws sparks, can send up flares, builds signal fires, causes proper matters to catch fire.

Clarissa Pinkola Estés

Brenda, an executive coaching client, was in her early thirties. She had recently been promoted as supervisor of a staff of ten people, and six of them had more seniority than Brenda. During our first session she shared the problems she was experiencing. I asked many questions about how she viewed each member of her staff and what efforts she had made to work with them.

She shared incident after incident. Her answers gave evidence that she did not know her staff. She believed she was to be in command, directing everyone's movement. Her staff was working for her—there to make her successful—and she had the right to say with her demeanor, choice of words, and tone of voice, "I'm the boss, that's why!"

There was also no indication that she supported, coached, and motivated her staff. She wanted to continue to do the work that she was comfortable doing—her previous job. She was not secure in her new position because she did not have the skills needed to engage her staff in meaningful ways. She was not alone. I recalled to her one recently-appointed manager who said, "You mean I have to talk to them!"

Like many who are promoted to the first level of management and beyond, she was promoted because she was good at her work, but she had no idea how to manage people. No problem. I was there to help.

During a pause moment, she said, "Do you think they don't respect me because I'm Black?"

I was unaware that she was Black, and even if I had known, I would not start there. Without hesitation, I asked, "Do you want to be known as a great manager or a black manager?"

I was shocked by my words. Just as had happened before, those words came flying out of my mouth. Not planned. No processing. And being an introvert, this blurting out is a double whammy! Those words crystallized for me something of which I was unaware until that moment.

I said, "When I started my own consulting firm, I was diving into an ocean of men—a male-dominated world. I would walk into a meeting, and most often they were all men. I never once thought, *Oh, I'm a woman, and they're going to treat me like I'm clueless or disrespect me, push me around, think I don't know what I am doing*, although that may happen. I walk in and own my being there. I come prepared so I feel confident in my abilities. That has the possibility of upending any preconceived notions anyone has.

"If you are secure in your position, confident, and reach out to your staff, you can establish a good working relationship with them. In time they may come to trust you and believe you are interested in their success. You can do that by inspiring and providing helpful feedback. Together all of you can achieve great things."

I explained that I never walk into any room thinking I am going to be treated differently or discriminated against because I am a woman or because of my age or stature. I always believe I have a place at the table, that I could express my thoughts and ideas. And if there were repercussions, I would handle them, but I would never call foul. It would just meet with resistance, and they would then know I was vulnerable.

Brenda had a *minority mindset*. Her response was based on her experiences and that of others. It was intensified because she was ill-prepared for her position. It may be true that some or all of her staff were prejudiced against her, but she had no proof. If she asked them, they might deny, and what would it have changed?

Believing that prejudice was the reason would not solve the problems. Just as my age or gender were not going to change, neither will her ethnicity, but her mindset can.

In a Taoist story a young man, Yen Ho, was about to take up his duties as tutor. He went to Ch'u Po Yu for advice. He said, *"I have to deal with a man of depraved and murderous disposition.... How is one to deal with a man of this sort?"*

"I am glad," said Ch'u Po Yu, *"that you asked this question. The first thing you must do is not to improve him, but to improve yourself."*

Most often blaming gender, skin color, age, or ethnicity does not get the desired results or at least a desired result that would not cause resentment and upheaval. And it definitely may not be one that would change the dynamics with her staff.

And blaming her employees is easy but short-sighted. Brenda would not have to do anything different. She would continue to be ineffective and frustrated. She would not have to look at her part in what was happening. She would stay stuck in the belief that she had done everything right, and it was someone else's fault. So, it was important for her to try a different approach.

In my coaching sessions with Brenda, she came to see how her behavior was being perceived. She realized her critical remarks at times, her lack of understanding of her staff, and her not engaging them in a meaningful way had left them without a leader. Her lack of direction, believing she could manage from a distance at her desk, and her employees' fear of negative repercussions rendered her ineffective.

So, instead of allowing the chasm between Brenda and her employees to get wider and wider, it was imperative that the issues be addressed but not in a hostile way. And if she did not address what her staff was experiencing, the problems would continue to fester and escalate.

We decided to convene several sessions with Brenda and her staff so they could get to know each other. Using different situations, they had an opportunity to observe the dynamics among the entire staff members. Through their interactions and the debriefing sessions, Brenda and her staff realized that their differences in style of work and how they communicated needed to be addressed so they could work together more effectively. No one was blamed.

I share that story because so often we run in the wrong direction. Someone slights us, speaks harshly, does not befriend us, and so on, and we assign motives, possibly believing they are doing so deliberately. And if the motives are accurate and justified, how are you going to change the situation if you get stuck in your *righteous right* and believe you have to do nothing?

Often, our silence, not addressing the issues, gives people permission to continue to avoid us, go around us, or just behave badly. Sometimes it is on purpose; other times they are at a loss as to what to do. Also, because Brenda felt insecure and inadequate, she put that on her staff. But if you want to change the situation, have the courage to engage them in a discussion and look at the situation from all perspectives.

And think about the possibility that people may look past age, gender, ethnicity when they are engaged in meaningful ways, when they believe the other person is vested in their well-being, and when they feel inspired. Not always a reality, but instead of staying stuck, consider taking another path.

Eight
Jealousy and Envy

"Some people will try to expose what is wrong with you because they can't stand what is right about you."
Unknown

Jealousy and envy are two words that are often interchanged, and topics that are rarely discussed, often ignored and cast aside. Maybe it is too hurtful to consider that someone has these feelings about you or you possess these feelings toward someone else.

Jealousy occurs when a person is protective of what they believe is theirs and fears someone may take it away. It appears if a relationship is under a threat by a third person. For example, you notice your daughter is more connected to your sister as time goes by. You are afraid of losing your daughter to your sister because she is yours. Being afraid of losing her love, you become jealous of your sister and denigrate her to your daughter.

It could also be the loss of your status, position, a relationship, or something of personal value. An employee may experience jealousy if a project he was promised was assigned to someone else. And a sibling may experience jealousy if she loses the attention of her parents to the baby.

Envy is a feeling of discontentment and resentment when someone desires what someone else already possesses, and they do not. That can include money, a nice house, beauty, confidence, reputation, education, title, and so on. You are not only covetous of possessing that something, but you also begrudge the person who has it. If you are driven by envy, you cannot let another person enjoy something because you are unable to enjoy it.

Zsa Zsa Gabor said, "Being jealous of a beautiful woman is not going to make you more beautiful." She misspoke. The word was "envy."

A few months before Mary passed, she told her daughter, Barbara, that she and her sister, Lois, would be estranged after she died. Shocked to hear that prediction, Barbara was silent. Hadn't her sister moved beyond her antagonism, jealousy, and envy that were so evident when they were children and into adulthood? Apparently not.

Then her mother blurted out, "She's jealous of you. Just like my family was jealous of me."

At the time Barbara did not ask her mother why she was saying that. We do not pry or delve into the meaning behind hurtful words. Maybe because we are frozen by the enormity of them. Or we fear the answer. We want to remain in the dark or do not want to face the reality. But on reflection, Barbara realized her mother must have been hearing things said by Lois against her, and her mother wanted to warn her.

The proof of jealousy and envy had been there all along, but Barbara had ignored the signs, not wanting to create upheaval. Barbara recalled a wall of pictures of Lois and her husband and children over the years. Also on the wall were pictures of Lois' brother-in-law and his wife and son, as well as both sets of parents. Barbara had noticed her absence but did not say anything.

Barbara could not make Lois care about her, and their history, riddled with Lois' assaults, spoke to Barbara. Saying anything would likely anger Lois. What would she say?

About fifteen years before this prediction-of-estrangement handed to Barbara by her mother, Barbara was living and working in Chicago—about five-hundred miles away from where she grew up. Moving to Chicago turned her life upside down, thrusting her into a journey she had never planned or imagined.

A few years after being in Chicago, at Lois' urging, Barbara shared stories about her big city life, her traveling, the places she was seeing. Barbara thought her sister was interested and cared about her, that they had bridged their differences, but then Lois yelled out, "You've always had everything. You…. You….

Lois could not hurt Barbara with her fists, something she did when they were children, so she used words. Barbara sat there holding the phone wondering what she had done to trigger this outburst. Thinking over that conversation, Barbara was surprised that she did not hang up, but she had yet to learn. Instead, she tried to explain.

What Barbara did not realize is that Lois did not hear her words. Her agenda was to lash out at Barbara, believing it was her right to do so.

If Barbara would have shared all the problems she was encountering in her new job, it would not have evoked any sympathy or understanding from Lois. If Barbara stated that she had worked hard to achieve her degrees and position—one of the many targets of Lois' envy—her words would only meet with silence and a lack of concern.

Barbara knew that because throughout their years Lois had never shown any concern about her. Yet, she expected Barbara to help her at every turn.

Barbara knew she was living her sister's dream and that all the other accusations were envy. As a young girl, Lois had wanted to move to Chicago and become famous. She was married with children, which she always said she wanted. Barbara was unmarried with no children. Her life had not been better. It had been different.

And envy and jealousy also rear their ugly heads in the workplace. An employee may lash out at their co-workers, and maybe not so directly. Maybe they spread rumors, degrade others, and undermine their colleagues' efforts. And this is often clandestine and not in the open. Remember my manager who took away my opportunity to speak.

Lois did not want to hear anything from Barbara. She only wanted to hurt her. By doing so, her envy would never go away. By blaming Barbara. Lois did not have to take responsibility for her own life. Her life was what she made it and not because Barbara had made a different life.

Barbara also came to realize that she had avoided conflict with her sister. "Keep the peace" being the motto. She had grown up watching her mother ostracized again and again by her family and how hurtful that had been. Barbara also did not want to put her parents in a position where they would have to choose.

But in time she also came to realize that her unwillingness to speak to Lois had given Lois control over her.

Barbara also learned by the change in her relationship with her niece and nephew that Lois had spoken against her to them. Her nephew told her that he had nothing against her, but his mother would not allow him to see her. After Lois ostracized Barbara from her family, she came to realize she had lost only the appearance of being part of a family, and a weight in time was lifted.

Years ago, I was taking a course at a Jung Institute. The instructor used a fairytale similar to Cinderella. Her words gave me a wake-up call. "If someone is jealous or envious of you, you have the problem."

I raised my hand. "Why would the envied have the problem? The other person has the deep-seated resentment."

"Although that may be true. The envied has the problem because there isn't anything she can do about it."

Oh my! Those words took me on a journey to understand more about jealousy and in time envy. What did I learn? Experiencing envy is painful. You are denounced and diminished and are rendered impotent, unable to change the situation. Whether jealousy or envy, both are distinguished by the sense of resentment.

Envy makes the envied feel utterly helpless. What can I do? The answer is usually nothing. Being kind and compassionate or doing a great job will only be met with disdain. "She thinks she is so nice. Well, I know better!" "She thinks she is so smart. Well, she's not!"

Barbara no longer existed as a person to Lois and her family. Her missing picture on the wall was evidence of that. She was being viewed through a distorted lens and was powerless against the assaults flung at her.

The story of Barbara and her sister demonstrates how the envied feels trapped and the assaults might even be unknown to the person who is envied.

So, what can be done? Her choices are few. If the relationship is important, and for reasons only known to the envied, she may not want conflict or doesn't want to sever the ties.

After their mother had passed away, Lois did not contact Barbara. If Barbara did not make the call, they did not speak, which was true of their entire adult life. Barbara decided to take responsibility one last time to change the relationship.

In many ways Barbara had fueled the difficulties because she never said anything. She decided to ask her sister to take responsibility for the relationship and not allow it to reside within her only. She was asking to be embraced by her family, to be respected and valued. Her sister's response: "Some sisters can't be close and that's fine with me."

Nothing was ever going to change the resentment Lois felt then and would in the future, so where was Barbara to turn? What can be done? Get angry and get even is one option. Barbara held many secrets that Lois would not want her children or husband to know.

After all, what did Barbara do to warrant these attacks? Usually, a person who is envied did nothing. And even if she did, why not discuss it with her, rather than demonizing her? Usually, the envied is helpful and supportive. Remember Cinderella! And getting angry and becoming vengeful are not natural for Barbara.

Barbara can change herself into someone else, but what changes would she have to make? Of course, Barbara could always try to become less talented, less successful, less kind, less, less, less.… but at what cost?

AND why should any of us have to become someone else or hide our light under a bushel to please another? And will the changes make a difference in the relationship or will they only render a woman more helpless? And isn't that what a lot of women do in relationships? Try to hide their wisdom, intelligence, knowledge….?

Another choice is to ignore the situation and persevere with the relationship, but what eggshells will she have to walk on again and again, how much of herself will she lose again and again? How much of herself had she already lost?

Barbara can leave the relationship, which in time may be the least painful. And a woman being passed over for promotion could do the same thing.

If you are envied, the answers are yours alone.

Now reflect on how women are regarded in a patriarchy. If I am jealous and envious of your ability and the gifts you have and afraid of your potential, I am going to paint you as inferior, lash out with lies and cause you pain, and ostracize you from taking a place at the table.

Envy and jealousy permeate any society, so are envy and jealousy what a woman faces in the workplace, within the family unit, with friends and men and society?

Are jealousy and envy two of the many roadblocks in the way of gender equality? Do women envy those women who make different choices, select a different path? Is that why they demean them and covet the patriarchy who are trying to deny them? ENVY!

Do men envy women's unique way of moving in the world, their compassion, intuition, curiosity, ability to relate to others in meaningful ways? Are they envious and jealous of women because as Jung said, "Women are magical," and they possess enviable gifts?

Is jealousy rearing its ugly head because men are afraid of losing what they have to women and other men as well?

Are they envious of the contributions of women, their way of solving a problem, the way they engage people?

Instead of railing against women, viewing them as the enemy, do what some men are doing who want to experience the gifts a woman brings to a relationship. They embrace them!

A woman can be a man's best friend, his confidant, and provide him with support and encouragement, and maybe, just maybe men could do the same in return.

Nine
Do it With Intention!

"Hope and wishes for all that delights will sour in the midst of action not taken and words unsaid."
Maximilian Degenerez

Instead of doing something with intention, how much of your life have you turned over to hoping and wishing? Clinging to hope and wishes is like throwing your life to the wind. Hoping and wishing gives your life over to *what* and to *whom* to do *what IT may.* And that is usually nothing.

Wishing and hoping conveys the belief you do not have any choices. It says you do not have to take any responsibility for your life. You do not have to do anything. Just wait and wait and wait! And although I do believe, from experience, that there are opportunities and signs that will come your way, they will not always give you what you wished and hoped for.

Hoping and wishing are such promising words; yet, hoping and wishing are blind and do not know where they are going. Hoping and wishing release you from doing or saying anything; free to dream. No action necessary. But what if wishing and hoping does not give you what you desire or gives you what you do not wish or want?

Hoping, wishing, praying, fantasizing, and daydreaming are telling you that something needs attention—YOUR attention. Hoping and wishing something or someone will intervene, fantasizing that the phone will ring, praying for your heart's desires are hollow endeavors, void of action on your part.

And, of course, we all hope and wish and daydream and pray, but don't stop there. Instead, pay attention and reach for the life you are meant to live.

It would be a wonderful gift to have a magic wand—a wand that will take away all the suffering, a wand that would eclipse all the hard work and struggles and heartache. But I do not have that magic wand and neither do you. But you do have passion and tenacity and courage. You do not have to waste energy complaining, blaming, wishing, and hoping.

But taking action takes courage. Often people do not act because they do not want to make a mistake. And if they do make a mistake, some excuse themselves by saying, "I'm unlucky!" Then, they don't have to take any responsibility and can blame it on the "God of Unlucky." The God of Unlucky just does not like you, so he penalizes you.

That way a person does not have to look at his part in what happened to him. But then nothing will change in the future. She will always believe she acted correctly, and she will never get off the merry-go-round of her life.

So, without a magic wand, how do we transform our lives? Transform into what you ask? Transforming your life into the one you desire—not the one you think or someone else believes you should live, but one that fills you with joy and contentment.

At the same time, by moving differently in the world, it would be transformational, not only for you but for society, our country, the world.

Transforming our country, our culture and ultimately the world must happen because our main purpose on this earth should NOT be to conquer, plunder, and rob people of a life—literally and figuratively.

Ten
That "Knowing"

"The intuitive mind is a sacred gift and the rational mind is a faithful servant. We have created a society that honors the servant and has forgotten the gift."
Albert Einstein

Have you said to yourself, "I knew better, but I did it anyway"? You denied that "knowing" because all around you people questioned you, poked fun. You were asked to prove something that can only be proven after the fact.

I was to travel to Moscow on a business trip. I wasn't making the plane reservations, and time was running out. I decided to trust my "knowing" and did not go.

When I spoke to my contact after the event, he told me how fortunate it was that I didn't make that trip. The ruble had fallen. People were waiting in line for food. There was no food at the hotel, and so on. I had no way of knowing that would happen, but I did know something wasn't right.

So, what is that "knowing?" Often intuition is defined as a hunch, a gut feeling, an ah-ha moment. That "knowing" just appears.

I liken it to connecting random bits and pieces unconsciously into the whole without my being aware of doing anything. There is no deliberation, no lock-step approach. Instead, that knowing appears without reflection or premeditation.

Jung identified intuition as one of the eight preferences that make up our psychological type—our personality. Intuition is different from thinking as defined and should not be considered the same as some have stated. Thinking is logic and analysis, weighing pros and cons when making a decision. Both thinking and intuition can work together in tandem or not. They may be in conflict. Logic could be saying "yes," and intuition could be saying the opposite. And often those who value their intuition will override their "thinking" function if that "knowing" is not in agreement.

During a management seminar, I was presenting the differences that affect our personality and communication. A male participant said. "Boy, do I understand that intuition thing. My wife would say to me, 'Harry, if you do that, this is going to happen.' I never heeded her advice, and what she predicted did happen. I hated that she was right and resented her for the longest time. Then one day, I realized she was a gift to me." Hoorah for Harry!

So, are women denying that knowing, their intuition? I say women because the saying "women's intuition," often said with a smirk, shrug, or snide remark, signifies that this phenomenon is observed in women more often than men, but men possess it too. Often, like some women, they want to override it with logic and reasoning or feelings. They believe they have to have more than a hunch.

Often intuition is disregarded and questioned when there is no concrete evidence to present. Has that caused women to doubt themselves and forced them to purge that knowing? Or has it allowed intuition to remain dormant?

Has the work that women have been *allowed* to do, such as administrative work, teaching, and nursing, overridden that knowing with detail-like work? Did their education, which is often detail-based (regurgitation of facts), win out?

Whatever the reason—claim your knowing back, own it, immerse yourself in it, and be grateful every day that you have it within you.

Eleven
Supporting Others

"For decades, women have been calling for the equality that is their right. And today, they are shaking the pillars of patriarchy.... Everywhere, women are saying 'the time is now': Time for equality and opportunity, respect, and equal representation. Time for an end to violence. Gender equality is the unfinished business of our time. And so, the time is now to change it."

Antonio Gutteres

Wouldn't it be a blessing not to have the gender debate, the race debate, the divisiveness, and instead accept our differences, celebrate them, and come together? Then, men would not have to live by the patriarchal dictates and be demeaned when they don't fit the mold.

Women could do whatever they wish without roadblocks and negative voices ringing in their ears. Wouldn't that be beneficial to the world, with less stress, fewer struggles and heartache?

So, what can we all do to support each other in the home and in the workplace and in our day-to-day lives? There are numerous ways--calling out demeaning comments, discussing biases, and reaching out and giving a helping hand. And this will matter, and you will matter.

There are some ways a man can support a woman, no matter what her heart and mind desires. And there are many ways we can support each other. And there are numerous ways we can do what needs to be done for ourselves.

Everything that I am suggesting applies to anyone who is being slighted, demeaned, and dismissed. They are not just recommendations for men but also for women.

When Sarah is experiencing a snide, belittling comment, you can speak out and possibly share a different perspective. "Wait a minute! Why kill the idea before we discuss it!" And Sarah could say, "Please hear me out and comment on my idea and not....?" And do so in a calm, even-toned voice but with confidence and no tentativeness.

Women are interrupted and talked over more often than men. A man or a woman could say, "Wait a minute, I want to hear what Lisa has to say." OR Lisa can say, "Please let me finish," Interrupt if you have to. You have been interrupted, so repay in kind. And do not stop until you are heard, no matter what words are thrown at you.

And why are women always the one who takes notes, makes copies, runs errands, plans the parties, and makes coffee at home and in the office? And by men allowing this, men are perpetuating the stereotype that women are their servants and do not have anything more important to do. A man could volunteer or a woman can rescue herself by saying, "Jim, could you take notes today?" "Mark, it's your turn to make breakfast," and so on. Women: Assign duties. Do not volunteer and do not wait for men to volunteer.

A common complaint I have heard for over thirty years is that women also are not always given credit for their ideas. Initially, it was dismissed and later brought up by a man or their boss took the credit. This can be corrected with some well-chosen words from a colleague, "Stop a minute! I want to hear more about Judy's idea!" Wouldn't you welcome that as well, so why not do so for a colleague? Or Judy could say, "Wait a minute. I would like you to consider my idea or tell me why not." OR "I just put an idea on the table, and I'd like your thoughts. I believe it has merit, so let's not dismiss it so quickly...."

If the idea has been passed over, and it is brought up again: Someone could say, "Didn't Judy mention that same thing the other day." OR "I'm glad you brought that up again. When Judy mentioned it the other day, it was dismissed...." Or Judy can say, "Jim, I'm glad you see the merits of that idea. I brought it up the other day. I'm glad you thought about it and now see it's worth considering...."

So often, a person whose idea did not get attention or was dismissed are frozen, not able to speak or afraid to speak. Maybe they walk away, complaining to others. That yields nothing, and if you do that, you are portraying yourself as a victim.

Yes, it is always a gift if someone helps you along the way. But often you need to do that for yourself, and you will be delighted that you did so. In time, taking care of your own issues will become a habit you will never wish to break.

We are all aware of the signals that diminish others and the challenges others face in their careers, so we can participate in a discussion about who gets assigned work that meets their abilities and whether they are receiving equal treatment.

Managers can ask an employee a myriad of questions and must be ready to take action. "What do you do that is boring? What do you do that excites you? Is the work using your talents?" Or a spouse to the other: "You've had a tough day. How can I help?"

When a man or woman witnesses a woman (man) experiencing sexism or being a victim of aggressive behavior, they can call it out, instead of standing there mute or chuckling to relieve the tension. "Wait a minute! Maybe you want to rephrase that?" using a calm tone of voice. And do not be afraid to do so.

Bullies are just that—bullies, and they must be stopped. And speaking out will encourage others to do so, and in time it may become the norm and not an outlier statement that surprises. That can reshape the workplace. Most importantly, everyone must take the time to listen and believe what they hear, even if it is about their own behavior.

Gathering a forum to discuss ways to be supportive can be helpful and eye-opening, revealing ways we may not have considered. Also, some people do not want to be rescued, and we need to be aware of that.

In the home, men can support their spouse by sharing the parenting duties and if possible, take parental leave. Yes, it would interrupt their career trajectory, but why should women bear all the responsibility of raising children and have their career interrupted again and again? And if your partner doesn't offer, ASK!

Women who have children and work are suffering from a deficit of time, and it may hold them back in their careers. A manager may think, "Oh, she has two children and won't commit herself if I promote her." Does he think that of a man?

A man who professes to love the mother of his children needs to show that love. He needs to lighten the parental and household chores by sharing the responsibilities. The doctor appointments, parent-teachers' meetings, doing homework and studying for exams, and playtime should not be only the mother's responsibility. And women, if they do not volunteer, ASK! And just because you can do something with less difficulty than a man doesn't mean you should do it.

A woman's job may not have the status or salary of a man's but that doesn't mean he shouldn't respect her contribution. He could show an interest, engage her in conversations about her work and future opportunities that she desires for herself. And, of course, she can do the same for him. Not just listen, but listen with intent, asking questions, and no interruptions PLEASE! Turn off the phone!

Despite the belief that women have made strides in the workplace, men hold the majority of management positions, and so they make the majority of the decisions. Men in these positions can advocate policies that support and benefit women and minorities. And everyone can support those who are struggling but who have tenacity and spirit.

These ideas are a touchstone, some ideas to take action to assist anyone who could benefit from support and guidance. And men speaking up for others in words and deed are laudable and appreciated, but women and minorities, anyone in the shadows struggling to be seen and heard, must learn to rescue themselves!

Twelve
Vive la Différence!

"I used to think I was introverted because I enjoyed being alone, but it turns out I really liked being at peace with myself and my surroundings and I am extremely extroverted with people who bring me comfort and happiness."

Anonymous

One of my coaching clients, Iris, had been put in charge of developing a team. Her manager, Luke, chose her because she had a good working relationship with her staff—something several of the other managers did not have.

Yet, Luke spoke negatively about Iris to me. She did not speak in meetings and did not keep him informed. He declared, "When I speak with her, she gets this glazed-over look. I want to knock on her head and ask if anyone is home!" Oh my!

In contrast, Luke was bombastic, talked about everything, approved of the managers who dropped in and spoke with him. In fact, he had an open-door policy, and the staff beat a path to his door with complaint after complaint.

One day Iris and I were meeting and discussing the progress she had made in putting together her team. I said, "What are you going to say at the staff meeting tomorrow?"

"I don't speak at meetings!" she pronounced.

"I know you don't. But you do have something to share about your progress with your team, so why not share it? If you don't share any progress, Luke will think you are not doing anything. I'm sure he would want to hear from you."

Knowing she would be more comfortable if she were prepared, we drafted some notes. I also encouraged her to share more, be more verbal, and drop into Luke's office occasionally and share what was happening with her staff.

I explained, "By not sharing and engaging others in conversation, they may not regard you positively, especially people who are looking for you to speak.

"It may be assumed that you are not accomplishing anything, are secretive, or not trustworthy. Luke may think you are hiding something or aren't enthusiastic about your work." I never revealed what Luke had said about her.

A year later, there were two management positions added, one rung up the ladder. Iris got one of the positions. Then I was asked to coach Lee, the other manager who was promoted. He said to me, "Do for me what you did for Iris!"

"What do you mean?"

"Everyone knows that once you started to work with Iris, she became a different manager."

And so, Lee and I began a wonderful relationship. He was one of the most enjoyable clients I ever had the pleasure of coaching. He was like a sponge.

Both Iris and Lee had made a difference in their own lives. In some ways, maybe I gave them permission to be who they were meant to be. But they were willing to look in the mirror, assess the way they interacted with others, and make needed changes.

In contrast, I worked with Kevin, another supervisor in the company. He arrived at our meeting angry with having been called on the carpet. Kevin told me that his manager said he was broken, and I was going to fix him. Oh no!

So, we started at a deficit. At the end of our first meeting, he said to me, "So, just tell me what I need to do, and I'll do it!"

My response, "Management is not like a coat you put on and then take off. You need to have a philosophy about how you want to work with your staff. Are you a manager for the title or did you become a manager to inspire and work with your staff?"

No response, so I continued, "It is important to be vested in your staff's success and for them to experience that. From what you have said, you view yourself as someone who is to correct your people's work, but what support or guidance do you provide?"

Needless to say, he wasn't having any of it. It was obvious after two more meetings that he was not willing to discuss how to work with his staff. I went to management and told them that I would no longer work with Kevin. Although I had a 20-hour contract, I was not going to go through the motions.

Kevin was surprised and so was management. His manager, upset by Kevin's unwillingness, said to me, "What can I do with him?" Unfortunately, I knew Kevin was not going to change his ways. He was in concrete, and I did not have enough dynamite.

I advised Luke that he consider putting Kevin in a position where the company could benefit from his obsession with detail and out of management until he demonstrated he was willing to work with people in a more positive way. Not everyone should be in management, even if that is a desire.

Too often, people wish to go into the position for the title, promotion, bragging rights, perceived power, money, and a window office and not a desire to guide, support, and inspire their staff.

Nancy had moved across the country because her son cajoled her into returning to where she once lived and he now lived. He insisted that he wanted his son to know his grandmother.

When she returned, she soon realized that the influence she expected to have on her grandson had been taken by the maternal grandparents. She did not have the money to compete and always felt like an outsider. Yet, her son insisted she attend events with his in-laws and with her former husband and his new wife again and again. He even invited all of them to a dinner she was hosting without her consent.

Her brother insisted she buy a house from him that he owned. It's a tiny house; her furniture is crammed into the space, and she hates the house. She left her life of twenty years and her friends to be miserable. To add to her misery, her male cousin, who she always regarded positively, said that the worst thing she did in her life was to move away from her family and stay away for twenty years.

After relating this tragedy of her life, she asked me why a strong, confident woman, who she once was, doesn't speak up and tell others how she feels.

I understood trying to please and not disappoint. Yet, there must be another way. But often we do not want to cause upheaval or conflict. We may fear the repercussions. But if you are already experiencing fear and upset, what is stopping you? To decide whether to take action, you have to assess what would you gain if you did not acquiesce? What would you lose?

Changing the dynamics in a relationship does not have to be confrontational. You can begin by setting boundaries, speaking calmly, without anger and outbursts. But most importantly, you have to change the dance.

With anyone in your life, there is a dance you do together. You say this, they do that, and so on. Those who wish to control your actions know how to get you to acquiesce or make you feel guilty if you do not, and so on.

To change the dance, your response has to be different. Questions are an exacting way to do that. That upends them, and they cannot continue to push and prod as they have done in the past.

It could also be as simple as giving yourself permission to say NO and believing you have the right to do so. I once said I missed my terrible TWOs. I had not learned that word, but when I did, it was freeing. And if you feel trapped, you too can be freed.

And if your response does cause conflict, the conflict that erupts is not about you. It's about that someone losing control over you, and conflict is often a necessary part of taking back your life.

Thirteen
A Rose by any Other Name

*"The healthy man does not torture others. Generally,
it is the tortured who turn into torturers."*
Carl Jung

The woman who was to introduce me at a national conference was asking about my credentials. I said, "Why not say, Here's Elizabeth," and chuckled. She was not amused.

I added, "My credentials do not matter. If I cannot speak and get my points across, then my credentials have no meaning. It's what I do in the next hour that gives me credibility. If I cannot persuade and inspire them to take action by my words, my title, degrees mean nothing."

That was a bridge too far for her, so I told her what she needed to introduce me. I share this happening to discuss "power." Every day people speak of power. Often the examples and words that follow are muddled and confusing. Substance is missing; abstract words rain down.

Most often power is confused with authority, which comes with a title that is endowed with certain rights. But most often power is confused with bullying and coercion, with dictatorial, tyrannical behavior, with might and right.... So, let's begin with a table rasa—a blank slate.

Power that is worthwhile and lasting manifests itself from what resides within you that connects with others. I have named that power *inherent power* because it is personal to you and who you are. You are authentic. You do not feign behavior, and you do not lie or bully or punish or reward.

Inherent power has the potential to inspire and transform others. You do not do for others or rescue them. Instead, your words and actions lift them up and give them the inspiration and wisdom to do for themselves.

No playbook! No template! No quick-fix! No promises! No deceit! No need to degrade and diminish another! No intimidation! No minimizing or lying to make a situation look better than it is. Your ego is in its proper place, so your unhealthy ego does not drive your actions and words.

Inherent power arises from your belief in yourself and your willingness to move in the world with courage and confidence, and act without fear. It arises from your ability to influence and persuade, motivate, and inspire, honestly and authentically. Not mouthing what you should say, but being honest, even if you think it will not be popular.

Those who embrace who you are and what you espouse will follow, not because you make promises, preach fear, and portray them as victims. Instead, you have a dialogue, explain issues, trusting that with knowledge, reasoning, and understanding, they can decide for themselves.

You listen, ask questions, and paint a vision of a future that is inclusive, free of hate and plunder, free of reciprocity, free of control and dictates. You are moral and ethical.

You inspire others to take part in the process and encourage them to take action for their well-being. You lift them up, so they can take flight. You do so with your honesty, your passion and compassion, and understanding. Not because you said what they want to hear, but because you have made a case for what they need to hear. No manipulation, no indoctrination, no dogma!

If you are credible, you can present your position, making it relatable and accessible, speaking with passion and logic. You may even be outspoken, without mincing words. And you can do so without any authority, without any title, without name calling, without harm or threats.

If you persuade and influence others by not bowing to their whims, not saying what will please, that is the only power that is worthwhile and authentic.

Coercion is not power because coercion is not sustaining. It fades, and once again you have to coerce—using rewards, punishments, intimidation, name-calling…. It is transactional and has no lasting effect because there is no ownership of an idea, a decision, solutions, a law, rules….

A title, such as supervisor, vice president…. gives you authority. And you can wield that authority by using rewards and punishment. You can treat others with respect or harm another by criticizing, denying an adequate raise or promotion. But carrying a big stick, punishing others, and iniquitous practices are coercive and harm others. You are fooling yourself if you think that it is power. It is not!

You can gain the opportunity to persuade and influence, but if you try to do so unethically, with force, with threats, by lying and making false promises, it is not only immoral, you will have to keep doing so again and again.

And we have seen on the world stage that those who do NOT have inherent power that is lasting have to threaten people, assault and accuse, name call, degrade others to elevate themselves, reward, make promises (which may not be kept), punish, cheat, lie, threaten, use unethical practices, and make people fear something or someone. They make others uncertain about their future and doubt they can do anything to change their situation on their own.

And they have to keep using those tactics again and again, signifying they have no sustaining ways to inspire followers. If they do not keep stirring the pot, saying what they believe will sway people, their followers would abandon them. To stay on that high, often they have to exercise their choice of poison again and again.

Now reflect on all of those whose words we quote and who we revere. Those who had no title, used no authority, used no coercion, performed no miracles, and did not demean others.

When my niece and nephew were five and seven, I had them visit me for a week. We were riding in the car to visit my parents for some fresh vegetables from my father's garden. Out of the blue, my nephew said to me, "Why don't you yell at us?"

I chuckled to myself. It was true. I spoke to them in a calm voice, and a day earlier they were fighting and both had come to me complaining about the other. I told them to go and figure it out. They made the problem, so they should make it go away.

So, when my nephew asked me why I did not yell, I wanted to give him an answer that he could understand and hopefully embrace.

I said, "If I yell at you or punish you when you do something wrong, I will always have to yell and punish. I don't want to do that. Do you want me to do that?" He shook his head NO.

"So, I want you to be good because you want to be good. And in time because no one is yelling at you, you will think well of yourself."

I looked at him, "Do you understand?"

He nodded, and I knew he did.

When we got back to the house, I told them they had to play together nicely and not disturb me. I had fresh sweet corn my father had given me to freeze and dinner to make.

Not having had kids in the house, it took some time to register that there was no noise. I raced into the living room. No kids. I looked outside. No kids! Into their bedroom. No kids, but their bed had been made. Surprise! Then I heard the television in my bedroom. I raced in. My bed had been made, and they were sitting there watching television.

That's what inherent power looks like? No coercion, force, hammer, and so on. And I believe that came about because I had always treated them with caring and compassion, spoke calmly, didn't favor one over the other, and whatever other tangibles they could only name.

So, why do people use coercion, punishment, and a carrot and stick? Because they know no other way, and they have to control others or the situation. Most often coercion is expedient—a fast resolution. However, these tactics are telling others they have no idea what they are doing.

If deep within, you act without malice but with compassion, have no need to control others and are mindful of what is best for all, contentment will surround you.

In the book, *A Simpler Way*, the author, Margaret Wheatley, tells of birds in the Galapagos Islands. Some have long beaks; others have short beaks. The birds with the long beaks eat the nectar deep within the flower, leaving the nectar at the surface for the birds with the short beaks. If birds know about interdependence, that we must take care of each other, not harm another, why don't we?

Nobody is free until we are all free. Nobody is safe unless everyone is safe. For any one of us to be free, to live without constraints and dictates, free to become who we are, you can no longer view the oppression of others as their problem alone.

At this time in our history may we believe we all deserve joy and the life we are meant to live. We are in a fight for survival of all of us—not the survival of the few!

Fourteen
The Elusive Authentic Life

"To be a soulful person means to go against all the pervasive, prove-yourself values of our culture and instead treasure what is unique and internal and valuable in yourself and your own personal evolution."
Jean Shinoda Bolen

Nietzsche said, *"So long as men praise you, you can only be sure that you are not yet on your own true path but on someone else's."* By conforming to someone's version of you, denying who you are, you are lying to yourself and to others. Pretending, conforming, hiding behind a mask are forms of deceit, trickery, and contribute to being inauthentic.

The good news: This mental clothing, such as the acquired mind and masks, can be purged. And I emphasize purged, not traded in for another form of deceit and lack of authenticity. Living authentically takes courage. It is necessary to silence the voices on the news, internet, friends, family, society, and so on, and step back and ask: What do I believe? What do I value?

Peter and his wife adopted a bi-racial son. He is meeting with some clients who make some negative comments about people of color. Although Peter is uncomfortable and wants to let them know he has a bi-racial child, he does not say anything. He wears the mask of agreement. He doesn't want to offend his clients, so he is silent. Silence is a conscious omission of what is true. Later Peter feels guilt, ashamed that he did not say anything.

To justify his silence and to attempt to alleviate any remorse, shame, and guilt he is experiencing, Peter denies that there was anything negative meant by what his clients said. He has gone from silence to guilt, remorse, and shame. Then to alleviate those feelings, denial. He is unable to face the reality or admit an obvious truth.

Yet, that may not be the end of his feelings of guilt and denial. And in time his clients and others may learn of his son if his wife shows up at the office with the little boy while his clients are there or he meets the couple in the park.

So, what could he have done? If he chooses to be honest and honor his son, he could have said in a calm voice, "Excuse me. My wife and I recently adopted a bi-racial boy. He's two and brings us such joy. We wanted a child for so long...." After Peter had his say, it would be best to pause briefly. And if it gets awkward, move on to the next topic.

Peter and his wife knew when they adopted a bi-racial child, they might hear snide remarks or notice side glances. Prejudice and bigotry are often out in the open, so why wasn't he prepared?

Often people stumble through life. The decisions you make and the actions you take affect those around you, so you must be prepared to handle the fallout.

If Peter and his wife had decided how they were going to respond to such situations, he could have been prepared to address these comments, instead of staying silent. He and his wife also might adopt the mindset that if there were negative repercussions to that adoption, they had done nothing wrong, so why hide their son.

They live in a bigoted world, and bigotry should not allow them to negate their son's existence. And if Peter is truly committed to his young son, maybe he should risk the loss of a client to honor his son and the decision he and his wife made to adopt him.

In time Peter and his wife need to prepare their son for what he might hear and then talk about what he can do if racial slurs are hurled against him. And yes, the discussion may be uncomfortable, but is it better to allow their son to figure it out for himself? And along the way, they must show him they never regret their decision, and maybe neither will he. Just an idea!

Living authentically demands that you get to know yourself, embrace your potential, admit to all your imperfections, and take responsibility for the choices you have made. Only then can you begin to chart your own course and be true to yourself and live a moral life.

At its bare bones, living authentically and morally gives you a sense of freedom. You do not have to pretend, and you do not have to bend.

Living an authentic life can be a difficult road if you have a strong need for approval, applause, and acceptance. It can be unwieldy if you measure your worth by the number of people in your life and those who praise you. It can be difficult if you have a strong desire to be part of a pack—any pack—and live in fear of being tossed aside.

You may become angry over time if those you spend time with have a need to control the pack's behavior and ostracize those who do not "jump to it."

The journey to become your unique self involves questioning the collective's idea of what you should and should not do. To escape, you must shut out those voices that say you must do this, you must do that. The acquired mind must be put in its proper place. The predators and slayers of your desires must be silenced. The masks must be ripped off.

Fifteen
Still Many Roads to Travel

"The woman who follows the crowd will usually go no further than the crowd. The woman who walks alone is likely to find herself in places no one has ever been before."

Albert Einstein

Have you lived your life embracing the ideal that men and women deserve the same opportunity?

Have you been chastised by those who dictated to you a different path, and you did not acquiesce?

Do you feel compelled to experience a life, free of being silenced and free of the ties that bind you?

Like some of you, I have lived and continue to live my life calling out the perpetrators of behaviors that disrespect and abuse women but also those who harm men and children and animals.

So, I ask you, does my willingness, does your willingness to tackle issues make us wrongheaded?

If we speak out against injustices with passion and conviction, should we be maligned?

If we call out behavior that harms others, should we be punished? Called foolish, aggressive, difficult, stubborn….?

What names are attached to any woman who speaks out and takes her place at the table? And any man?

What does it take deep within to speak out, without concern for being labeled, threatened, punished, ostracized, and chastised?

Do people think if they live in the middle of the road, they are safe?

Don't bathe in your fears. Naming them makes them real. Then you can focus on the work you are meant to do.

Silence, agreeing, or compromising do not guarantee you will escape harm or conflict or heartache. It does not mean you will be accepted.

But by silence and going along, you are disrespecting and diminishing who you are, and it definitely does not garner a lifetime of contentment if you feel trapped and struggling with pretense.

A woman in her seventies told me that she does not speak out on issues. She was taught not to offend people.

I asked her, "And what has that gotten you?"

Her immediate reply, "Stepped on!"

I then asked her who taught her to be silent. She looked at me, stunned by the question. She shrugged and finally said, "It was a long time ago."

Maybe no one person taught her; predators are all around. They taught her.

Think of how many years she has remained silent!

Sixteen
Go Find Your Life

"The authentic self is the soul made visible."
Sarah Ban Breathnach

Imagine going through life like a cart with one broken wheel, hobbling along—not in balance, not content, struggling to find your way. Then one day, you may start to question your choices.

You desire a new challenge, a new adventure, do something you have been denying yourself.

You want to stop making the same mistakes, the same questionable choices.

You realize your life has been put on hold or maybe is spinning out of control.

You have agreed to live a life that others have mapped out for you.

You thought it was easier to give up your life to someone else. But now you realize you gave up the life you desired and chose one you thought you should desire.

You have not had the courage to question or admit that you were unsettled, unhappy, maybe filled with sorrow.

Prior to this time, you may have had certainty, a definite idea of who you are and what you wanted to do. Now you find yourself out on a limb, alone, confused.

You now believe, as Carl Jung did, that the privilege of a lifetime is to become the unique individual that you are. You are now asking yourself, "Who is this person I've become?" "Who am I deep within?" "What is next?"

The urge to discover your potential can be a compelling force. And awakening to the realization that you want to take a different path can be frightening. Consider doing it anyway! And please know I am not denying the struggles of doing so, but sometimes in life you have to LEAP! And once you take flight, wondrous gifts may await you.

If you look to the outside, approval will come from outside forces. That validation often comes with strings attached. If you seek the answers from within—make conscious the unconscious—you will awaken and discover your true self. And the approval will come from within you.

Everyone's path will be different. There is no formula. You can begin by discovering who you are without dancing to the tune of those forces in the outside world. Ask yourself what is important to you and only you. "If no one were looking, who would you be?" and "What would you do?"

Demanding your silence is a hurtful game people play. Your silence gives others permission to dictate to you. Your silence is also a testimony to a lack of courage.

Obedience and conformity may make a good son, a favored son, but it is a recipe for living a tragic life.

Obedience and conformity may make a good daughter, a father's daughter, but it is a recipe for living a tragic life.

To be that voice of fire requires you to advocate what is just and compassionate. It requires you to speak out. But it also requires purging fear and hatred and bigotry and not choosing what is self-serving. Doing so with calm and confidence, with words that inspire will get you heard. It can be rewarding and bring you contentment and possibly joy.

To start your journey, I do believe you have to silence the voices of hate; purge the unhealthy ego, ask questions continually about your choices, take responsibility for your words and actions, and question the actions of others and the events in the world. And keep asking how do you want to live this one life?

Every day is a challenge. Instead of getting wrapped up in upset and irritation, enjoy the thrill of those challenges.

If you have ever felt judged, denied, disheartened….

If you ever felt you do not belong or are not enough….

If you are finding it difficult to find your pack, those who embrace you as you are….

Know that there are people out there for you. Maybe you have been looking in all the wrong places. Maybe you have been unwilling to reach out. Maybe….

I did not write this book because I have the answers and never made a mistake, and I definitely do not have the answers for you. No one does. But I did desire to make you reflect and challenge you to think.

No path that any one of us travels is easy, but why make it more difficult by bowing to the dictates of others? And remember you are not done yet. There are many paths to travel, no matter your age.

In the movie, *The Help*, Skeeter finds those who she enjoys spending time with and listening to their stories. They are the maids of Louisiana. They were not the women she grew up with, and the people she was expected to embrace. They were not her pack, and she chose to distance herself from them and travel her own path.

At the end of the film Abelene, a maid with courage, says to Skeeter, *"Go find your life, Miss Skeeter."* And the journey of finding the life you are meant to live, although never-ending, can free you.

Remember the answers are within you, but you must be willing to listen. Go find your life and blessings on your journey!

Author's Notes

I have lived most of my life keeping my own counsel and sharing my thoughts and knowledge with friends and in classrooms and workshops. The thoughts in this book have been swirling in my head for decades and finally coalesced. Putting my words on paper, releasing them into the universe, was a joyous and fulfilling experience.

I do not consider this a book for women. It is a message for anyone who wants to break the chains that keep any one of us shackled to a life that does not fulfill our desires.

For years, I have been disheartened and horrified by the injustices throughout the world and those that have been leveled at women for centuries. Women were not allowed to read, and a woman could be sent to an asylum for daring to express an opinion and not bowing down to her husband or father. Women have been paid less and denied the ability to reach for opportunities they desire. At the same time, the injustices to the laborers, immigrants, and minorities are also horrifying, filled with hubris and greed.

There are times I have quoted people in articles but have not mentioned their names because I did not want to make them the issue. My goal was to focus on the rhetoric and use that as examples to analyze and question.

You are welcome to reach out to me. You can contact me at elizabethrodenz@gmail.com

Wishing you the blessings you desire, but only you can make them come true!

Acknowledgments

Writing is a very solitary endeavor, which makes the support of family and friends more special. Fortunately, I was blessed with parents who supported me on my journey. Though they are no longer walking beside me, their love and caring and regard for me sustains and inspires me daily.

My husband walked into my life as my parents were about to make their exit. From the moment we met, he never once has hesitated in his support, no matter what adventure I wish to embark upon. He believes in me and is my counsel.

There is much gratitude within my heart for those who have touched my life in innumerable ways and supported me throughout my journey.

I am thankful to the participants in workshops and students in my classes who challenged me.

I am thankful for the support and inspiration of my friends and readers who encouraged me to put down these words and to get it published, especially Sarah Moreno, David Baker, Pat Sandrue, and Linda Mracko who blessed me with their support and counsel.

The works of so many that I have mentioned in this book, teachers and professors, and many others have enlightened my life. They provided a springboard for me to integrate my life experiences and thoughts into the words in this book.

I was thrilled that the artist Lin Shih agreed to creating the cover design. I am grateful for his support and guidance.

I am grateful for Kelly Barnhill whose book *The Girl Who Drank the Moon* crystallized for me the *Sorrow Eaters*. We never know where we will find that nugget of gold.

About Elizabeth

Elizabeth writes from her heart and soul to educate and inspire. She writes to expose the injustices to animals, women, minorities, immigrants—anyone marginalized.

Like her many interests and writings, Elizabeth has had an eclectic career as an educator, editor in a publishing company, and an entrepreneur with her own management consulting and executive coaching firm.

For the last twenty years she has taught courses and conducted workshops on psychological types, archetypes, wholeness journey, and fairytales. She also conducts workshops and speaks to libraries and historical museums on the topics: *When Coal Was King* and *Immigration, Unionization, and Chaos During the Industrial Age.*

She is the author of *Josephine: A Woman of Indomitable Spirit*, a literary/historical novel inspired by the life of her maternal great-grandmother that traces the Industrial Age in the coal patches of western Pennsylvania.

The Adventures of Samson and Delilah, is a memoir of two beagles Elizabeth and her husband rescued in New York City. The sequel, *The Adventures of Samson and Delilah Plus Twenty*, continues the journey of those two loveable beagles who welcomed twenty foster dogs into their home.

Odd Ducks and Birds of a Feather: A Mystery of Type is a fictional tale to teach personality types based on Carl Jung's work.

My Distinctive Father is a memoir of the heart that captures the bonds between a daughter and her father and will be published in the fall 2026.

Website: elizabetrodenzauthor.com

Recommended Books

There are many books I could recommend, but if you read just the books listed below, your world will expand.

Goddesses in Every Woman, Jean Shinoda Bolen

Gods in Every Man, Jean Shinoda Bolen

Women Who Run with the Wolves. Clarissa Pinkola Estés

Memories, Dreams, and Reflections, Carl Jung

The Invention of Wings, Sue Monk Kidd

The Girl Who Drank the Moon, Kelly Barnhill

Lying with the Heavenly Woman, Robert Johnson

Femininity Lost and Regained, Robert Johnson

A Simpler Way, Margaret Wheatley

The Chalice and the Blade, Riane Eisler

Anima and Animus, Emma Jung

Josephine: A Woman of Indomitable Spirit, Elizabeth Rodenz

Odd Ducks and Birds of a Feather, Elizabeth Rodenz

www.ingramcontent.com/pod-product-compliance
Lightning Source LLC
Chambersburg PA
CBHW070822110726
47973CB00003B/32